Rediscovering Political Economy

Rediscovering Political Economy

Edited by
Joseph Postell
Bradley C. S. Watson

LEXINGTON BOOKS

A division of
ROWMAN & LITTLEFIELD PUBLISHERS, INC.
Lanham • Boulder • New York • Toronto • Plymouth, UK

Published by Lexington Books
A division of Rowman & Littlefield Publishers, Inc.
A wholly owned subsidiary of The Rowman & Littlefield Publishing Group, Inc.
4501 Forbes Boulevard, Suite 200, Lanham, Maryland 20706
www.lexingtonbooks.com

Estover Road, Plymouth PL6 7PY, United Kingdom

British Library Cataloguing in Publication Information Available

Library of Congress Cataloging-in-Publication Data

Rediscovering political economy / edited by Joseph Postell, Bradley C. S. Watson.
p. cm.
Includes bibliographical references and index.
ISBN 978-0-7391-6659-8 (cloth : alk. paper) — ISBN 978-0-7391-6660-4 (pbk. : alk. paper) — ISBN 978-0-7391-6661-1 (ebook)
1. Economics. I. Postell, Joseph, 1979–. II. Watson, Bradley C. S., 1961–.
HB75.R4426 2011
330—dc23 2011018244

™ The paper used in this publication meets the minimum requirements of American National Standard for Information Sciences—Permanence of Paper for Printed Library Materials, ANSI/NISO Z39.48-1992.

Printed in the United States of America

For Robert and Betty Postell

Contents

Part II: Political Economy and American Economic Experience

Preface

The Forgotten Field of Political Economy

We are not only experiencing an economic crisis; it may be said we are in the midst of a crisis of economic understanding. The two crises are not unrelated. The economic crisis is in some ways easy to apprehend: human hardship abounds, and there is general disquiet about the size, scope, and competence of government. But few people, even in high political or administrative office, grasp the causes of the present problems, or see clearly how to build sounder economic and political foundations for the future. Even economists are often unable to agree on what, exactly, has happened to our economy, and what needs to be done to fix it.

The confusion stems from the fact that different economists bring different presuppositions to the data they measure and manipulate—and economics as a discipline does not have the capability of adjudicating between the presuppositions the economists bring to their task. This points to the necessity of rediscovering political economy. Thomas Carlyle famously dubbed economics "the dismal science," and it is a name that has stuck, due in part to the fact that economics deals necessarily with the production and consumption of goods and services, and its purview cannot be broader than this. It cannot, in itself, guide us toward human happiness. Yet the proper understanding of economic principles can contribute to our striving for happiness, in the form of playing an appropriate, if limited, role in achieving the best possible political order.

There remains a disconnection between the study of economics and politics. Economists and politicians often talk at cross-purposes, or simply past each other. And much fault can be laid on both sides. The result is that the greatest insights of the discipline of economics often have scant influence on public policy or public opinion. Economists are often ill equipped to present their ideas to non-economists, and political actors remain in a fog about basic economic principles, and indeed tend to exist within an incentive framework that encourages such ignorance.

It need not be this way, and indeed one might argue that it hasn't always been. Some of the greatest champions of free market economics, from Adam Smith, to Friedrich Hayek, to Milton Friedman, wrote books that were explicitly political rather than economic. Friedrich Hayek's classic work *The Road to Serfdom* opened with the frank admission that it was a political book rather than a treatise on economics. Today, we have lost sight of the integral relationship between economics and politics. The evidence is manifold: Politicians are lauded for seeking to alter fundamentally our economic system—and with it our way of life—as leaders in both major political parties advocate bailouts, stimulus spending, and a government seemingly unlimited in principle.

It is time for a restoration of political economy. Political economy represents a field of inquiry wherein political and economic ideas mutually inform each other, providing a way to reconnect economics to the human good, rather than merely confine it to mathematical formulas purportedly conducive to the maximization of material prosperity.

What is the human good? This is a question that scientific economics cannot answer. Our political and moral principles—including our Constitution—must once again inform our thinking about economic policy. Economic thinkers and political actors need once again to consider how the Constitution and basic principles of our government might give direction and discipline to our thinking about economic matters, and to the economic policies we choose to implement.

Our intent with this book is to begin to reunite economics—the study of how goods and services are produced and distributed—with politics and moral philosophy, in order to place economics, once again, in service of the human good. The contributors are experts in economic history, and the history of economic ideas. They address basic themes of political economy, theoretical and practical: from the relationship between natural law and economics, to how our Founding Fathers approached economics, to questions of banking and monetary policy. It is our hope that their insights will serve as trusty guides to future generations, as well as to our own.

Joseph Postell, Colorado Springs, Colorado
Bradley C. S. Watson, Latrobe, Pennsylvania

Acknowledgments

This book is based on papers presented by leading economic thinkers at a conference held at Saint Vincent College in Latrobe, Pennsylvania. The conference was co-sponsored by the Heritage Foundation, of Washington, D.C., and the Center for Political and Economic Thought, an interdisciplinary public affairs institute of Saint Vincent's Alex G. McKenna School of Business, Economics, and Government. The Center combines the resources of the college's political science and economics departments. It was founded in 1991 to sponsor research and educational programs in politics, economics, and culture. It seeks to advance a free and well-ordered society in the American and Western traditions.

We at the Center are grateful to Saint Vincent College as a whole for providing a wonderful environment for our extensive program of conferences and lectures, all of which deal with the conditions necessary for a free and decent political, social, economic, and moral order. The Benedictine Order did much to preserve and transmit classical learning and thereby lay the foundations for Western civilization. Saint Vincent, America's first Benedictine college, today remains open and receptive to the conversation about ideas that is so central to that civilization. Special mention should be made of the Rt. Rev. Douglas R. Nowicki, O.S.B., the archabbot of Saint Vincent Archabbey and chancellor of the seminary and the college; Mr. Jim Towey, former president of Saint Vincent College; Br. Norman W. Hipps, O.S.B., the current president of the college; and Dr. John Smetanka, vice president for academic affairs and academic dean of the college.

As editors, we owe a great deal of thanks to the foundations and individuals that support us. The conference would have been impossible without the confidence and generous support of The Heritage Foundation, particularly the

B. Kenneth Simon Center for American Studies, and, at Saint Vincent, the Sarah Scaife Foundation and the Philip M. McKenna Foundation.

We have also enjoyed the personal support and encouragement of Matthew Spalding, the Director of the B. Kenneth Simon Center; Gary M. Quinlivan, the co-director of the Center for Political and Economic Thought and dean of the McKenna School; and T. William Boxx, the Center for Political and Economic Thought's senior fellow. Their ideas and encouragement ensured the success of the conference on which the book is based. We are also indebted to many other individuals who assisted with the conference and book, in ways large and small. Prime among them is Kim Shumaker, the Center's program coordinator, who handled the daunting logistical tasks associated with staging a major academic conference attended by hundreds. Eva Kunkel, assistant to the dean of the McKenna School, has provided invaluable aid with many of the tasks associated with publishing this volume. The student staff of the Center aided us in ways too numerous to count.

We are grateful too to the editors and staff at the Rowman & Littlefield Publishing Group and its scholarly imprint, Lexington Books, whose efficient decision and production timelines should be a model for academic publishing.

And of course, we are deeply indebted to the contributors themselves, who remind us of the importance of the sometimes forgotten subject of political economy. We also owe thanks to our families, whose futures will be profoundly affected by how we, as citizens and policy makers, come to recapture a proper understanding of that subject.

Part I

THEORETICAL FOUNDATIONS OF POLITICAL ECONOMY

1

The Moral Basis for Economic Liberty

Robert A. Sirico

In his widely discussed treatise *The End of History and the Last Man*,[1] Francis Fukuyama predicts that democratic capitalism has won out over its competitors and that it will soon be universally recognized as the most desirable organizational principle of society, economy, and politics. What is left to us in the 21st century, he suggests, falls largely under the rubrics of management: improving the administration of public policy, debating spending priorities, fine-tuning regulations, and sustaining an appropriate mix of liberty and equality that satisfies the most urgent demands of both. The big battles over ideas are over, Fukuyama argues. Capitalism is here to stay, and all that remains to be decided is how to make it run most efficiently.

Few would dispute that events of the past several decades have shown the practical desirability of markets over socialism, and in this, the "end of history" thesis seems correct. Even those who advocate for a great degree of government intrusion into and regulation of our economic life recognize the unreplicable ability of free markets and free enterprise to create widespread prosperity.

Yet there is good reason to doubt that this victory is total. In fact, we have more recently witnessed a resurgence of the old view that a centrally planned economy is desirable. Despite the efforts of many great economists, political philosophers, and historians, economic liberty is far from having captured the moral high ground in public debate.

Perhaps more alarming is the fact that many of those who defend economic liberty do so on a questionable basis. If economic liberty is valued by its defenders, it is rarely because it is considered more just or more proper than any alternative. Today, those who defend free markets and capitalism often do so solely on the kinds of managerial and technical grounds that Fukuyama suggests will consume our efforts in the post–Cold War world.

We freely argue about how many "jobs" this or that piece of legislation creates, but we are squeamish about asking whose property will be used to create these jobs or whether it is better to have property commandeered by political authority or put to voluntary use by market participants. An argument over whether there ought to be ceilings on corporate remuneration typically centers on whether high salaries are economically justifiable, not on whether government ought to have say over such matters in the first place. We might dispute a proposal to force private business to add another function to its list of mandated benefits on grounds of cost, but not on grounds of the right and wrong uses of private enterprise.

Consider the opinions of men and women whose work affords opportunity for philosophical reflection on morality, the two most prominent being academics and ecclesiastics. How many among them can offer—or would even be willing to try—a moral defense of private property and free markets? A safe answer is precious few. And how can the institutions of liberty survive and flourish so long as the moral opinion-makers are so overwhelmingly sympathetic to only one side of the debate?

It is my contention that the loss of a normative defense of liberty introduces a certain instability into the social order. The "efficiency defense" of economic liberty is not enough, and management of a libertarian society without reference to morality will ultimately prove injurious to liberty itself. To ensure that free markets are preserved as much as possible by our public policies, as Samuel Gregg has argued, we must provide "a robust explanation of their moral value."[2]

So long as economic liberty—and its requisite institutions of private property, free exchange, capital accumulation, and contract enforcement—is not backed by a generally held set of norms by which it can be defended, it cannot be sustained over the long term. Into the moral vacuum left by capitalism's defenders rush notions hostile to economic liberty, notions drawn largely from the values and vocabularies of interventionism and socialism.

Further, if a principled defense of markets based on the sanctity of private property and the virtue of voluntarism is absent from public life, it is very likely that the moral center of the buying public has begun to slip as well. In any market, the kinds of goods and services producers provide reflect the values of the consuming public. What consumers are willing to purchase will determine what kinds of goods and services are most prominent in the market.

That is both the virtue and the vice of the consumer sovereignty inherent in market transactions where the consumer is king. Where the values of the buying public are disordered, the products available in the market will be disordered as well. On the other hand, where a free people's actions and preferences are informed by spiritual concerns, market activity and wealth accumulation present no danger in themselves.

But as Wilhelm Roepke has argued, institutional virtue and public virtue are codependent.[3] Societies that have a deep and unyielding respect for the sanctity of private property have traditionally fostered institutions that we associate with a vibrant social and cultural life: for example, intact families, savings and deferred gratification, cooperative social norms, and high standards of morality. Similarly, cultural decadence, family collapse, and widespread secularization have corresponded with statism and socialism more times than an essay of this length could name.

The link is more than suggestive; it is direct. Economic liberty needs a moral defense. This defense must start by making important distinctions between natural rights and government privileges, between natural and positive rights, and between societies which operate through voluntary exchange and collectives which operate through coercion.

Most important, we must begin to rediscover the inherent relation between economic liberty and moral virtue and to see that they are mutually reinforcing. For, historically, the first thinkers who made the argument for free markets were rooted in the moral and religious tradition of Scholasticism. By thinking about economic liberty in this way, we will be able to see clearly the two alternatives we face today: namely, entrepreneurship versus the welfare state.

CRUCIAL DISTINCTIONS

Many of the confusions of our age rest on a loss of certain crucial distinctions. Therefore, we must begin by drawing a few important distinctions which will help us understand the connection between morality and economic liberty more adequately.

Rights Versus Privileges

The most apparent distinction that we fail to make in contemporary politics is the distinction between rights and privileges. John Hospers, my philosophy professor at the University of Southern California, used to say we have undergone a "rights inflation." As in a monetary inflation, the value of the common unit of measurement has been drastically watered down. For all the talk about rights, we lack a clear understanding of what constitutes meaningful rights.

Rights are the claims which the individual has against others. An example is the right to life, which is another way of saying that any one person has a just claim not to be injured by another. Rights represent more than a legal claim. In order for rights to be inalienable, as Jefferson proclaimed them to be, they must exist prior to and independent of any legal or institutional rules, such as the Bill of Rights. Laws and institutions may obfuscate, violate, or protect an individual's rights, but they can neither grant nor remove rights. Rights, in order to be claims which are inalienable and fundamental, must exist independent of the coercive apparatus of the state. In order for rights to be all that we have just said, they must derive from the nature of the case, which is to say that the human person must possess rights by virtue of his or her very nature.

Many of today's so-called rights have nothing to do with this older idea. Most often, they are the consequence of the political process, as if legislators and civil servants are capable of conferring immutable claims on groups. In the place of natural rights, which are possessed by human beings by virtue of their nature, we have substituted government-created and government-granted rights, which are provided at the whim of the political process.

Furthermore, these government-created rights are often at odds with the natural rights that were defended by the American Founders. We may speak, for example, of the right to cosmetic surgery on demand at a low price. If we assert this right, we are implicitly denying the long-accepted right to the security of private property one has in one's just earnings, that they not be taken by others through force, for the payment of cosmetic services rendered at a low price must be fulfilled by taking the property holdings of members of the general public. It is a right that contradicts other rights and thus cannot be considered a "natural" right, one that flows from our nature as acting human persons.

Government Versus Society and Commune Versus Collective

Another basic distinction is that which exists between a community or a society and a government or political order. A society may exist with or without a particular political arrangement. The Philippine society continued to exist despite the deposition of the Marcos political regime. Even a regime as brutal as that of Soviet Russia left behind a Russian society that has a legitimate claim to continuity with the pre-Soviet one.

Similarly, a community is distinct in that its members hold certain values, mores, customs, and culture in common, but it is not marked by legal recognition or coercive capacity. Yet today, the term "community" is often used to put a humanitarian gloss on what used to be called a political pressure group.

We can make a further distinction between commune and collective. By a commune I simply mean a group of people voluntarily associating in an organization where goods are shared. People can enjoy a life in common, sharing values, homes, property, and philosophy in common, without the requirement that it be held together by force or the threat of force. Collectives are something different in this taxonomy because they require coercion to enact and sustain, typically through legal and governmental means.

The family is the best example of the commune. Property is more or less held in common, and its distribution is handled not by the price system, but by a natural authority. That is why the family cannot be used as an appropriate metaphor for political organization, which relies on the distinctive traits of the state and its monopoly on the legal use of aggressive force.

These distinctions are not simply semantic; they go to the heart of defining the natural order of liberty. Individual rights, civil society, and voluntary community are all part of this order. Government-bestowed privileges, political order, and the state—the institutions with which these are usually conflated—are distinct from this natural order of liberty. They are not, of course, entirely separate, but it is essential to understand the difference so that rights do not turn to privileges and become self-devouring.

Further, our concept of community has degenerated into warring political interest groups. What is done by political means, particularly regarding the distribution of wealth, is confused with what should be done by social means.

To understand the difference requires recognizing the difference between a voluntary, freely chosen action and an action enforced by coercive edict. There is no need to enter the debate on what precisely constitutes a freely chosen act; the commonsense understanding will suffice: A free act occurs in the absence of an aggressive use of force, coercion of the kind that can be exercised by both private criminals and public officials in their various capacities. A social and economic order dominated by a voluntary exchange matrix, the essence of the business economy, is a free social order.

On the other end of the spectrum is the social order dominated by networks of regulators, revenuers, monetary managers, and state social workers. The most extreme form of the latter culminated in the socialist experiment in the Soviet Union and Eastern Europe. These societies were not free in the sense I use the term.

Most systems of government today represent a combination of these polar opposites, and much of modern political dialogue consists in conflating the two different philosophies. But that does not diminish their usefulness as ideal types—free versus controlled—especially in providing indicators of the appropriate direction of change.

THE INTERRELATIONSHIP BETWEEN FREEDOM AND VIRTUE

In the same way that economic liberty lacks a widely accepted moral defense, we are too casual about individual liberty. It is fashionable, of course, in many circles to defend personal liberties, even when these have been misnamed. The content of the singer's song or a writer's text is often denounced and even censored, but the broadly defined right of free speech is rarely objected to in principle. But when it comes to the right of traders to trade what they wish, how they wish, and buyers to buy what they wish in a manner they think right and proper, many people see this as another matter altogether.

The objections mount if we speak of the right of businessmen to make as much money as they wish and to accumulate wealth to any extent they wish. Far from being a human right, it is considered to be a right of society to tax them and redistribute their earnings. The degree of vehemence directed at wealth is sometimes qualified by the nature and source of one's earnings. For instance, a wealthy physician is sometimes seen as less objectionable than a wealthy stock trader.

Nonetheless, the connection between economic and personal liberty should be clarified. It matters little to writers to be told they have the right to write what they wish if they are not permitted to buy a typewriter or computer, or if they do not have the right to sell their works to anyone who will buy them. Likewise, the freedom to exchange information and to promote one's talents—which is in essence what advertising is and, for that matter, what trading itself is—displays the connection between the personal and the economic.

The curtailment of economic liberty leads easily to a curtailment of personal liberty in much the same way that the enhancement of economic liberty may lead to the enhancement of personal liberty, as Milton Friedman argued.[4] Indeed, a cogent argument can be put forth making the case that a significant reason for the rapid collapse of Communism in Eastern Europe had to do with the progress made in economic liberty via communications technology. Computers have made the exchange of information easier, and economic progress became dependent in part on the exchange of information. This made it considerably more difficult for totalitarian regimes to effectively control other means of information, such as political ideas and dissenting opinions.

Rightly understood, personal liberty is also tied to the freedom to act based on religious and moral conviction and for those convictions to take on a social dimension. No civilization in history has survived or flourished without a religious foundation. Nor have great classical liberal thinkers neglected the spiritual dimension of man. From the writings of the late Scholastics to 18th-century British economists, they have always discovered a linkage between faith and freedom.

It is an unfortunate consequence of the growing secularism of our time that "religion" and "oppression" are two words somehow linked in the public mind. The authentic expression of religious values and high moral principles requires that political oppression be minimized. As F. A. Hayek said:

> Freedom is the matrix required for the growth of moral values—indeed not merely one value among many but the source of all values. . . . It is only where

> the individual has choice, and its inherent responsibility, that he has occasion to affirm existing values, to contribute to their further growth, and to earn moral merit.[5]

The term "values" assumes many meanings within the modern political context. Although the word has normative overtones, its technical meaning is simply a ranking, suggesting a subjective preference revealed in thought or action with no inherent moral content. What Hayek is suggesting, however, is that good choices and rightly ordered values can have a transcendent meaning only if freely chosen. Liberty is the source of all values because values cannot have concrete meaning in the absence of the freedom to demonstrate them in action. One's values cannot be measured if one's actions are coerced, because there is no way of determining whether that person's choice is a reflection of what he values.

Personal values will always be diverse, in both economics and personal morality. They are variously acquired on the basis of philosophy, family, culture, religion, personal preference, and the like. What we need is a political and economic system that allows for the free exercise of those values in a manner not inconsistent with the equal right of others to pursue theirs.

Forcing one view of proper values through political means has the consequence of purging the moral substance of goodness. Can a person be said to be noble or heroic if his or her action was not a freely chosen action that displayed either nobility or heroism? Hayek's phrase "earn moral merit" is particularly appropriate, because no heroic act is considered as such if compelled by a third party. In short, in the absence of liberty, virtue or good action is extraordinarily difficult.

It is, of course, possible and even praiseworthy for people to make moral choices under coercion as an act of resistance, as a martyr accepts death rather than moral compromise. It would, however, be absurd to hold the ethics of resistance as a guidepost to the right ordering of public life.

The relevant question is whether virtue itself can be the product of force. In the authentic sense, it cannot. When freedom is absent from the context of ideals like morality, nobility, compassion, or heroism, the result is to strip the action of its meritorious component. A morality that is not chosen is no morality at all. Only human beings with volition can be said to be moral, and in order to act in a moral way, one must have liberty. Liberty is not so much a virtue by definition, but the essential social condition which makes virtue possible.

Considered another way, a close connection exists between the spiritual and physical. These two aspects of the human character are what make up the human reality: Human beings are flesh and spirit. We are not like angels, who have no bodies; we are not like beasts, who have no conscience. Animals are bound by instinct; humans are related to things by reason because we are self-reflecting. It is the rational relationship between the human person and nature that gives rise to the desire to assume dominion over the resources given to us by God in the world and to transform them as God transformed nothingness into the physical world at the creation (*ex nihilo*). Liberty, therefore, is a product of our unique capacity to reason, which sets us apart from beasts but which also calls upon us to exercise our judgment responsibly.

What, then, is the appropriate and legitimate use of coercion in social intercourse? It is widely understood that individual physical aggression against person or property is wrong. Difficulties arise, however, when the same moral criterion is extended to society at large.

Despite conventional wisdom, an act that is wrong does not become right simply because it is performed at the political level by the state. Physical violence against person or property should not be used as an act of aggression in any context; physical violence may, however, be used in defense, particularly in defense of the rights of person and property, to enforce restitution for crimes committed, and to satisfy the demands of justice (classically defined as giving to each his due). Everything else in life is best left to the noncoercive sphere where additional and effective norms apply.

All of this flows from the principle that voluntary action is more suited to moral action than coercion. Lord Acton offered this succinct expression of this view of politics: "Liberty is not a means to a higher political end. It is itself the highest political end."[6] Lord Acton did not argue that personal liberty is itself the highest end of man, which would be a kind of hedonism. The kind of liberty Acton is upholding is not unrestricted. We are not speaking about free love or free thought. His emphasis is on the political, the sphere in which the distinguishing feature is the legal use of aggressive force.

Insofar as we concern ourselves with the proper function of the state, Acton's dictum is correct. Rights are best protected by strictly limiting the state's power to use aggressive force. When the state is used for wealth redistribution, unjust wars, inflation, and confiscatory economic regulation, the state comes up against Acton's dictum about the political order: Its primary purpose is the advancement of liberty. Beyond that, the promotion of virtue is best left to the natural order of liberty, meaning church, family, community, and tradition.

AUTHORITY AND FREE MARKETS: THE MIDDLE GROUND BETWEEN LAWLESSNESS AND ABSOLUTE POWER

In the same sense that upholding freedom is not sanctioning moral license, neither is liberty inconsistent with rightly exercised authority. "Authority," writes Robert Nisbet, "is rooted in the statutes, functions, and allegiances which are the components of any association. Authority, like power, is a form of constraint, but, unlike power, is based ultimately upon consent of those under it; that is, it is unconditional."[7] It is often thought that the opposite of power is antinomianism, as if anarchy reigns where the state does not interfere. This supposes that where there is no coercive power over human beings, they will not conform their actions to law or principle. Nisbet is suggesting that a middle ground exists between lawlessness and power, namely, the structures of authority offered under liberty.

Contrary to conventional wisdom, authority is found in the free market, which both produces prosperity and serves as a moral tutor for entrepreneurs. The facts of scarcity, human frailty, and original sin are existential realities from which only the Kingdom of God can ultimately deliver the human race. Freedom can make no such claim, but what freedom *can* do (indeed, what history attests the freedom of exchange has done with remarkable proficiency) is to maximize human resources to their fullest, to the greatest benefit of humankind.

As most entrepreneurs realize, the free market functions as a moral tutor by fostering rule-keeping, honesty, respect for others, and bravery. Markets and the entrepreneurs who enable the market to function do this because they require, in the first place, a certain moral context in which to exist and function smoothly. Firms cannot long exist without a reputation for honesty, quality workmanship, and, in most cases, civility and politeness. Given the fact that a free market depends on voluntary exchange to operate, if some of the virtues are lacking, consumers are the best judge of when to end the relationship.

In fact, the practical intelligence of the market is its most obvious virtue. It can be seen both by the consumer looking for a good deal and by the business person who must be other-regarding by tending to the needs and desires of the consumer. In this respect, the system in which the entrepreneur must operate requires and promotes altruistic behavior, as George Gilder has argued.[8]

In the promotion of traditions, manners, ethics, and virtue, voluntary institutions are more trustworthy than the state, and more effective as well. These matters are too important to be entrusted to bureaucrats and politicians. The opposition here is not to social authority but to coercive power, especially when it becomes centralized. What Nisbet calls intermediary institutions, social arrangements of authority that provide a buffer between the individual and the state, are critically important.

In the development and flourishing of these institutions, private property—in the means of production, distribution, and exchange—is a necessary foundation, but private property and wealth do not exist in a state of nature. They require a government to establish and enforce basic rules. They come about when people decide that the creation of a civilized community requires some agreement about what is mine and what is thine. It is not enough to wander from place to place and take from others as the moment calls for; there must be rules of who owns what and what the terms of agreement and exchange will be. The defense of the right of property ownership should be seen as the defense not of detached material objects in themselves, but of the dignity, liberty, and very nature of the human person. The right to own and control justly acquired property is an extension and exercise of authentic human rights.

RELIGION AND LIBERTY

We must recognize the importance of religion to the preservation and defense of economic liberty. Religion has been central in human history in providing a higher moral reference point to which human beings conform their behavior. Furthermore, religion's role in laying the groundwork for economic liberty is not often appreciated.

The religious tradition to which I refer defended the importance and dignity of the individual, as well as the family as a voluntary means of providing for the needs of the community. More specifically, the ideas of liberty and free-market economics was developed within the medieval religious tradition, through the late Scholastics who were heavily indebted to Thomas Aquinas's teaching on the natural law. In sum, religion gave us the ideas of morality, natural law, individual dignity, and free-market economics that serve as the basis for economic liberty. Rather than attacking those foundations, religion is a necessary support for economic liberty.

No society could be held together very long without some kind of higher reference point, lest individuals find themselves vulnerable to the excesses of the stronger against the weaker. We find in the Jews the rudimentary notion that a high morality is a prerequisite for ordered liberty to flourish. When we look back two thousand years to the center of the civilized world, we observe how those seeds sprouted in the Christian idea.

From the Christian perspective, the most important events in human history are the incarnation, death, and resurrection of Jesus Christ. These events represent a deepening appreciation in human consciousness of the sacredness of the individual. They happen, after all, to an individual and for other individuals. In the last analysis, the purpose of Christ's appearance in human history is to redeem concrete human beings, not abstractions.

The Christian message employs the model of the family, not the state, as the ideal human community. It emphasizes love rather than power as the distinguishing mark of the true believer and the binding force of the community.

As Alexander Ruestow observes, "in its doctrine of immortality and of the infinite worth of each human being as a child of God" and "in placing every individual human soul in direct relation to God," Christianity furnished "a strong counterweight to its other components of restraint and conscience." It was this that gave rise to antidomination tendencies and forms the "roots of individualism and liberalism."[9]

Medieval Economic Thought: A Prelude to Free-Market Economics

Saint Thomas Aquinas brought the mightiest mind of the Middle Ages to bear on the question of human rights and liberty. By synthesizing Aristotle with Christianity, Saint Thomas developed the theory of natural law, which he described in the following manner:

> Now, among, all others, the rational creature is subject to Divine providence in the most excellent way, in so far as it partakes of a share of providence, by being provident both for itself and for others. Wherefore it has a share of the Eternal Reason, whereby it has a natural inclination to its proper act and end; and this participation of the eternal law in the rational creature is called natural law.[10]

Regarding the impact of natural law on human law, Thomas says: "Consequently, every human law has just so much of the nature of law, as it is derived from the law of nature."[11]

The resiliency of natural law throughout the centuries is seen in the name of the endeavor. Natural law is resilient because it accounts for and makes sense of reality. The coherence of natural law is twofold: It coheres with experience and with reason. It establishes a reference point, as did the Law and the Prophets for the Jews, outside of institutional dictate. And most important for the development of liberty, and especially economic liberty, it establishes the sanctity of the individual as a rational being who can interpret the relationship between the individual and the community in terms of free association and contract.

Emerging from this concept of human beings as free persons, autonomous yet in relation to one another, the disciples of Saint Thomas went on to apply their moral theory and deductive methodology to the realm of economics. In a systematic sense, these scholars, the late Scholastics, founded the discipline of economics long before the time of Adam Smith.[12] In his massive treatise on the history of economic thought, Joseph Schumpeter writes that "it is within their system of moral theology and the law that economics gained definite if not separate existence, and it is they who come nearer than does any other group to having been the 'founders' of scientific economics."[13]

A comparison of the thinking of many of these medieval Scholastics on economic liberty with modern free-market proponents reveals an astonishing harmony.[14] The similarities begin at the justification of property and exchange, continue through the analysis of value and economic growth, and extend all the way to money, banking, and the theory of interest rates. Even the analysis of taxation and regulation bears a striking similarity, given the many centuries that separate modern free-market thought from these disciples of Saint Thomas.

Unlike more positivist schools of economic thought, these approaches emphasize the centrality of the acting person; the subjective will, and all that this implies, is the driving force behind economic life. The intellectual tradition beginning in Scholasticism ran through the Late Scholastics and was recovered in late-19th century Vienna and the Austrian School of economics. This tradition was reintegrated into modern Catholic social teaching by Pope John Paul II.

In particular, the "personalism" in Late Scholastic economic thought was central to the Austrian School. The personalism of the Late Scholastics argued that the way to understand economics was by reflecting on the preferences, purposes, outlook, and intentions of economic actors themselves rather than the things that the economy produced.

Beginning with Saint Thomas, Scholastic economic thought became progressively liberal and refined, culminating in the 16th century School of Salamanca in Spain. First, the Franciscan San Bernardino of Siena raised the status of businessmen to a higher moral plateau, rejecting the idea that business was intrinsically immoral. Later, Thomas Cajetan articulated new theories of monetary theory that would be central to a free market. Francisco de Vitoria, the founder of Salamancan economics, contributed the idea that the "just price" was the common market price, furthering the argument that the value of a thing was influenced by the preferences of economic actors. Finally, Domingo de Soto affirmed that a man can "donate or transfer the things he legally owns in any way he wants" as a matter of "natural right."

In all, the School of Salamanca phenomenon represents a major episode in the history of economic thought, which deserves closer study today. The link between the Late Scholastics and the late-19th century Austrian School is the theory of economic value. The value of any good or service, by implication, resides not in the objective qualities of the good itself, but rather in how people personally regard the good. That is, economic value derives from individual impressions and intentions and is ultimately subjective. This necessarily precludes the idea that outside parties, including governments, can better impose prices and plans than those intended by individual economic actors themselves.

The Church's Contemporary View of Economics

These arguments, to repeat, have been renewed by the modern Catholic view of economics. For example, *Centesimus Annus*, written by Pope John Paul II, recaptures the Scholastic economic tradition for modern Christians.

Exactly what the Pope's economic influences were in preparing the encyclical are impossible to determine. Prior to the promulgation of the document, the Vatican met with a series of mainstream Western economists, among them Kenneth Arrow, Hirofumi Uzawa, Anthony Atkinson, Jeffrey Sachs, Hendrick Houthakker, Amartya Sen, Robert Lucas, and Edmond Malinvaud. But their influence is far less evident than the schools representing a more explicitly free-market brand of economic thought: for example, the monetarist, supply-side, public choice, and Austrian schools of modern economics.

In general, these latter schools argue that the free-market economy is a process of discovery that carefully balances the scarcity of the world's resources with unlimited demands of consumers and that the free-market mechanism is superior to any alternative in performing this task. They regard the pursuit of private interest, in the context of freedom of contract and private property, as serving both individual good and the good of society as a whole; as a corollary, they do not overlook the private interests of individuals in the state sector and regard them as largely destructive social forces. The allocation of resources, they argue, should be taken care of by the price system because it is more reliable than government macroeconomic management.

Centesimus Annus echoes these themes in many passages. The occasion of the encyclical was the 100th anniversary of *Rerum Novarum*, but the collapse of socialist central planning in Eastern Europe—what Pope John Paul II calls the "events of 1989"—is also placed at the center of the document.

A profound understanding of the importance of the division of labor is present in the encyclical. The Pope points out that "goods cannot be adequately produced through the work of an isolated individual; they require the cooperation of many people in working towards a common goal." To coordinate the division of labor requires "initiative and entrepreneurial ability."[15] He correctly says that, while not everything man needs is provided through economics, "the free market is the most efficient instrument for utilizing resources and effectively responding to needs."[16] The word "profit" is not used derisively in the Pope's text:

> The Church acknowledges the legitimate role of profit as an indication that a business is functioning well. When a firm makes a profit, this means that productive factors have been properly employed and corresponding human needs have been duly satisfied.[17]

He has recognized the distinctively human part of the calculation process and the glory of markets in that they can both satisfy individual interest as well as that of the entire community. The profit is a measure of that satisfaction.

On the development of the Third World, he especially calls for a "breakdown" of "barriers of monopolies which leave so many countries on the margins of development," thus correctly realizing the primary problem of less-developed countries. He asks:

> Can it perhaps be said that, after the failure of Communism, capitalism is the victorious social system, and that capitalism should be the goal of the countries now making efforts to rebuild their economy and society? Is this the model which ought to be proposed to the countries of the Third World which are searching for the path to true economic and civil progress?

The Pope says yes, if by capitalism we mean "an economic system which recognizes the fundamental and positive role of business, the market, private property and the resulting responsibility for the means of production, as well as free human creativity in the economic sector."[18]

The religious concept of God's creation of the human family in his own image, and hence with an intrinsic dignity, has made a significant contribution to the modern understanding of the limitations of power in social and political relationships and the need for human beings to enjoy legitimate autonomy. Political and economic liberty is misunderstood, however, if it is seen as resulting in a completely secularized and libertine society or if it entails the notion that citizens animated by religious ideals may not be permitted to have an impact on their communities. Political liberty does not demand theological or moral relativism. It merely guarantees that moral and religious ends are not achieved by political means: that is, that they are not coerced by the state.

The process of extracting the church from the direct responsibility of ordering the political arrangements of each country to a religious end has been a long and arduous one, and it is not completely finished. John Courtney Murray, the American Jesuit whose work on religious liberty and American pluralism contributed greatly to the historic shift in the Catholic Church's understanding of religious freedom as a human right, said, "in all honesty it must be admitted that the church is late in acknowledging the validity of the principle."[19]

Yet through Murray's work, the theme of toleration is picked up in *Dignitatis Humanae*, the Vatican II document on religious liberty, which outlines a legitimate sphere of political liberty without compromising the truth-claims of the Christian faith. The document draws the following distinction:

> This sacred Synod likewise professes its belief that it is upon the human conscience that these obligations [to seek truth] fall and exert their binding force.

> The truth cannot impose itself except by virtue of its own truth, as it makes its entrance into the mind at once quietly and with power.[20]

The current Pope—Pope Benedict XVI—furthers this movement within the Church. In his much-anticipated third encyclical, *Caritas in Veritate* (Love in Truth), Pope Benedict XVI does not focus on specific systems of economics. He is not attempting to shore up anyone's political agenda. He is rather concerned with morality and the theological foundation of culture. The context is, of course, a global economic crisis: a crisis that has taken place in a moral vacuum, where the love of truth has been abandoned in favor of a crude materialism. Yet his encyclical contains no talk of seeking a third way between markets and socialism. Words like "greed" and "capitalism" make no appearance here. People seeking a blueprint for the political restructuring of the world economy won't find it here.

He constantly returns to two practical applications of the principle of truth in charity. First, this principle takes us beyond earthly demands of justice, defined by rights and duties, and introduces essential moral priorities of generosity, mercy, and communion—priorities which provide salvific and theological value. Second, truth in charity is always focused on the common good, defined as an extension of the good of individuals who live in society and have broad social responsibilities. Several commentators have worried about his frequent calls for wealth redistribution. Benedict does see a role for the state here, but much of the needed redistribution is the result of every voluntary and mutually beneficial exchange.

This encyclical is a theological version of his predecessor's more philosophical effort to anchor the free economy's ethical foundation. Much of it stands squarely within a long tradition of writings of a certain "classical liberal" tradition, one centered on the moral foundation of economics, from Saint Thomas Aquinas and his disciples, Frederic Bastiat in the 19th century, Wilhelm Roepke, and even the secular F. A. Hayek in the 20th century. It also clearly resonates with some European Christian democratic thought.

Religion and Centrally Planned Socialism

Perhaps the greatest example of an organized political system of intolerance that both religious and secular societies have had to endure was that of centrally planned socialism, but this should not surprise us. It is consistent for a regime which believes it can plan the entire economy, which means to dictate the economic decisions of every citizen, to find little room in society for religious freedom. By attempting to own and control private property and to suppress religious and political expression and the freedom of association, the totalitarian rulers of Central and Eastern Europe in the late 20th century hoped to produce a society sanitized of any reference to God, or at least a God which transcended the pronouncements of the political ruler.

Certainly, many factors went into the astounding and rapid demise of Communism, but it would be an oversight to neglect the role of religion—Catholic, Protestant, and Jewish—in finally undermining the illegitimate authority the state had claimed for itself. It would also be an oversight to neglect the role of religion in providing a secure moral foundation for freedom so that liberty may be used properly and defended in moral terms. The contributions of religion to the development of the free society and the further implications for our future understanding of political liberty have only begun to be explored.

ENTREPRENEURSHIP VERSUS THE WELFARE STATE

Having defined the terms of the debate in the first part of this essay, defended the idea that freedom is an essential condition for the exercise of virtue in the second part, and traced the religious foundations of liberty in the third part, a discussion of two contemporary ideas should help to clarify the principles of liberty. Those ideas are entrepreneurship, which rests on voluntarism and creativity, and the welfare state, which rests on state interventionism. The current moral terminology used to discuss and evaluate the two institutions is gravely deficient and in need of radical corrections.

The experience of totalitarian societies has taught us the need to be wary of the power of the state and to be more tolerant of what is often called "diversity." The word "diversity" also implies a recognition that there are differences between people. While we may all labor under the same rules, the kind of work we do and what we produce will differ according to our different temperaments and talents. In economic thought, the resulting matrix of individual differences is called the division of labor.

It is an unfortunate holdover of old socialist notions that the religious community is not yet entirely comfortable with the concept of the division of labor. Religious leaders are not prepared to grant that all economic actors can also be moral beings. The capitalist is not given the same moral status as the laborer, for example. The person who lives off investment income is not considered as morally upright as the wage earner. And the replacement worker is not considered as virtuous as the striker.

Yet all of this is confusion. If a person is using his or her talents in a peaceful manner, if an assumed position in the division of labor does not conflict with moral teaching, there is no reason to condemn any occupation.

In the free market, all persons occupy a position in the economy according to particular individuals' strengths, and all can use their respective positions for good or ill.

With few exceptions, the religious establishment views entrepreneurs (people whose profession requires risking scarce capital in markets to create future goods and services) as one of the least favored groups in society. One sees evidence of the prejudice against the entrepreneur everywhere. Books, television programs, films, cartoon strips, and sermons all convey the same message: What he does is rapacious, greedy, and socially destructive. Business may be a necessary evil, says reigning opinion, but the entrepreneur should never be given a moral sanction. That is conventional wisdom as proclaimed by the opinion-molding classes.

This fundamentally reflects a bias against capitalism and has spiritual consequences. As a priest, I often find entrepreneurs who are disenfranchised and alienated from their churches. All they hear from their churches is that the path to personal redemption is to give up all their money. But religious leaders display very little understanding of the vocation called entrepreneurship, of what it requires in the way of personal sacrifice, and of what it contributes to society. In virtually all the seminaries with which I am acquainted, there is no course on economics, which, unfortunately, has not kept religious leaders from pronouncing on economic matters.

In addition, the lack of understanding most often comes from people who operate from a distributivist economic model. On Sunday morning, a collection basket is passed. On Monday, the bills are paid and acts of charity are attended to. If the money is short, they appeal for more. There is nothing wrong with this model, but it tends to foster a view of the economic world as a pie that needs to be divided. Those who take a large piece are forcing small pieces on others.

The entrepreneur operates on an entirely different model. He or she talks of making money, not collecting it; of producing, expanding, not redistributing, wealth. He or she must consider the needs, wants, and desires of consumers, because the only way to get money peacefully and without charity is to offer something of value in exchange.

A more proper economic analysis teaches that entrepreneurs are impresarios, visionaries who organize numerous factors, take risks, and bring resources into connection with each other to create something greater than the sum of the parts. They drive the economy forward by anticipating the wishes of the public and even creating new ways of organizing resources.[21] They are the men and women who create jobs, reduce human suffering, discover and apply new cures, bring food to those without, and help dreams become realities

This creative aspect of the entrepreneur is akin to God's creative activity as it appears in the book of Genesis, as Michael Novak has argued. In order to carry out this creative enterprise, entrepreneurs must have access to the material factors of production; they must be permitted to acquire and trade property. They must act in an atmosphere of freedom. They should not have to suffer slights from religious leaders who do not approve of the talents and gifts that God has given them.

Does this elevate the entrepreneurial technique above the spiritual dimension of man? Not at all. As Etienne Gilson put it, "technique is that without which the most fervent piety is powerless to make use of nature for God's sake."[22]

What is ultimately extraordinary about the institution of entrepreneurship is that it requires no third-party intervention to make it come into being and thrive. It requires no government program or government manuals. It does not require even special low-interest loans, special tax treatment, or public subsidies. It does not even require a specialized education or prestigious degree. Entrepreneurship is an institution that grows organically from the natural order of liberty. Those with talent, even the calling, toward economic creativity are compelled by nature to enter it and lead society in the creation of wealth.

What does this call mean to those in the vocation of enterprise? It means that they must strive to be more fully what they are; to display more fully the virtue of inventiveness; to act more boldly with the virtue of creativity; to continue to be other-regarding as they anticipate market demands, as they develop in themselves and school others in the virtue of thrift. They should not merely share their wealth with those in need, but also act as tutors to others by example and mentorship. They must teach others to become independent and to produce wealth themselves.

Truly, the gifts that entrepreneurs offer society at large are beyond anything they themselves and others can completely comprehend. The entrepreneur is the source of more social and spiritual good than is recognized. In contrast, the welfare state is too often thought of in morally favorable terms, but its social consequences, however well-intended, can be largely damaging.

For decades, the "provider state" has been thought to be an effective compromise between the oppression of full-blown socialism and the alleged uncertainties and rigors of free markets. This provider state offers a variety of extra-market provisions of goods and services. Today, many people of many different political stripes agree that the present welfare system does not work. The consensus for radical reform is growing. Yet public representatives of religious bodies and institutions have proved largely unable to adjust to the modern realities of the social welfare state. Sincere and well-thought-out plans to change the incentives of a program or cut government welfare spending—

even when it would thereby leave more money for private charity—are often denounced as lacking compassion and even being ill-intended.

The moral high ground on this question is occupied entirely by defenders of welfare redistribution—on the fairly crude premise that Christian charity and coercive wealth transfers are morally identical. Of course Christians have a moral obligation to minister to the poor, for what we do to the least of Christ's brethren we do to Christ Himself. Church leaders, however, have too often conflated Christian duty to help the poor with a supposed moral duty to support the trillion-dollar enterprise we call the welfare state.

Far from ameliorating poverty, many of these programs have the perverse effect of further subsidizing the initial conditions of eligibility, whether single motherhood, poverty, homelessness, or joblessness. Thus, they create and further the conditions they profess to cure. They foster a debilitating sense of dependence.

Religious traditions have always stressed the centrality of the family, yet there is no more effective an opponent of marriage and the family than a government bureaucracy that provides financial incentives against getting married and establishing a family. In many cases, the welfare state has decreased the sense of marital obligation and eroded the values that sustain families. When the state provides for the old and the young, it takes away moral responsibilities from people in the prime of their lives to administer charity to family. Without such responsibilities, people can too easily fall into consumerism, precisely the condition anti-capitalists profess to oppose.

When religious people think about poverty, it is too often in materialist terms. Yet the problem of poverty is not so much one of poor people getting material assistance. It is a problem of establishing human bonding. Marvin Olasky, in his challenging book *The Tragedy of American Compassion*, reminds us that compassion means to suffer with another.[23] Bureaucratize compassion, and it becomes simply giving to another, and that tends to create depersonalized dependence. What we need instead is a greater sense of bonding with those who are in need. In this way, we provide role models and incentives for those who want to find their way out of economic deprivation.

Some say that economic redistributionism is a matter of social justice, but if all social relations are based merely on a state-enforced vision of justice, the virtues of love and compassion lose their meaning. Charity is supposed to represent obedience to the dictates of conscience; its character changes when it disintegrates into simple obedience to government agencies.

There are other dangers that priests, rabbis, and ministers face in promoting the government as the resource of first resort. They reduce the incentive of people in the pews to become personally involved in needed projects. People in the pews might think: "Why do I need to get involved in helping people who are suffering, feeding the poor, or caring for my neighbor?"

There is nothing wrong with churches involving themselves in political activities, and, indeed, sometimes religious people must enter political battles out of moral obligation. But the church's mission should not be relegated to the role of lobbyist; that deprives the church of the spiritual nourishment that comes with actually performing acts of mercy. Political activity also implies a moral obligation to be informed about economics and the consequences of certain kinds of statist policies.

We must wisely consider the most appropriate ways in which our obligations to the poor are carried out. From the earliest Christian reflection on aid to those in need, this obligation was never an unconditional one. While Saint Paul encouraged the early Christian community to remember those in need, he was also prudent and realistic. "If a man does not work," he said, "neither let him eat."[24] Christianity insists on love as a fundamental virtue, but it never advanced the notion that we must subsidize those who can be, but refuse to be, responsible for their own lives.

The modern welfare state is simply incapable of making the kinds of distinctions that Saint Paul insists are necessary in administering charity. The centralized state, by its nature, administers programs on the assumption that people are identical and can be shaped according to an inflexible central plan. Private charity may not be able to do all the work that is necessary, but where and when it is allowed to work, it does a better job than the public sector. It is also based on the principle of voluntary action as opposed to state coercion, which gives it a morally superior status.

In *Centesimus Annus*, Pope John Paul II expressed reservations about the welfare state, especially the modern one which tries to provide cradle-to-grave public support. "Malfunctions and defects in the Social Assistance State are the result of an inadequate understanding of the tasks proper to the State," he writes. The alternative principle he advances is the notion of subsidiarity: "a community of a higher order should not interfere in the internal life of a community of a lower order, depriving the latter of its functions."[25]

Americans are mostly unfamiliar with the term, much less the substance of, the principle of subsidiarity. Europeans know it well, but in the context of the debate surrounding the power of the European Union. In that debate, the subsidiarity principle is supposed to serve as public reassurance that the new European government in Brussels will not interfere in the affairs of other states when it is not necessary. (It has taken on special meaning with regard to central banking and monetary policy.)

The downside of viewing the term in this context is the implication that subsidiarity is about relations between different levels of government. This is far from the case. It is instead about relations between all spheres of life. The first units in society are individuals. They own property, and they form families. These families form communities, and communities group together in localities. The circles of authority expand to the state, the region, and the nation. Each circle has its own form of government.

The subsidiarity principle tells us that lower orders ought to perform social functions when they can. Only when failure is evident and it has been thoroughly established that shifting to higher orders would result in an actual improvement should functions undergo a transfer. The modern central state has assumed responsibilities not only when it cannot undertake them in a better fashion than lower orders, but also when the failures of lower orders are not even evident.

The principle is thus much more widely applicable than the debate over subsidiarity in Europe suggests. The issue is not which government we should trust to take care of us; it points to a mandate for decentralizing economic and political functions from the center to the local and individual levels. Here are the principles:

- Property owners should be the producers of first resort.
- Families are the primary government.
- Local politics is apt to be more consistent with community concerns than are distant bureaucracies.

This is the way subsidiarity works itself out in a social and normative sense.

What does the principle of subsidiarity imply that we should do about the poor? "It would appear," the Pope argues in *Centesimus Annus*, "that needs are best understood and satisfied by people who are closest to them and who act as neighbors to those in need."[26] This matches our daily experience. If a family member is in trouble, the family has the first responsibility to help. The family member also wants to help and knows best how to help. The same is true of the relevant community and locality. People throw themselves most fully into projects closest to home, where they can monitor the way resources are used and even view the results.

We have learned that government employees do not have the incentive or knowledge to deal with problems of poverty all over vast masses of land and population. It is absurd for the central government to have presumed to undertake such a job. It is as implausible as socialism itself, under which government mandated five-year production plans and fixed every price. And the experiences and lessons that surround the history of socialism are very similar to the ones the welfare state is teaching us today. No one group of planners, no matter how wise and sensitive to human needs they may be, can see the deepest needs of the human soul, which are so frequently at the root of economic problems.

Central planning boards, whether at the Politburo or the various ministries of modern Western governments, rarely improve society and most often interfere with the public's ability to uncover relevant knowledge about local circumstances to address them efficiently. If they were partially deprived of the power and funds to administer poverty programs, resources and capital would be freed to solve local problems locally.

The time has come for religious leaders to abandon the orthodoxy of more and more government programs. Instead of erecting more bureaucracies, they should take back from the state their rightful positions as the primary ministers of the welfare of the poor.

THE ETHICS OF CAPITALISM

Far from having achieved victory, the economic order of liberty is in a precarious position. Its utility has been demonstrated time and again, and very few responsible intellectuals or clergymen are willing publicly to support concrete and radical alternatives to the market economy. If democratic capitalism has won the day, so be it. The big battles over ideology may be over, though recent policy proposals that centralize and increase government control suggest that the question is not entirely settled in our politics. This much we can know: The big battles over morality in public life have just begun.

It is, moreover, entirely evident that in this debate on the morality of economic systems, the advocates of the market economy do not yet have the upper hand. Too often, economists refuse to speak in normative terms, and they often act as if they should not. Those who are charged with pronouncing on morality in public life do not have strong sympathies with the ethic of capitalism—if they are sympathetic to it at all. Most people are content to settle with a system that seems to reconcile the "ethics" of socialism with the productivity of capitalism.

Yet political economy and ethics should be and must be reconciled. If we continue to promote an "ethics" of socialism, it will eventually endanger institutions that support the productive capacity of capitalism. It is not a trivial fact that every step away from the free market is a step away from voluntarism and that every step toward interventionism is a step away from liberty. It speaks to the essence of what it means to act virtuously.

A moral argument for economic liberty should not shrink from its own logical implications, however politically unfashionable. An imperative against theft and in favor of the security of private property must also suggest caution about taxes above the minimal level necessary for the rule of law. Freedom of contract must include the freedom not to contract. Freedom of association must include the freedom not to associate. Toleration of individual differences must include tolerances for the inequality in wealth that will be the unavoidable result. And a morality that favors virtue in the context of liberty must allow room for personal moral failure and an understanding of the difference between vice and crime.

It is sometimes said that no one dreams of capitalism. This too must change. Rightly understood, capitalism is simply the name for the economic component of the natural order of liberty. It means expansive ownership of property, fair and equal rules for all, economic security through prosperity, strict adherence to the boundaries of ownership, opportunity for charity, wise resource use, creativity, growth, development, prosperity, abundance. Most of all, it means the economic application of the principle that every human person has dignity and should have that dignity respected. It is a dream worthy of our spiritual imaginations.

NOTES

1. Francis Fukuyama, *The End of History and the Last Man* (New York: Free Press, 1992).
2. Samuel Gregg, "Economic Liberalism and Its Discontents," *The Public Discourse*, November 13, 2009, at *http://www.thepublicdiscourse.com/2009/11/1013.*
3. Wilhelm Roepke, *The Humane Economy* (South Bend, Ind: Gateway, 1960).
4. Milton Friedman, *Capitalism and Freedom* (Chicago: University of Chicago Press, 1962).
5. F. A. Hayek, "The Moral Element in Free Enterprise," in *The Spiritual and Moral Significance of Free Exercise* (New York: National Association of Manufacturers, 1961), 26–27.
6. Lord John Acton, "The History of Freedom in Antiquity," in J. Rufus Fears, ed., *Selected Writings of Lord Acton* (Indianapolis, Ind.: Liberty Fund, 2002), 1:22.
7. Robert Nisbet, *The Quest for Community: A Study in the Ethics and Order of Freedom* (San Francisco: ICS Press, 1990), xxvi.
8. George Gilder, *Spirit of Enterprise* (New York: Simon and Schuster, 1984).
9. Alexander Ruestow, *Freedom and Domination* (Princeton, N.J.: Princeton University Press, 1980), 250.
10. *Summa Theologica*, I–II, q. 90, art. 2.
11. *Summa*, I–II, q. 95, art. 2.
12. See Alejandro Chaufen, *Christians for Freedom: Late Scholastic Economics* (San Francisco: Ignatius Press, 1986).
13. Joseph Schumpeter, *History of Economic Analysis* (New York: Oxford University Press, 1954), 97.

14. Chaufen, *Christians for Freedom.*

15. *Encyclical Letter Centesimus Annus of the Supreme Pontiff John Paul II on the Hundredth Anniversary of Rerum Novarum*, 1991, para. 32.

16. *Centesimus Annus*, para. 34.

17. *Centesimus Annus*, para. 35.

18. *Centesimus Annus*, para. 42.

19. John Courtney Murray, "Contemporary Orientation of Catholic Thought on Church and State in the Light of History," *Theological Studies*, Vol. X (June 1949), 181.

20. Documents of the Second Vatican Council, *Declaration on Religious Freedom* (*Dignitatis Humanae*), para. 1.

21. See Joseph Schumpeter, *The Theory of Economic Development* (Cambridge, Mass.: Harvard University Press, 1949).

22. Etienne Gilson, "L'intelligence au service du Christ-Roi," in *Christianisme et Philosophie* (Paris, 1936), 155–156.

23. Marvin Olasky, *The Tragedy of American Compassion* (Washington, D.C.: Regnery Gateway, 1992).

24. 2 Thessalonians 3:10.

25. *Centesimus Annus*, para. 48.

26. *Centesimus Annus,* para. 48.

2

Restoring Sound Economic Thinking

What Natural Law Taught Us

John D. Mueller

The logical and mathematical structures of scholastic, classical, and neoclassical economics differ fundamentally. The first part of this chapter, "a brief, structural history of economics," summarizes the differences in economic theory and their underlying worldviews. It will show that the most important element of scholastic economics—final distribution (comprising Augustine's theory of personal distribution and Aristotle's theory of distributive justice)—has been missing from economic theory since its deliberate omission by Adam Smith. Unlike the scholastic theory of utility, which Smith also dropped, final distribution has not yet been generally readopted, though it is necessary to solve several major problems with today's neoclassical economics. In short, rediscovering economic concepts in Aristotle, Augustine, and Aquinas will help us restore sound economic thinking in the aftermath of this most recent economic crisis.

The second part of the chapter illustrates one such problem that can be solved by the concept of final distribution, by showing that empirical data from the American National Election Studies (ANES) contradict the predictions of the neoclassical "theory of public choice" but confirm those of the neoscholastic "theory of American public choice." In coming decades, neoscholastic economists building on the original scholastic outline will supersede neoclassical economists for the same reason the latter supplanted classical economists starting the in 1870s: Having one more indispensable explanatory element, their theory is more comprehensive and empirically more accurate.[1]

A BRIEF STRUCTURAL HISTORY OF ECONOMICS

Economic theory has been taught continuously at the highest university level since the mid-thirteenth century, when it was first fully integrated within the scholastic natural law. Yet we must begin with two simple but widely overlooked facts: First, the logical and mathematical structures of scholastic, classical, and neoclassical economics differ fundamentally. Second, few economists today are aware of these differences, in large measure because American university economics departments, led by the University of Chicago in 1972, abolished the requirement that students of economics master its history before being granted a degree.[2] This requires a brief structural history of economics, as shown in Table 2.1.

What is economics *about*? Jesus once noted (as an astute empirical observation, not divine revelation) that since the days of Noah and Lot people have been doing, and until the end of the world presumably will be doing, four kinds of things. He gave these examples: "planting and building," "buying and selling," "marrying and being given in marriage," and "eating and drinking" (Luke 18:27–28). In other words, we humans *produce, exchange, give,* and *use* (or *consume*) our human and nonhuman goods.

That's the usual order in our action. But as Augustine first explained, the logical order is different in our planning. First we choose *For Whom* we intend to provide; next *What* to provide as means for those persons.[3] Finally, as Aquinas would later elaborate, we choose *How* to provide the chosen means, as described by Aristotle's theories of production (always) and exchange (almost always). Thus *economics is essentially a theory of providence*: it describes how we provide for ourselves and the other persons we love, using scarce means that have alternate uses.

Scholastic "AAA"[4] economics (c. 1250–1776) began when Thomas Aquinas first integrated the four elements of production, exchange, distribution, and consumption, all drawn from Aristotle and Augustine, into an outline of personal, domestic, and political economy, both positive and normative, within the natural law.[5]

POSITIVE SCHOLASTIC THEORY

To explain the Two Great Commandments,[6] Augustine had started from Aristotle's definition of love—*willing some good to some person*[7]—but drew an implication that Aristotle had not: every *person* always acts for the sake of some *person(s)*. For example, when I say, "I love vanilla ice cream," I really mean that I *love myself* and *use* (consume) vanilla ice cream (in preference,

Table 2.1. The Origins and Historical Structure of Economic Theory

Common-sense meaning	*Gifts (or Crimes) & Distributive Justice*	*Consumption*	*Production*	*Justice in Exchange*
Generic meaning	1. Preference for persons as ends	2. Preference for scarce means	3. Actualization of means: a.	4. Actualization of means: b.
Element of Economic Theory	Final Distribution (social unit described)	Utility (type)	Production (factors assumed to vary)	Equilibrium (type)
Source	Augustine, *On Christian Doctrine* I, 26 (person); Aristotle, *Ethics* V, 3 (household, business, government)	Augustine, *City of God* XI, 16 (ordinal: 1st, 2nd, 3rd, etc.)	Aristotle, *Politics* 1, 4 (none)	Aristotle, *Ethics* V, 5 (partial)
Period				
Scholastic (1250–1776)	Yes (all: personal, domestic, & political)	Yes (ordinal)	Yes (none)	Yes (partial)
Classical (1776–1871)	No	No	Yes (tangible human)	Yes (partial)
Neoclassical (1871–c. 2000)	No	Yes	Yes	Mixed
School: *British*	"	" (cardinal: 1, 2, 3, etc.)	" (tangible nonhuman)	Yes (partial)
Austrian	"	" (ordinal)	" (" ")	No (Mises)
Walrasian	"	" (ordinal)	" (" ")	Yes (general)
Chicago (1920–1960: like British) (1960–)	"	" (cardinal)	(All: tangible & intangible human & nonhuman)	Yes (partial)
Neo-Thomist (Pesch: 1900–)	Mixed (domestic & political only)	Yes (cardinal)	Yes (tangible human & nonhuman)	Yes (partial)
Neoscholastic (c. 2000–)	Yes (all)	Yes (ordinal)	Yes (all)	Yes (general)

Source: John D. Mueller, *Redeeming Economics: Rediscovering the Missing Element* (ISI Books, 2010), Table 5-1, pg. 130

say, to strawberry ice cream or Brussels sprouts) to express that love. Augustine also introduced the important distinction between "private" goods like bread, which inherently only one person at a time can consume, and "public" goods (like a performance in an ancient amphitheater, a modern radio or television broadcast, national defense, or enforcement of justice) which (at least within certain limits) many people can simultaneously enjoy because they are not "diminished by being shared."[8]

In other words, Augustine's crucial insight is that we humans always act on two scales of preference—one for persons as ends and the other for other things as means: personal love and utility, respectively. Moreover, we express our preferences for persons with two kinds of external acts. Since man is a social creature, Augustine noted, "human society is knit together by transactions of giving and receiving."[9] But these outwardly similar transactions may be of two essentially different kinds, he added: "sale or gift."[10] Generally speaking, we *give* our wealth without compensation to people we particularly love,[11] and *sell* it to people we don't, in order to provide for those we do love.[12] Since it's always possible to avoid depriving others of their own goods, this is the bare minimum of love expressed as *benevolence* or goodwill and the measure of what Aristotle called *justice in exchange*.[13] But our positive self-love is expressed by the *utility* of the goods we provide ourselves, and our positive love of others with *beneficence*: gifts. Hate or *malevolence* is expressed by the opposite of a gift: *maleficence* or crime.

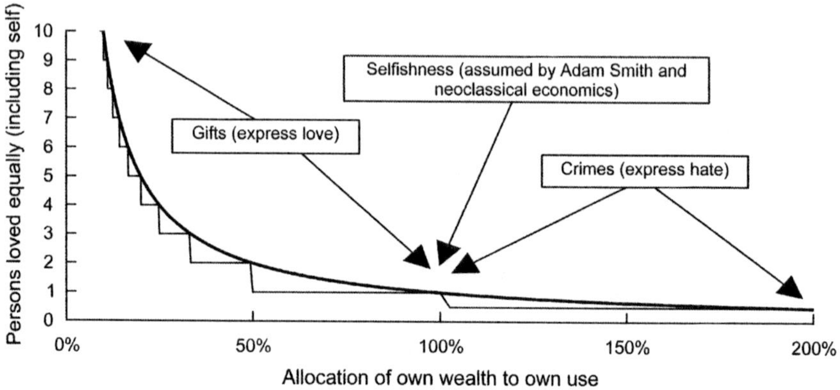

Figure 2.1.

The social analog to personal gifts is what Aristotle called *distributive justice,*[14] which amounts to a collective gift: it is the formula social communities like a family or nation under a single government necessarily use to distribute their common (jointly owned) goods. Both are a kind of "transfer payment"; both are determined by a geometric proportion that matches distributive shares with the relative significance of persons sharing in the distribution; and both are practically limited by the fact of scarcity. That is "positive" scholastic economics in a nutshell: describing *what is*, not necessarily what ought to be.

"NORMATIVE" SCHOLASTIC THEORY

We naturally love ourselves, Augustine pointed out. All other moral rules are derived from the Two Great Commandments because these measure the degree to which our love is "ordinate": rightly ordered.[15] If a good were sufficiently abundant we could and should share it equally with everyone else. But with such goods as time and money, which are "diminished by being shared"[16] (i.e., scarce), this is impossible. Therefore "loving your neighbor *as yourself*" can't always mean *equally with* yourself: "Since you cannot do good to all," Augustine concluded, "you are to pay special regard to those who, by the accidents of time, place, or circumstances, are brought into closer connection with you."[17]

Aquinas extended Augustine's insight to Aristotle's corresponding analysis of all communities: Common goods are necessary to the existence of both families and governments. But the fact of scarcity requires that most common goods be owned by families, not governments, because of the two advantages noted by Aristotle (greater social peace and productivity) and the third added by Aquinas (greater order).[18]

Political distributive justice and/or justice in exchange are violated by what Aristotle described as, and James Madison later termed, "faction." Each faction has an ideology, which Hannah Arendt succinctly defined as a worldview that requires its adherents to create a "fictitious world" that distorts reality to the advantage of its members.[19] For example, Karl Marx's collectivist ideology collapsed all justice to distributive justice, as if all goods were both common and political; Smith's individualist ideology collapsed justice to justice in exchange, as if all goods were personal, private, and never given or shared.

The scholastic economic system is comprehensive, logically complete, mathematical, and empirically verifiable. It was taught at the highest university level for more than five centuries by every major Catholic and (after the Reformation) Protestant economic thinker—notably Lutheran Samuel von Pufendorf, whose work was used by Adam Smith's own teacher to teach Smith economics and was also highly recommended by Alexander Hamilton.[20]

CLASSICAL ECONOMICS (1776–1871)

Classical economics began when Adam Smith cut the four elements to two, trying to explain specialized production (which he called "division of labor") by production and exchange alone. Smith and his classical followers undoubtedly advanced those two elements. But Smith also dropped Augustine's theory of utility (which describes consumption) and replaced Augustine's theory of personal distribution (gifts and their opposite, crimes) and Aristotle's theory of domestic and political distributive justice with the (often false) assumption that every individual intends only his own gain.[21]

Three keys are necessary to understanding Smith's revision of scholastic economics: his moral Newtonianism, his philosophical Stoicism, and his rhetorical Sophistry. First, Smith wanted to do for moral philosophy what he believed Isaac Newton had done for natural science: to reduce all its phenomena to a single familiar principle, like gravity. He was always aiming, as he put it in a Glasgow University lecture, "to see the phenomena which we reckoned the most unaccountable all deduced from some principle (commonly a well-known one) and all united in one chain."[22] Second, having rejected his Christian baptism well before writing the *Wealth of Nations,* Smith was a wholehearted convert to Stoic philosophy—and Stoics are pantheists.[23] Third, Smith's view of rhetoric resembled that of the Sophists who opposed Aristotle by placing a higher value on whether a statement is useful to the speaker than whether it is an accurate description of reality.[24]

Smith's moral Newtonianism induced him to oversimplify the scholastic economic theory he had inherited. Just as in his earlier *Theory of Moral Sentiments* he had tried to reduce all morality to the single principle of "sympathy," Smith attempted in the *Wealth of Nations* to explain all economic behavior by the single principle of "labor." (He never reconciled these two all-explaining principles.) Smith's philosophical Stoicism accounts for his rejections of some elements of the scholastic outline of economics and his retention of others.[25] In the *Theory of Moral Sentiments,* Smith rejected the scholastic theories of final distribution and utility on the grounds that they presume rational, purposive behavior.[26] In Smith's view—and here the pantheism becomes apparent—decisions about ends and means, rather than being decided *by* human beings, are ultimately *dictated to* them by an inscrutable Stoic version of providence, which engages the vast majority of humankind in a "deception" about the "real satisfaction" afforded by economic goods.[27] Smith's rhetorical Sophistry accounts for his one-sided presentation. For example, in the *Wealth of Nations*, he dismisses the scholastic theory of utility with his "paradox of value"—though he had easily solved it for his students at the University of Glasgow by applying the same theory of utility.[28]

NEOCLASSICAL ECONOMICS (1872–C. 2000)

Neoclassical economics began when three economists dissatisfied with the practical failure of Smith's classical outline (W. S. Jevons in England,[29] Carl Menger in Austria,[30] and Leon Walras in Switzerland[31]) independently but almost simultaneously reinvented Augustine's theory of utility, starting its reintegration with the theories of production and exchange.[32] They abandoned Smith's revised outline mostly for three related reasons: without the theory of utility classical economists were unable to answer some important questions (for example, why goods that can't be reproduced with labor have value); made predictions about others that turned out to be spectacularly wrong (notably the "iron law of wages," which predicted that rising population would prevent rising living standards); and directly fostered Karl Marx's disastrously erroneous economic analysis. Though schools of neoclassical economics have since multiplied, all are derived from these three.

NEOSCHOLASTIC ECONOMICS (C. 2000–)

In *Redeeming Economics: Rediscovering the Missing Element,* I predict that Neoscholastic economics will revolutionize economics once again in coming decades by replacing its lost cornerstone, the theory of distribution: simply because, as with the theory of utility, including the element does a far better job of empirical description.

Thus Adam Smith's chief significance lay not in what he *added to*, but rather *subtracted from* economics. As Schumpeter (1954) demonstrated, "The fact is that the *Wealth of Nations* does not contain a single *analytic* idea, principle or method that was entirely new in 1776."[33] The facts about the development of economics seem to indicate that a re-evaluation is overdue and quite likely for both Augustine and Adam Smith, particularly since Smith essentially "de-Augustinized" economic theory to its detriment. Though far from exhaustive, this brief structural history of economics explains why scholastic economics contained four, classical only two, and neoclassical economics three basic elements: Neoclassical economists restored one element dropped by Smith, utility, but not the other, final distribution. (The differences in economic theory are summarized earlier in this chapter, in Table 2.1. A more detailed technical comparison of the (neo-) scholastic, classical, and neoclassical models is presented in *Redeeming Economics*.)

However, these three approaches to economic theory also express three distinct worldviews, the confrontation of which goes back nearly two millennia. When the Apostle Paul preached in the marketplace of Athens, he prefaced the Gospel with a biblically orthodox adaptation of Greco-Roman natural law. The evangelist Luke tells us that "some Epicurean and Stoic philosophers argued with him" (Acts 17:18). The same dispute has continued among scholastic, classical, neoclassical, and now neoscholastic economists.

In (neo-) scholastic natural law, economics is a theory of rational providence, describing how we rational, matrimonial, and political animals choose both persons as "ends" (expressed by our personal and collective gifts) and the scarce means used (consumed) by or for those persons, which we make real through production and exchange. By dropping both distribution (the choice of persons as ends) and consumption (the choice of other things as means), Smith expressed the Stoic pantheism that viewed the universe "to be itself a Divinity, an Animal"[34] with God as its immanent soul, so that sentimental humans choose neither ends nor means rationally; instead, "every individual . . . intends only his own gain . . . and is led by an invisible hand to promote an end which was no part of his intention."[35] By restoring utility (the choice of means) but not final distribution (the choice of persons as ends), neoclassical economics expressed the Epicurean materialism that claims humans somehow evolved as merely clever animals, highly adept at calculating means but having no choice other than self-gratification, since "reason is, and ought only to be, the slave of the passions," as Hume put it.[36]

The notion that Adam Smith invented or is somehow indispensable to understanding economics might be called "Smythology" (with two y's; Smithology as mythology). By far the most influential piece of Smythology was Milton Friedman's argument linking Adam Smith's philosophy with the meaning of the American Declaration of Independence: "The story of the United States is the story of an economic miracle and a political miracle that was made possible by the translation into practice of two sets of ideas—both, by a curious coincidence published in the same year, 1776." According to Friedman, "the fundamental principles of our system [are] both the economic principles of Adam Smith . . . and the political principles expressed by Thomas Jefferson."[37]

Like many others I found Friedman's argument persuasive, and incorporated it for many years into my own worldview. But the "choice of 1776" was actually a divergence, not a convergence, and of three, not two worldviews. The third symbolically significant event of 1776 was the death of Smith's dear friend, the Epicurean skeptic David Hume.

THE THEORY OF AMERICAN PUBLIC CHOICE

The neoscholastic model is a powerful tool of analysis at every level: personal, domestic, and political. Several promising applications are suggested in *Redeeming Economics*. For example, strong evidence for the existence of Augustine's "distribution function" is evident in the strong tradeoff between economic fatherhood and the homicide rate. This relationship incidentally overturns Steven D. Levitt's famous assertion that legalizing abortion must have reduced crime rates 16–20 years later. Employing the distribution function also makes it possible to correct serious gaps in the neoclassical theories of fertility and the family.

The theme of the present volume is "rediscovering political economy." The neoscholastic approach offers explanations for the sharp commodity-led price inflation of 2003–2008 and the recession of 2008–2009. However, the last part of this chapter will focus instead on the neoscholastic "theory of American public choice," because it provides strong empirical evidence for the neoscholastic as opposed to the neoclassical approach to political economy. Without the theory of final distribution, neither classical nor neoclassical economics can fully describe *any* state of equilibrium. The necessity of describing all four facets of any economic event with at most three explanatory equations has condemned classical and neoclassical economists frequently to resort to circular logic and/or empirically false assumptions.

Implicit throughout the history of American political economy is what might be called the "theory of American public choice." This theory, originated *by* the American Founders, has three basic premises: as James Madison put them, first, that "[j]ustice is the end of government";[38] second, that "as a man is said to have a right to his property, he may be equally said to have a property in his rights";[39] and third, that "the most common and durable source of factions, has been the various and unequal distribution of property."[40] Meanwhile, Hamilton distinguished true public goods, which benefit all citizens equally, from "quasi-public goods," which benefit many but not all citizens.[41] Combining Madison's theory of faction with Hamilton's distinction between public goods and quasi-public goods, the corresponding theory of American political distributive justice implies that true public goods should be financed by equiproportional taxation of income from all sources of property, but quasi-public goods should be financed by taxation on the class of citizens that benefits.

Among the competing theories of public choice, the leading libertarian neoclassical version holds (as Anthony Downs put it): first, that rather than justice, "the goal of government is attaining the income, power, and prestige that go with office";[42] second, that partisan voting is essentially unrelated to voters' economic interests (which also seems to obviate the second premise of the theory of American public choice).[43] I will show with empirical tests that only the neoscholastic version fully explains certain fascinating questions of American political life, including why there are two major American parties, who identifies with them, and how American voters' views of political distributive justice are reflected in the federal budget.

The differences in worldview among the scholastic natural law, Stoic pantheism, and Epicurean materialism are *not* matters about which reasonable people can disagree, because those differences concern precisely whether (and to what degree) humans are rational. In the same way, the corresponding differences among the scholastic, classical, and neoclassical economic theories cannot be settled within either classical or neoclassical economic theory, because their logical incompleteness often renders both unfalsifiable. Yet the differences can be settled empirically to any reasonable person's satisfaction by applying the neoscholastic economic theory, because it is both logically complete and empirically verifiable.

APPLYING THE THEORY OF AMERICAN PUBLIC CHOICE

In the realm of political economy, the American National Election Studies (ANES) are reasonably well suited to test the alternative theories, since they have surveyed American voters' economic and demographic characteristics, the issues they consider most important in national elections, and their national voting back as far as 1948 or 1952, depending on the question.[44] Also, the survey ranks voters' characteristics such as family income according to percentiles derived from a normal curve, according to which just over two-thirds of any population should fall within one standard deviation above or below the mean.

Because the libertarian theory of public choice presumes that voters' issue concerns are essentially identical apart from random variation, it treats voters' concerns as essentially random, and therefore argues that these interests should be "peaked"—that is, clumped—around the mean. But if they are not random, voters' interests should at least clump around *some* pronounced maximum or minimum, without which, according to the libertarian theory, no stability of government is possible.

The theory of American public choice, which is intuitively grounded in neoscholastic insights, distinguishes among public goods properly so called, which concern everyone about equally regardless of income or party affiliation; and quasi-public goods, about which voters' interests should vary systematically, particularly according to the allocation of their family income between labor and property compensation. Moreover, those objectively grounded differences in voters' issue concerns should explain the continuity in partisan ideologies under the American federal system, because the fact that each party needs a majority to win the White House or either house of

Congress will force the parties to adjust the positions of their dominant faction in order to win.

If we begin with the single issue that voters identify as most important in each election, looking cumulatively over the whole period for which data are available, we find that voters' issue concerns can be categorized rather neatly under the categories suggested by the theory of American public choice. First, there are public goods like national defense and domestic public order, for which concern is nearly identical regardless of family income. And second, there are quasi-public goods of which the appeal varies systematically both by voter family income and by party affiliation. Concerning quasi-public goods, there is interest at each income level, but issues involving social welfare programs and labor are linearly and inversely related to income, while those involving such broadly economic issues as taxation, business, agriculture, consumer safety, and natural resources are linearly and positively related to voter family income.

Thus, American voters' concern for both domestic and international public goods behaves according to the theory of American public choice, which suggests that everyone will support public goods that benefit everyone in almost equal proportion, but in being almost absolutely flat rather than "peaked," it contradicts the prediction of the libertarian theory of public choice.

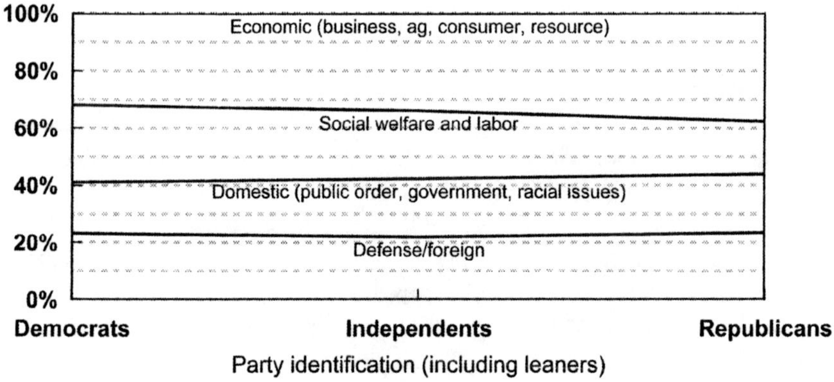

Figure 2.2.

When we range voters according to their identification with political parties rather than family income, a similar pattern is revealed. The interest of Democrats, Republicans, and Independents in both domestic and international public goods is nearly identical regardless of family income, while Democrats are more interested in quasi-public goods involving social welfare and labor issues, and Republicans more interested in all other quasi-public goods, with Independents in between. Yet voters at every income level and of every political party affiliation are interested in all of these goods, and perhaps surprisingly, voters' interests appear to differ somewhat more by income level than by partisan self-identification. This suggests that rather than viewing each voter as having a single dominant interest, all voters are best viewed as sharing the same interests to about the same degree for public goods, but for quasi-public goods in degrees that differ systematically with the level and source of their family income.

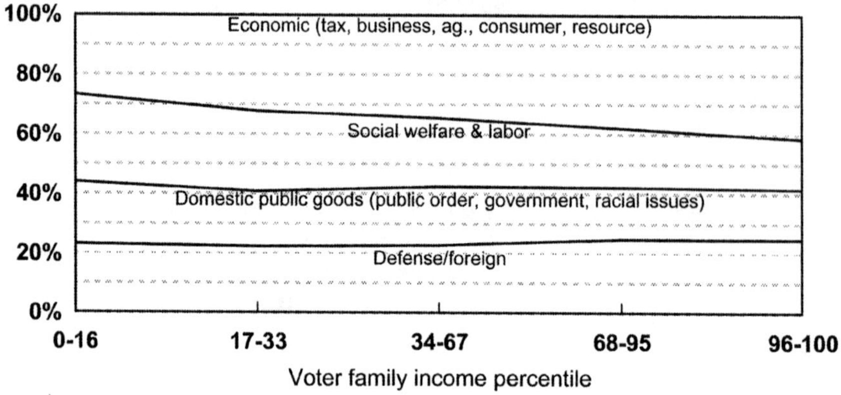

Figure 2.3.

While casting serious doubt on the claims of the libertarian neoclassical theory of public choice, particularly its presuppositions about the supposed randomness of voters' views, and while supporting one feature of the neoscholastic theory of American public choice—its distinction between public goods and quasi-public goods—the evidence just presented is far from confirming the latter theory. For one thing, the neoscholastic version emphasizes not the relative *levels,* but the relative *sources* of family income, which the ANES data do not provide; for another, looking at all American voters' behavior cumulatively in postwar national elections ignores how voters' views and behavior change from election to election; and finally, it reveals no discernible influence of the presidency, let alone of individual presidential candidacies or administrations.

The first shortcoming can be remedied by combining the ANES data for voter family income with methods (described in the next section of this chapter) that trace all family income to its sources in labor and property compensation. The percentiles of income obviously stay the same even when absolute incomes change.[45] Combining the two confirms a hypothesis of James Madison's (which he derived from Aristotle): "Different interests necessarily exist in different classes of citizens,"[46] and "the most common and durable source of factions, has been the various and unequal distribution of property."[47] As Figure 2.4 indicates, the data confirm that the Democratic Party attracts voters whose income (before taxes and transfer payments) is disproportionately labor compensation—the return on their investment in "human capital." The Republican Party, on the other hand, attracts voters whose income is disproportionately property compensation—the return on investment in nonhuman capital. The family incomes of Independent voters, meanwhile, have been between those of Republican and Democratic voters.

The same figure indicates why, even though the dominant faction in each major party is constantly lobbying for preferential treatment—for labor compensation in the Democratic Party and for property compensation in the Republican Party—the failure of such policies to win voter approval has forced both parties' leaderships repeatedly back toward policies that treat labor and property income alike.

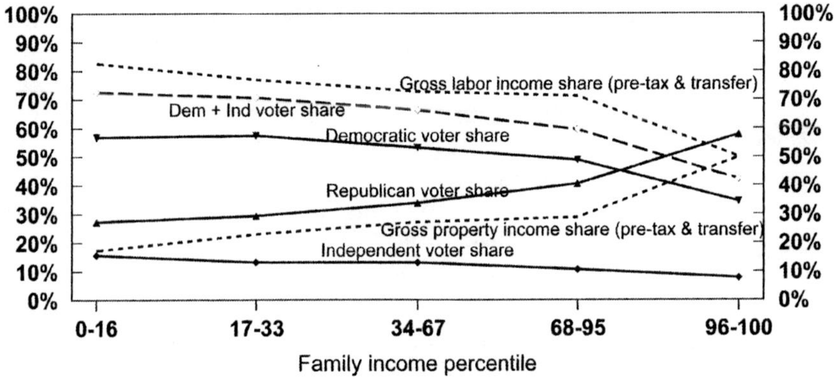

Figure 2.4.

As Figure 2.4 indicates, Democratic vs. Republican partisan self-identification parallels the shares of labor vs. property compensation in voter family income before taxes and transfer payments. Yet partisan economic programs do not result from a kind of osmosis. Instead, they are initiated primarily by candidates for president, since the holder of that office will be at the same time the nation's chief executive and (if an effective president) the undisputed leader of a major political party. The ANES data reflect the importance of this dual role if we view shifts in partisan allegiance over time and policies initiated by pivotal presidents. Pivotal presidential elections typically are won by small majorities or pluralities (e.g., Lincoln, Kennedy, Reagan), while successful first terms are rewarded by a step-change in voter partisan allegiance beginning with that president's reelection.

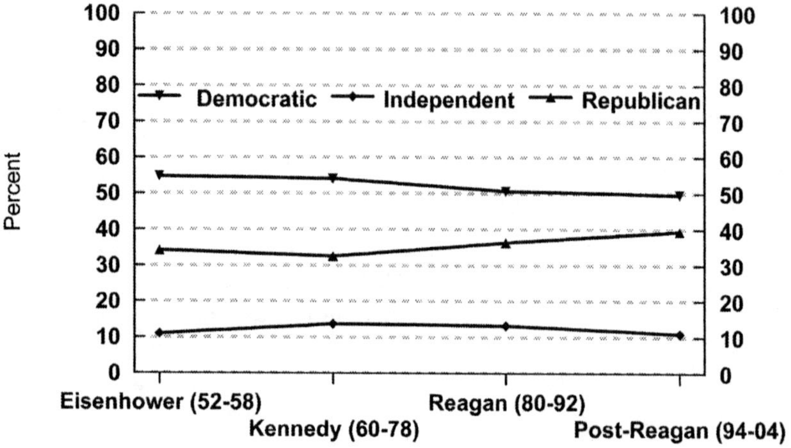

Figure 2.5.

The ANES data cover the Eisenhower, Kennedy-Johnson, and Reagan eras. Eisenhower was a popular Republican president at a time when nearly 55 percent of all American voters identified themselves as Democrats and only 34 percent as Republicans. After Kennedy's 1960 election, Democrats lost about 1 percentage point and Republicans about 2 percentage points, while the ranks of Independents grew nearly 3 percentage points. Reagan's policies caused over 3 percent of voters to stop identifying themselves as Democrats and 4 percent to identify themselves as Republicans, while the share of Independents fell slightly. Under Bill Clinton and George W. Bush, Democratic Party self-identification fell another 1 percent and Republican self-identification rose 3 percent, while Independents fell 2 percent.[48]

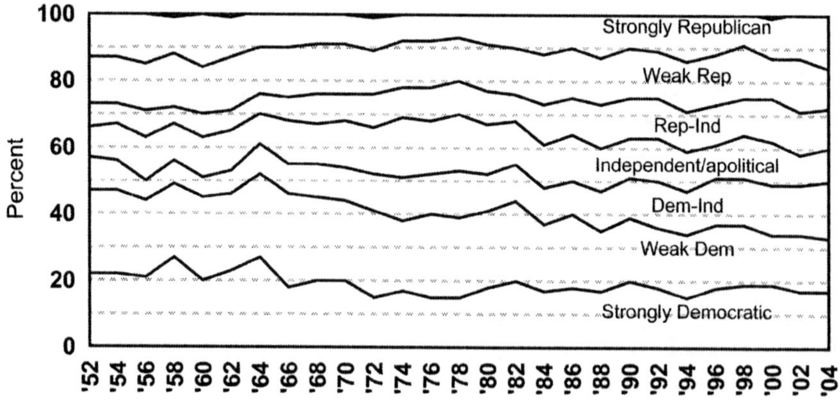

Figure 2.6.

Thus, at the start of the twenty-first century about 50 percent of American voters identified themselves as Democrats, about 40 percent as Republicans, and about 10 percent as Independents, and the latter identified themselves slightly more with Democratic than Republican positions on economic issues (while being more secular than either as measured by the rate of religious worship). Our empirical comparison therefore strongly rejects the predictions of the libertarian neoclassical theory of public choice (that voters' interests should vary randomly and be unrelated to partisan ideology). At the same time, it confirms three important hypotheses of the theory of American public choice: first, that voters' interests and opinions vary systematically with the shares of labor and property compensation in family income; second, that voters respond positively to economic policies that treat labor and property income equally, notwithstanding the extreme reluctance of the dominant factions in both the Democratic and Republican parties to offer such policies; and finally, that the president, as the only official elected by a national majority of voters, plays a decisive role in the delicate balance of American political power, and presidents have achieved greatest political success by proposing and enacting such policies.

CONCLUSION

As historian of economics Henry William Spiegel noted of the "marginal revolution" that ended classical and launched neoclassical economics in the 1870s, "Outsiders ranked prominently among the pioneers of marginal analysis because its discovery required a perspective that the experts did not necessarily possess."[49] I don't underestimate the time or effort it will take. But I predict that in coming decades "neoscholastic" economists familiar with the natural law of Aristotle, Augustine, and Aquinas will similarly prevail because they are more orthodox—not in a religious but rather in the strict etymological sense of having *right opinion*: an economic theory both more complete and empirically accurate.

NOTES

1. Other than Viner (1978), few academic economists so far have recognized the systematic differences between classical, neoclassical, and neoscholastic economics. An important recent exception is Aguirre, 2006; see also Aguirre, 2004. Also deserving special mention for insights drawn from scholastic theory are Worland (1967), Chafuen (1986), Chafuen (1993), Morse (2001), Piedra (2004), and Yuengert (2004). Aguirre and Morse have begun the necessary rewriting of the neoclassical economic

theory of the family. Though similarly inspired by scholastic theory, Mueller (1996) was still formally neoclassical. Warning to theologians: "neoscholastic" has nearly opposite meanings in theology and economics. In 19th- and 20th-century theology it essentially meant equating Aquinas with Aristotle and removing Augustine's fundamental insight that all persons (human or divine) are motivated by love for some person(s), and all personal love is expressed with a gift. In 21st-century economics "neoscholastic" theory restores that insight to its central role.

2. This change culminated a long campaign that George J. Stigler had started in 1955. "In 1972, he [Stigler] successfully proposed that the history of thought requirement be dropped at Chicago. Most other economics departments later followed suit. . . . At the same meeting Stigler unsuccessfully proposed that the economic history requirement also be dropped." Leeson (1997), endnote 62. Leeson (1997) was subsequently incorporated into Leeson (2001). In his campaign for the change, Stigler rejected Aquinas' view that a scientist is defined by whether he understands his subject rather than having a degree. Stigler claimed instead that every science is continuously defined by a self-governing elite calling themselves scientists. From this sociological definition, Stigler said it was obvious that "one need not read in the history of economics—that is, past economics—to master present economics." Instead, "the young theorist . . . will assume . . . that all that is valid in earlier work is present—in purer and more elegant form—in the modern theory," and that "the history of the discipline is best left to those underendowed for fully professional work at the modern level." But as the text indicates, the young economist who assumed this would be underendowed for fully professional work because he wouldn't know his subject (Stigler, 1969, reprinted in Stigler, 1982, p. 107).

3. Among prominent modern economists, only Jacob Viner (1978) seems correctly to have identified Augustine's main technical contribution to economic theory, distinguishing separate scales of preference for persons (love and justice) and non-persons (utility), and both of these from the absolute metaphysical scale of being: Augustine deals "simultaneously with three scales of value, relating to order of nature, utility, and justice." Viner (1978), p. 55.

4. In his otherwise magisterial *History of Economics Analysis,* Schumpeter (1954) incorrectly wrote that Augustine "[n]ever went into economic problems" (p. 72) and Aquinas' economics was "strictly Aristotelian" (p. 93). As we'll see, Aquinas not only combined Aristotle's contributions with but also subordinated them to Augustine's, in both "positive" or descriptive and "normative" or prescriptive theory.

5. On Augustine's theory of personal distribution, see Augustine (396/397) and Augustine (395/396), cited below; Aristotle's social distribution (distributive justice): *Ethics* V,3 in Aristotle 1954 (350 BC); Augustine's theory of utility (consumption): *City of God* XI,16 in Augustine 1984 (413, 426, 427); Aristotle's theory of production of people and property: *Politics* I,4 in Aristotle 1962 (c. 350 BC); Aristotle's justice in exchange (equilibrium): Ethics V,5. In Aquinas, three of these four elements (the distribution function, the utility function, and the equilibrium conditions) are described (and the production function implied) in Aquinas 1993 (1271–1272). Personal distribution: Book V Lectures IV–IX, pp. 293–318; social distribution: p. 294; the "equilibrium conditions": pp. 294–296 and pp. 297–299; the "utility function" and analysis

of money: pp. 312–315. The production function is described in his commentary on Aristotle's *Politics* I, 1–3: Aquinas 2007 (1271–1272). The same analysis is also scattered throughout his *Summa theologiae* in Aquinas 1981 (1271–1272), especially in his commentary on the seventh commandment.

6. "You shall love . . . God with all your heart . . ." (Deut. 6:5) and "love your neighbor as yourself" (Lev. 19:18).

7. Aristotle (1932 [335–322 BC]), p. 2, p. 4, pp. 102–103.

8. Augustine (395–396), viii, 19, p. 146. Private goods are now sometimes called "rival" goods. The formulation "diminished by being shared" is from Augustine (396/397), I, 2.

9. Augustine (397), p. 398.

10. Augustine (395/396), p. 131.

11. To be more precise, love with both benevolence and beneficence.

12. Or rather, love only with benevolence but not beneficence.

13. Aristotle 1954 (c. 350 BC), V, v; pp. 117–122.

14. Aristotle 1954 (c. 350 BC), V, iii; pp. 112–114.

15. For example, the first three commandments of the Decalogue specify in greater detail how we should love God and the others how we should love of our neighbor; the rest of the natural law proceeds in turn from the Decalogue: all as a matter of reason, not just faith.

16. Augustine (396/397), I, 1.

17. Augustine (396/397), I, 28.

18. "If the responsibility for looking after property is distributed over many individuals, this will not lead to mutual recriminations; on the contrary, with every man busy with his own, there will be increased production all round," Aristotle (1962 [c. 350 BC]), p. 63. Aquinas listed these two and added a third, greater order resulting from the efficient use of specialized knowledge: peace ("a more peaceful state is ensured to man if each one is contented with his own"); productivity ("every man is more careful to procure what is for himself alone than that which is common to many or all"); order ("human affairs are conducted in more orderly fashion if each man is charged with taking care of some particular thing himself, whereas there would be confusion if everyone had to look after any one thing indeterminately"), Aquinas 1981 (1271–1272), II–II, Q66, A2.

19. Arendt (1967), p. 438.

20. According to Ross (1995, pp. 53–54), Adam Smith's teacher Francis Hutcheson taught him from an annotated edition of Pufendorf (1991 [1673]). As with Aquinas and the earlier scholastics, Pufendorf's Protestant version of the natural law contains all four basic elements of economic theory, organized according to personal, domestic, and political economy, and integrating prescriptive with descriptive theory by the Two Great Commandments. Personal distribution, Pufendorf, (1991 [1673]), pp. 64–67; social and political distribution, ibid., p. 32 and pp. 61–63; utility, ibid. pp. 94–96; production of and by human and nonhuman factors, ibid., pp. 84–89; society organized around family household, ibid., pp. 120–131; justice in exchange or equilibrium equating product values and factor compensation, ibid., p. 31 and pp. 94–95. The Two Great Commandments integrating description and

prescription, ibid., 11–12. The fact that Pufendorf was a Lutheran who wrote a critical history of the Catholic Church and that his theories were taught at the Calvinist University of Glasgow demonstrates that the scholastic outline of economic theory was broadly known and accepted. Pufendorf was widely read in the American colonies and recommended by Hamilton (1775). Hamilton penned two-thirds of the *Federalist* papers and as first Treasury Secretary would reject Smith's specific economic advice in the *Wealth of Nations* to the United States (Smith [1966 (1776)], Book II, Ch. 5); Hamilton (1791).

21. By adopting special assumptions that are often empirically false, Smith altered the meaning of "distribution" and conflated two elements recognized in the scholastic system as distinct: distribution proper and justice in exchange. Smith's elimination of Augustine's theory of personal distribution from the outline of economic theory is signaled in the passage that includes his famous declaration: "It is not from the benevolence of the butcher, the brewer, or the baker, that we expect our dinner, but from their regard to their own interest. We address ourselves not to their humanity but to their self-love, and never talk to them of our necessities but of their advantages." Smith (1966 [1776]) I, II: Vol. I, p. 17. In Augustine's theory, the main reason the brewer or baker doesn't serve his customers from *beneficence* is not exclusive self-love, but rather that each is faced with the fact of scarcity: If the baker shared his bread equally with every customer instead of charging for it, he would leave himself and his family too little to live on. Augustine's theory also explains why the brewer or baker shares with his family or friends but not with his business customers: he loves his customers only with benevolence (wishing good to them) but his family with both benevolence and beneficence (doing good to them). He sells his product to customers to earn the means to provide for himself and the rest of his family. Augustine's theory of personal distribution explains the essential difference between a gift and an exchange, and provides a measure of how far each of us actually is motivated by self-love and how much by love of neighbor. Smith fails to grapple with the fact that charitable behavior simply does not fit into a theory that reduces all human transactions to exchange and self-love. He never explains why the butcher's customers *never* expect their dinner from his *beneficence*, yet his friends sometimes and his children *always* do.

22. Smith, 1985 (1762). Lecture XXIVth. Accessed from http://oll.libertyfund.org/title/202/55538/918007 on 2009-11-30. Smith's audience understood that this was what he was attempting. As one former student summarized: "His Theory of Moral Sentiments founded on sympathy, a very ingenious attempt to account for the principal phenomena in the moral world from this one general principle, like that of gravity in the natural world." Smith (1982 [1759]), *TMS,* 3; accessed from http://oll.libertyfund.org/title/192 on 2009-08-21. See also Hetherington (1983). Though it was generally agreed that Smith's attempt was ingenious—it involved redefining sympathy from the usual sense of compassion to the ability to imagine and judge the feelings of others—it was not generally agreed that Smith had succeeded. "I conceive this meaning of the word Sympathy is altogether new & that if one had not a hypothes[is] to serve by it he would never have dreamed that it is Sympathy that makes us blush for the impudence and rudeness of another," remarked Thomas

Reid, who succeeded Smith as professor of moral philosophy at Glasgow: Stewart-Robertson and Norton (1984), 314.

23. As the editors of Smith's *Theory of Moral Sentiments* observe, "Stoic philosophy is the primary influence on Smith's ethical thought. It also fundamentally affects his economic theory"; "Stoicism never lost its hold over Smith's mind"; Smith (1976 [1759]), Raphael and Macfie, eds., op. cit., 5, 6. Accessed from http://oll.libertyfund.org/title/192/200027/3301053 on 2009-09-14. The sixth and final edition of *TMS* (1790) begins with an advertisement featuring its expanded explication of "that famous sect"; ibid., 3, http://www.econlib.org/library/Smith/smMS0.html; accessed 15 September 2009; the dismissive contrary opinion about Smith's Stoicism in Rothschild 1994 and Rothschild 2001 often ignores the plain sense of Smith's writing and contemporary accounts. This recalls the pattern Jacob Viner had noted among professors of economics and of ethics: "If perchance Adam Smith is a hero to them, they follow one of the other of two available methods of dealing with the religious ingredients of Smith's thought. They either put on mental blinders, which hide from their sight these aberrations in Smith's thought, or they treat them as merely traditional and in Smith's day fashionable ornaments to what is essentially naturalistic and rational analysis, especially where economic matters and the *Wealth of Nations* are in question," Viner (1972), pp. 55–85; pp. 81–82. By the time he wrote the *Wealth of Nations*, Smith was openly hostile to the Christian faith in which he had been baptized. In a letter dated August 14, 1776, which he caused to be published, Smith wrote: "Poor David Hume is dying very fast, but with great chearfulness and good humour and with more real resignation to the necessary course of things, than any Whining Christian ever dyed with pretended resignation to the Will of God," Smith (1976 1759]), op. cit., 19, accessed from http://oll.libertyfund.org/title/192/200035/3301093 on 2009-09-14. Moreover, Smith's opinion was recognized by those who knew him well. James Boswell recorded that "it was strange to me to find my old Professor in London, a professed infidel with a bag wig" (Ross, *The Life of Adam Smith,* op. cit., 251).

24. According to Aristotle, the purpose of rhetoric "is not to persuade, but to discover the available means of persuasion in a given case." Why? "In Rhetoric, as in Dialectic, we should be able to argue on either side of a question; not with a view to putting both sides into practice—we must not advocate evil—but in order that no aspect of the case may escape us, and that if our opponents make unfair use of the arguments, we may be able to refute them." Aristotle, *Rhetoric I, 1;* (1932 [335–322 BC]), 6. Smith taught his students: "The Rhetoricall [discourse] again endeavours by all means to perswade us; and for this purpose magnifies all the arguments on one side and diminishes or conceals those that might be brought on the side contrary to that which it is designed that we should favour," Smith (1985 [1762]), 62, accessed from http://oll.libertyfund.org/title/202/55525/917785 on 2009-11-30.

25. The history of the "Adam Smith problem"—scholars' puzzlement over how the same man could have written the *Theory of Moral Sentiments* and *Wealth of Nations*—is summarized in Peters-Fransen (2000).

26. *Theory of Moral Sentiments* IV.1; op. cit., 179–187; http://www.econlib.org/library/Smith/smMS4.html; accessed 15 September 2009.

27. *TMS*, IV.I.9, ibid., 183, http://www.econlib.org/library/Smith/smMS4.html#IV.I.9

28. Smith (1896 [1763]), p. 178; accessed from http://oll.libertyfund.org/title/196/55650/920617 on 2009-11-30.

29. W. S. Jevons, *The Theory of Political Economy* (London: MacMillan, 1871).

30. Carl Menger, *Principles of Economics* [Grundsätze der Volkswirthschaftslehre] (New York: New York University, 1871).

31. Walras, L. (1954 [1874]). *Elements of Pure Economics, or the Theory of Social Wealth* [Éléments d'économie politique pure, ou théorie de la richesse sociale]. (Tr.) Jaffe, W. Homewood, IL: Richard D. Irwin.

32. Jevons (1871); Menger (1871); Walras (1874).

33. Schumpeter (1954), p. 184.

34. Smith (1982 [1795]), para. 274.

35. Smith (1966 [1776]), Bk. IV, Ch. 2; Vol. 2, p. 35.

36. Hume (1740), II, III, iii.

37. Friedman, M., and Friedman, R. (1979), 1–2.

38. Madison, J. (1788), p. 271.

39. Madison, J. (1792).

40. Madison, J. (1787), p. 44.

41. Among true public goods, for which government is instituted, Hamilton, A. (1788) listed "the duties of superintending the national defence, and of securing the public peace against foreign or domestic violence" (p. 151), accessed from http://oll.libertyfund.org/title/788/108619/2274086 on 2009-09-11. In Hamilton (1788a) he added also what might be called "quasi-public goods," which benefit many but not all classes of citizens equally: "the encouragement of agriculture and manufactures." Such public and quasi-public goods "will comprehend almost all the objects of state expenditure," ibid., p. 165, accessed from http://oll.libertyfund.org/title/788/108625/2274123 on 2009-09-11.

42. Ibid., p. 150.

43. "In reality party ideologies probably stem originally from the interests of the persons who found each party," Downs conceded. "But, once a political party is created, it takes on an existence of its own and eventually becomes relatively independent of any particular interest group," Downs, (1957), 142n. Presumed randomness is reflected in the theory's prediction that voters' interests will follow the "normal" (i.e., bell-shaped) curve associated with random variations: according to Downs, "stable government in a two-party democracy requires a distribution of voters roughly approximating a normal curve. When such a distribution exists, the two parties come to resemble each other closely," Downs (1957), ibid., p. 143.

44. American National Election Studies (ANES), Stanford University and the University of Michigan, with funding by the National Science Foundation, http://www.electionstudies.org/, retrieved 4 September 2009.

45. For example, the ANES data indicate that 13 percent of American voters in 1948 and 11 percent in 2004 were in the 96th–100th percentile of family income; rather than proving that income inequality was greater in those years, they merely reflect the fact that those were the smallest samples. The shares of family income

originating as labor and property compensation are based on figures for the year 2000. The total shares of labor and property compensation in gross national income can be determined from the National Income and Product Accounts, and are quite stable from year to year.

46. Madison, J. (1788), p. 270.

47. Madison, J. (1787), p. 44.

48. The ANES data for the 2006 and 2008 elections were scheduled for release after publication of this book. But according to exit polls, the decisiveness of economic issues in defeating Republicans suggests that the results will confirm rather than disprove the connection between sources of family income and partisan voting. "Campaign 2008," www.pollingreport.com, retrieved 1 September 2009.

49. Spiegel (1971), p. 507.

REFERENCES

Aguirre, M.S. (2004). The Family and Economic Development: Socioeconomic Relevance and Policy Design, in Love, S. (Ed.), *Family and Policy*, World Family Policy Center.

Aguirre, M.S. (2006), Marriage and the Family in Economic Theory and Policy, *Ave Maria Law Journal* 4(2), 435–465.

American National Election Studies (2009). Stanford University and the University of Michigan, with funding by the National Science Foundation, http://www.electionstudies.org/, retrieved 4 September 2009.

Aquinas, T. (1993 [1271–72]). *Commentary on Aristotle's Nicomachean Ethics*. (Tr.) Litzinger, C.I., O.P., Notre Dame, IN: Dumb Ox Books [1964 Henry Regnery Company].

Aquinas, T. (2007 [1271–72]). *Commentary on Aristotle's Politics*. (Tr.) Regan, R.J., Indianapolis and Cambridge: Hackett Publishing.

Aquinas, T. (1981 [1265–72]). *[Summa Theologiae] Summa Theologica*, 5 vols. (Tr.) Fathers of the Dominican Province, 1948, New York: Benziger Brothers. Reprinted in Westminster, MD: Christian Classics.

Arendt, H. (1967). *The Origins of Totalitarianism*, Allen & Unwin, London.

Aristotle (1954 [c. 350 BC]). *The Nicomachean Ethics of Aristotle*. (Tr.) Ross, W.D.; Oxford: World's Classics, Oxford University Press. Retrieved on April 15, 2009, from http://www.constitution.org/ari/ethic_00.htm.

Aristotle (1962 [c. 350 BC]). *The Politics*. (Tr.) Sinclair, T.A., Baltimore: Penguin Books.

Aristotle (1932 [335–322 BC]). *The Rhetoric of Aristotle*. (Tr.) Cooper, L. New York: Appleton-Century-Crofts.

Augustine, A. (395/6). On Free Will, in (Tr. & Ed.) Burleigh, J.H.S. (1953), pp. 102–217.

Augustine, A. (396–397). On Christian Doctrine. Grand Rapids, MI: Christian Classics Ethereal Library (CCEL). Retrieved on January 9, 2002, from http://www.ccel.org/a/augustine/doctrine/doctrine.html.

Augustine, A. (397). To Simplician—On Various Questions, in (Tr. & Ed.) Burleigh, J.H.S. (1953), pp. 370–406.

Augustine, A. (401). Of the good of marriage. (Tr.) Cornish, Rev. C.L., from Nicene and Post-Nicene Fathers. First Series, Vol. 3. (Ed.) Schaff, P. (Buffalo, NY: Christian Literature Publishing Co., 1887). Revised and edited for New Advent by Kevin Knight. Retrieved on February 2, 2005, from http://www.newadvent.org/fathers/1309.htm.

Augustine, A. (1984 [413–426/427]). *Concerning the City of God Against the Pagans*. (Tr.) Bettenson, H., (Ed.) O'Meara, J. New York: Penguin Classics.

Becker, G.S. (1974). A Theory of Social Interactions, *Journal of Political Economy* 82(6), pp. 1063–1091, reprinted in Becker (1991), pp. 253–281.

Becker, G.S. (1976). *The Economic Approach to Human Behavior*, Chicago: University of Chicago Press.

Becker, G.S. (1991). *A Treatise on the Family*, enlarged edition. Cambridge MA: Harvard University Press.

Becker, G.S. (1996). *Accounting for Tastes*. Cambridge, MA: Harvard University Press.

Black, D. (1948). On the rationale of group decision making. *Journal of Political Economy* 56: pp. 23–34.

Buchanan, J.M., and Tullock, G. (1962). *The Calculus of Consent: The Logical Foundations of Constitutional Democracy,* University of Michigan Press.

Buchanan, J.M. (1988). Précis of *The calculus of consent. Current Contents 2:16* (Jan. 11). Intercollegiate Studies Institute.

Buchanan, J.M. (2003). Public Choice: The Origins and Development of a Research Program. Center for Study of Public Choice. George Mason University. Fairfax, VA.

(Tr. & Ed.) Burleigh, J.H.S. (1953). *Augustine: Earlier Writings*. Philadelphia: Westminster Press.

(Ed.) Carey, G. W. (2001 [1818]). *The Federalist*. (The Gideon Edition). Liberty Fund. Indianapolis. Accessed from http://oll.libertyfund.org/title/788 on 2009-11-01.

Chafuen, A. (1986). *Christians for Freedom: Late Scholastic Economics*. San Francisco: Ignatius Press.

Chafuen, A. (2003). *Faith and Liberty: The Economic Thought of the Late Scholastics*. Lexington Books.

Donohue, J.J., III, and Levitt, S.D. (2001). The Impact of Legalized Abortion on Crime, *Quarterly Journal of Economics*, 116 (2: May), pp. 379–420.

Downs, A. (1957). An Economic Theory of Political Action in a Democracy. *Journal of Political Economy* 65 (2: April), pp. 135–150.

Downs, A. (1957a). *An Economic Theory of Democracy*. Harper, New York.

(Eds.) Forget, E.L. and Peart, S. (2000). *Reflections on the Classical Canon in Economics: Essays in honor of Samuel Hollander*. London, and New York: Routledge.

(Ed.) Forte, D. (1998). *Natural Law and Contemporary Public Policy*. Washington, D.C.: Georgetown University Press.

Friedman, M., and Friedman, R. (1979). *Free to Choose: A Personal Statement*, New York and London: Harcourt Brace Jovanovich.

Hamilton, A. (1775). The Farmer Refuted. *The Works of Alexander Hamilton I,* (Ed.) Lodge, H.C. (New York: G.P. Putnam's Sons, 1904). Retrieved from http://oll.libertyfund.org/Home3/Book.php?recordID=0249.01.

Hamilton, A. (1788). Federalist No. 31. In (Ed.) Carey, G.W. (2001 [1818]). Accessed from http://oll.libertyfund.org/title/788/108619/2274086 on 2009-09-11.

Hamilton, A. (1788a). Federalist No. 34. In (Ed.) Carey, G.W. (2001 [1818]). Accessed from http://oll.libertyfund.org/title/788/108625/2274123 on 2009-09-11.

Hamilton, A. (1791). *Report on Manufactures* in 4 *Works of Alexander Hamilton.* (Ed.) Lodge, H.C. Retrieved at http://oll.libertyfund.org/Home3/HTML-voice.php?recordID=0249.04.

Hetherington, N.S. (1983). Isaac Newton's Influence on Adam Smith's Natural Laws in Economics. 44 *Journal of the History of Ideas* 3:495–505 (Jul.–Sep.).

Hume, D. (1740). *A Treatise of Human Nature.* Retrieved on June 30, 2009, from http://www.gutenberg.org/dirs/etext03/trthn10.txt.

(Eds.) Hutchinson, W.T., et al. (1962–). *The Papers of James Madison.* Chicago and London: University of Chicago Press, 1962–77 (Vols. 1–10); Charlottesville: University Press of Virginia, 1977– (vols. 11–).

Jevons, W.S. (1871). *The Theory of Political Economy.* London: Macmillan.

Langholm, O. (1982 [1979]). *Price and Value in the Aristotelian Tradition: A Study in Scholastic Economic Sources.* Universitetsforlaget, Bergen.

Langholm, O. (1983). *Wealth and Money in the Aristotelian Tradition: A Study in Scholastic Economic Sources.* Universitetsforlaget, Bergen.

Langholm, O. (1984). *The Aristotelian Analysis of Usury.* Universitetsforlaget, Bergen.

Langholm, O. (1992). *Economics in the Medieval Schools: Wealth, Exchange, Value, Money and Usury According to the Paris Theological Tradition, 1200–1350.* Universitetsforlaget, Bergen.

Langholm, O. (2003). *The Merchant in the Confessional: Trade and Price in the Pre-Reformation Panitential Handbooks.* Leiden, Boston: Brill.

Leeson, R. (1997). The Chicago Counter-Revolution and the Sociology of Economic Knowledge. Working Paper 159, Murdoch, WA, Australia: Economics Department, Murdoch University (July).

Leeson, R. (2001). *The Eclipse of Keynesianism: The Political Economy of the Chicago Counter-Revolution,* New York: Palgrave Macmillan, 2001.

Levitt, S.D., and Dubner, S.J. (2005). *Freakonomics: A Rogue Economist Explores the Hidden Side of Everything.* New York: William Morrow (HarperCollins).

Madison, J. (1787). Federalist No. 10. (Ed.) Carey, G.W. (2001 [1818]). Accessed from http://oll.libertyfund.org/title/788/108577 on 2009-11-01.

Madison, J. (1788). Federalist No. 51. (Ed.) Carey, G.W. (2001 [1818]). Accessed from http://oll.libertyfund.org/title/788/108659/2274491 on 2009-09-11.

Madison, J. (1792). Property. (29 Mar.) (Eds.) Hutchinson et al. (1962–77), pp. 266–68, at http://press-pubs.uchicago.edu/founders/print_documents/v1ch16s23.html.

Menger, C. (1976 [1871]). *Principles of Economics* (Grundsätze der Volkswirthschalftslehre). New York: New York University Press. Online at http://mises.org/etexts/menger/principles.asp.

Michael, R. T., and Becker, G.S. (1973). On the New Theory of Consumer Behavior, *The Swedish Journal of Economics* 75(4), pp. 378–395, reprinted in Becker, G.S. (1976), pp. 131–149.

Morse, J.R. (2001). *Love and Economics: Why the Laissez-Faire Family Doesn't Work.* Dallas: Spence Publishing.

Mueller, J.D. (1998). Taxation, in (Ed.) Forte (1998), pp. 219–279.

Mueller, J.D. (2006a). How Does Fiscal Policy Affect the American Worker? *Notre Dame Journal of Law, Ethics and Public Policy* 20(2), pp. 563–619. Retrieved from http://www.eppc.org/publications/pubID.2671/pub_detail.asp.

Mueller, J.D. (2006b). Dismal Science. *Claremont Review of Books* 6(2), pp. 47–48 (Spring). Retrieved from http://www.eppc.org/publications/pubID.2608/pub_detail.asp.

Mueller, J.D. (2008). Infant Industry: The Past and Future of the American System. Lehrman American Studies Center Summer Institute Seminar Paper, pp. 1–35 (June 17). James Madison Program in American Ideals and Institutions and Intercollegiate Studies Institute (ISI). Princeton University, Princeton, N.J. Retrieved from http://www.eppc.org/publications/pubID.3926/pub_detail.asp on 30 October 2009.

Mueller, J.D. (2010). *Redeeming Economics: Rediscovering the Missing Element.* Wilmington, DE: ISI Books.

Olson, M. (1965). *The Logic of Collective Action,* Harvard University Press.

Peters-Fransen, I. (2000). The canon in the history of the Adam Smith problem, in (Eds.) Forget, E.L. and Peart, S. (2000), pp. 168–184.

Piedra, A.M. (2004). *Natural Law: The Foundation of an Orderly System.* Lexington Books.

Polling Report, Inc. (2008). Campaign 2008. Retrieved from http://www.pollingreport.com/wh08.htm on 30 October 2009.

Pufendorf, S. (1991 [1673]). *On the Duty of Man and Citizen According to Natural Law.* (Tr.) Silverthorne, M. (Ed.) Tully, J. Cambridge, UK: Cambridge University Press.

Röpke, W. (1963 [1937]). *The Economics of the Free Society.* Chicago: Henry Regnery.

Röpke, W. (1991 [1942]). *The Social Crisis of Our Time.* New Brunswick, NJ: Transaction Publishers.

Röpke, W. (1996 [1948]). *The Moral Foundations of Civil Society.* New Brunswick, NJ: Transaction Publishers.

Röpke, W. (1960). *A Humane Economy: The Social Framework of the Free Market,* South Bend, IN: Gateway Editions.

Ross, I.S. (1995). *The Life of Adam Smith*, Oxford: Clarendon Press.

Rothschild, E. (1994). Adam Smith and the Invisible Hand. 84 *American Economic Review* 2:319–322 (May).

Rothschild, E. (2001). *Economic Sentiments: Adam Smith, Condorcet, and the Enlightenment.* Harvard University Press.

Rueff, J. (1948). L'Ordre Social. Editions Paris: Genin.

Rueff., J. (1977). *De L'Aube au Crepuscule: Autobiographie.* Paris: Plon.

Rueff., J. (1977–1981). *Oeuvres Complètes.* Paris: Plon for The Lehrman Institute.

Schumpeter, J. (1954). *History of Economic Analysis.* (Ed.) Schumpeter, E.B., New York: Oxford University Press.

Smith, A. (1896 [1762]), *Lectures on Justice, Police, Revenue and Arms delivered in the University of Glasgow by Adam Smith, reported by a student in 1763 [sic].* (Ed.) Cannan, E. Oxford: Clarendon Press. Available online in a different edition, *Lectures On Jurisprudence*, ed. R. L. Meek, D. D. Raphael and P. G. Stein, 5 Glasgow Edition of the Works and Correspondence of Adam Smith (Indianapolis: Liberty Fund, 1982) at http://oll.libertyfund.org/title/196.

Smith, A. (1982 [1759]). *The Theory of Moral Sentiments.* (Eds.) Raphael, D.D. and Macfie, A.L. *I Glasgow Edition of the Works and Correspondence of Adam Smith* (Indianapolis: Liberty Fund). Retrieved on April 15, 2009, from http://oll.libertyfund.org/title/192.

Smith, A. (1985 [1762]). *Lectures On Rhetoric and Belles Lettres*, ed. J. C. Bryce, 4 Glasgow Edition of the Works and Correspondence of Adam Smith (Indianapolis: Liberty Fund). Accessed from http://oll.libertyfund.org/title/202 on 2009-11-30.

Smith, A. (1966 [1776]), *An Inquiry into the Nature and Causes of the Wealth of Nations.* London: W. Strahan and T. Cadell, 2 vols. Facsimile published by Augustus M. Kelley Publishers, New York, 1966. The definitive Cannan edition is available online: Smith, A., *An Inquiry into the Nature and Causes of the Wealth of Nations.* (Ed.) Cannan, E., 1904. Library of Economics and Liberty. Retrieved April 15, 2009, from http://www.econlib.org/library/Smith/smWN.html.

Smith, A. (1982 [1795]). *Essays on Philosophical Subjects.* in (Ed.) Wightman, W. P. D. and Bryce, J. C. Vol. III of the Glasgow Edition of the Works and Correspondence of Adam Smith (Indianapolis: Liberty Fund, 1982). Chapter: *SECTION IV: The History of Astronomy.* Retrieved on April 15, 2009, from http://oll.libertyfund.org/title/201/56020/916315.

Spiegel, H.W. (1971). *The Growth of Economic Thought.* Durham, NC: Duke University Press.

Stewart-Robertson, J.C., and Norton, D.F. (1984). Thomas Reid on Adam Smith's Theory of Morals, *Journal of the History of Ideas* 45, 314.

Stigler, G.J. (1958). Ricardo and the 93 Per Cent Labor Theory of Value. *The American Economic Review.* Vol. XLVIII (June 1958), reprinted in Stigler 1965, pp. 326–342.

Stigler, G.J. (1969). Does Economics Have a Useful Past? *History of Political Economy* 1, reprinted in Stigler, G.J. (1982), pp. 107–118.

Stigler, G.J. (1965). *Essays in the History of Economics.* Chicago: University of Chicago Press.

Stigler, G.J. (1982). *The Economist as Preacher and Other Essays.* Chicago: University of Chicago.

Tullock, G. (1959). Problems of majority voting. *Journal of Political Economy* (67: Dec.), pp. 571–79.

Tullock, G. (1967). The welfare costs of tariffs, monopolies, and theft. *Western Economic Journal* (5: June), pp. 224–32.

Viner, J. (1972). *The Role of Providence in the Social Order: An Essay in Intellectual History.* Philadelphia: American Philosophical Society.

Viner, J. (1978). *Religious Thought and Economic Society: Four chapters of an unfinished work.* (Eds.) Jacques Melitz and Donald Winch. Durham, NC: Duke University Press.

Walras, L. (1954 [1874]). *Elements of Pure Economics, or the Theory of Social Wealth* [Éléments d'économie politique pure, ou théorie de la richesse sociale]. (Tr.) Jaffe, W. Homewood, IL: Richard D. Irwin.

Worland, S.T. (1967). *Scholasticism and Welfare Economics.* Notre Dame, IN: University of Notre Dame Press.

Yuengert, A. (2004). The *Boundaries of Technique: Ordering Positive and Normative Concerns in Economic Research*. Lanham, MD: Lexington Books.

3

The Idea of Commerce in Enlightenment Political Thought

Alan Levine

In 1770 the Abbé Raynal (1713–96) asked the fundamental moral questions about commerce. In his *L'Histoire philosophique et politique des établissements et du commerce des Européens dans les deux Indes*, the eighteenth century's best selling and most highly regarded book on the discovery of the New World, Raynal declared the inauguration of (to use a current phrase) the age of globalization.[1] "No event has been so interesting to mankind in general, and to the inhabitants of Europe in particular," he wrote, "as the discovery of the New World, and the passage to India by the Cape of Good Hope,"[2] because these discoveries initiated an age of global commerce that was destined to forever change the world:

> [These discoveries] gave rise to a revolution in the commerce, and in the power of nations; as well as in the manners, industry, and government of the whole world. At this period, new connections were formed by the inhabitants of the most distant regions, for the supply of wants they had never before experienced. The productions of climates situated under the equator, were consumed in countries bordering on the pole; the industry of the north was transplanted to the south; and the inhabitants of the west were clothed with the manufactures [*le luxe*] of the east; a general intercourse of opinions, laws and customs, diseases and remedies, virtues and vices, was established among men.[3]

Like many people today, Raynal was ambivalent about the benefits of globalization. While it seemed good to him to acquire the "virtues" and "remedies" of other societies, getting their "vices" and "diseases" surely was not. Raynal wondered if it was good for the West to cultivate a taste for the luxuries associated with Eastern despotisms. Similarly, he reflected on whether the mixing of "opinions, laws and customs" was beneficial or if the destruction of local manners and traditions was to be lamented. These ruminations led Raynal in poignant fashion to pose the moral questions inherent in global commerce. Although he powerfully chronicled the horrors of European conquest and colonization, the deepest issues for Raynal had to do with the moral and political consequences that result from globalization itself. Raynal formulated the problem and question as follows:

> [With global commerce] every thing is changed, and must change again. But it is a question, whether the revolutions that are past, or those which must hereafter take place, have been, or can be, of any utility to the human race. Will they ever add to the tranquillity, the happiness, and the pleasures of mankind? Can they improve our present state, or do they only change it?[4]

Everyone sees that the spread of commerce, or what Schumpeter later termed the "creative destruction" of capitalism, leads to upheavals in the world.[5] The deeper question is whether these changes overall harm mankind, as Marx and traditional religious and political authorities have proclaimed, or whether global commerce benefits the world.

This chapter takes up Raynal's question about the economic, moral, and political consequences of commerce by examining the views of the Enlightenment philosophers who lived through the dawn of the age of global commerce. I argue that these Enlightenment thinkers made a complex and coherent case for commerce, and one that is still instructive today. The most prominent recent philosophical defenders of political and economic liberty, such as Robert Nozick, build their arguments on specifically moral claims about the human right to do what we will with ourselves and our property. Nozick effectively gives a Kantian or *deontological* defense of human liberty: human beings ought always to be treated as ends in themselves and never as means.[6] But while the dominant strand of thinkers examined in this essay were not unsympathetic to the moral case for commerce, their arguments were quite different. In addition to their more high-minded moral concerns, they also made a *prudential* case for the benefits of commerce, and they never lost sight of the need to address the self-interest of their audiences—including that most important audience, political sovereigns. In contemplating the complex pros and cons of the case for commerce today, we would do well to pay attention to the prudential arguments for commerce as well as the more familiar moral claims for human liberty.

The heart of this chapter examines the views of the revolutionary group of Enlightenment philosophers who first argued that commerce is a great good for mankind, which was the dominant Enlightenment position. Next the chapter turns to the views of their contemporaries who held the opposite view that commerce was to blame for most of our modern ills. The paper concludes by briefly tracing these views in the American Founders' (particularly Hamilton's) views of commerce. The way the Founders of the United States dealt with their economic situation—and the way that we deal with our economic situation—could not have happened without the Enlightenment philosophers who radically re-conceptualized commerce's benefits and harms. To understand what these thinkers hoped to gain from commerce, however, we must first look at what they rejected, both in theory and in practice.

ANCIENT AND MEDIEVAL VIEWS OF COMMERCE

Although commerce is as old as civilization itself, in ancient and medieval times it was not highly valued. This is clear in each epoch's theory and practice.

No major ancient or medieval philosopher celebrated commerce as a choice worthy or laudable of human endeavor. Ancient philosophers were either hostile toward commerce or accepted it merely as necessary. For example, in Plato's *Republic* tradesmen and traders are relegated to the lowest of the city's three classes. According to Plato's Socrates, craftsmen who make and traders who move products do so for wealth and money in order to attain pleasure. Anyone who lives merely or even primarily for riches and pleasure, he avers, has a soul dominated by desires (as opposed to reason or spiritedness [*thymos*]).[7] People whose souls are dominated by desire cannot help but use whatever powers they have in order to sate themselves, even if what they desire is unjust or their actions cause other people to suffer. They cannot control themselves and thus cannot be trusted with power, political or military. Plato deems the disease of improperly regulated desire to be rooted in the particular nature of the soul of each of these individuals and thus he views it as un-eliminable for them. These people are thus relegated by him to the ideal city's lowest class. They are there given wide rein to pursue wealth and sate themselves in *private* activity, so long as they stay away from political and military activities, in which their participation jeopardizes others.

Similarly, in Aristotle's *Politics*, economics and commerce are viewed as activities for supplying necessities and luxuries for the body but not the most important things. Economics is for life—mere or material life—not the good life. The good life, according to Aristotle, is found in the higher activities of soul, politics and philosophy, which he deems higher because only by participating in these activities does one reach the highest human potential of reflection on the good and the just. Those who spend their lives focusing merely on wealth and necessities do not therefore live fully human good lives. As with Plato, Aristotle aims to persuade the reader away from dealing merely with material things and to focus on what he deems to be a higher life of justice and the good.

Christianity similarly aims to turn people away from the material concerns of this life and toward a spiritual concern for the next. Its chief concern is the salvation of souls and getting to heaven. It extols virtues such as faith, piety, and charity—not acquisition in this world. For example, Augustine denounces lust for money and possessions as among the three principal sins of fallen man (along with lust for power and sexual lust).[8] In short, the great minds of the ancient or medieval worlds did not theoretically sanctify a life of commerce.

Ancient and medieval *societies* did not in practice value commerce much more than their *philosophers* did. Ancient republics were warlike. They valued freedom, but for the polity as a whole, not the individual. The individual existed for the common good, not vice versa. The virtues celebrated by these societies included military valor and self-sacrifice for the state.[9] A commercial life was tolerated in Athens but despised in Sparta. The warrior and civic-minded ethos of successful states such as Rome liked possessing goods, but they thought the best way to acquire them was through conquest, not commerce. A life of commerce was not particularly celebrated in medieval practice either. Wealth went to the Church and a few lords, but aside perhaps from in a few monasteries, the higher classes considered it unworthy of their status to work the land, make products, or trade them. In tension with its espoused Christian virtues, the aristocratic and feudal ethos of medieval society also valued chivalric honor and martial skills. While the spiritual and secular powers fought with and attempted to overcome each other throughout the medieval period, neither side celebrated commerce.

The social valuation of commerce began to change in the Renaissance as individuals, families, and even whole states began to get rich through commercial trade; but few, if any, of the great thinkers of the Renaissance, such as Dante, Machiavelli, or Boccacio, celebrated commerce as a way of life. Machiavelli asserts that "it is a very natural and ordinary thing to desire to acquire, and always, when men do it who can, they will be praised or not blamed," but he promotes the attainment of power and glory much more than the acquisition of commercial wealth.[10] Italian city-states benefitted from the wealth and luxury that trade enabled, but their thinkers nonetheless withheld from it their highest esteem.

It is generally acknowledged that the moral revaluation of commerce began in the Protestant Reformation, particularly in Calvin's reinterpretation of the prohibitions against lending money at interest.[11] The groundwork for this was laid in Calvin's justifications of economic inequality as religiously warranted. Beyond Calvin's particular religious justifications for commerce, however, for a broader, secular, full-blown, philosophical affirmation, commerce had to wait for the Enlightenment.[12]

THE ENLIGHTENMENT'S PRO-COMMERCE VIEWS

The philosophical revaluation of commerce was one of the Enlightenment's most revolutionary innovations. It was argued for powerfully and systematically by a number of great thinkers. The arguments articulated by them are just as valid today, so by examining their views we gain clarity on our own.

Locke's Defense of Property Rights and Commerce

The philosophical turning point in the Enlightenment's revaluation of commerce first came in the writing of John Locke (1632–1704). Moral arguments for commerce cannot exist without the prior conception that there is legitimate property that can be traded, so before examining the Enlightenment philosophers' views of the benefits of commerce it is worth our while to examine the fundamental Enlightenment justification for property which is most famously made by Locke. Locke argues that in the state of nature one attains the property right to a thing by mixing one's labor with it. When we mix our labor with a thing it becomes ours.[13] This is so, Locke asserts, because almost the entire value of a thing results from the labor that is mixed with it: "Nature and the Earth furnished only the almost worthless materials" (§ 43); "'Tis labor then which puts the greatest part of value upon land" (§ 43).[14] This is what scholars call Locke's "labor theory of value." Indeed, in the course of a few pages Locke increases the value added by labor from 9/10 to 99/100 to 999/1,000 (§ 40, 43). Essentially this means for Locke that fruit growing on a tree is nearly worthless until you pluck it and put it into your mouth. Until then, regardless of what the tree, the sun, and God have done, the fruit has no usefulness or nutritional value *to you*. To get that value, you have first to mix your labor with the thing. The mixing of the labor makes it yours and gives the thing its value. In the state of nature everything belongs to all in common until someone mixes his labor with a thing, as long as when he does so he satisfies two conditions. First, there must be enough left as good for others (§ 27), so hoarding is impermissible. Second, one must use what one takes. If something one has gathered is going to spoil, the property right to it is lost (§ 31). The second condition is a dictate of self-interest. Why would one labor for something that one would not use? Such activity would be irrational. The first condition seems to imply that Locke's state of nature requires a world of plenty.

Locke's conception of property leads to two main arguments in favor of commerce. First, Locke argues that commerce improves the condition of all. While the taking of a thing might seem to make everyone else poorer insofar as they no longer have a right to it, Locke argues that this is a false impression. He illustrates his claim using the example of farming. An acre of land on its own might produce X bushels of crop, but if one fences that land off and mixes his labor with it by seeding, fertilizing, and watering it, by chasing away the birds, etc., it might produce ten, one hundred, or one thousand times as much crop. So a farm of one acre is not stealing X bushels from the world. Rather, insofar as it is more productive and produces 10, 100, or 1000 X bushels, it gives the world a net surplus of 9, 99, or 999 X bushels as the case may be. Counterintuitively, then, property is not a net *taking from*—but a net *giving to*—humanity. However, this is only true if there is some mechanism for getting those additional bushels into the world. At minimum, one could argue that the farm decreases competition for other bushels in the state of nature from the farmer (and his family), but Locke's argument goes further. If the farmer cannot eat the entirety of his crop and cannot let it spoil, he has an incentive (and a duty) to trade it to others. Others will only pay a price that to them seems less of a cost than procuring that crop for themselves, so they get that crop at less cost to themselves and are thus better off. Locke's theory of property combined with minimal (perhaps only barter) trade argues that commerce enriches the world. Thus, the first benefit of commerce for Locke is the production of wealth.

In making what is perhaps the earliest complete philosophical argument for capitalism, Locke is clear in describing both this major benefit of commerce and a major cost. While commerce makes humanity as a whole better off, Locke is clear that everyone is not *equally* better off. In *absolute* terms, commerce either benefits or does not affect people, but Locke acknowledges that commerce can cause the *relative* inequality between them to grow.[15] Locke unblinkingly justifies this inequality. Locke's famous example to illustrate the merits of property and commerce, despite their compounding of relative inequality, is found in his contrast of the relatively worse condition of a king among the American Indians in comparison to a day laborer in England:

> There cannot be any clearer demonstration of any thing, than several Nations of the Americas are of this, who are rich in land, and poor in all the Comforts of Life; whom Nature having furnished as liberally as any other people, with the materials of plenty, i.e., a fruitful soil, apt to produce in abundance, what might serve for food, raiment, and delight; yet for want of improving it by labor, have not one hundredth part of the conveniences we enjoy: and a King of a large fruitful Territory there feeds, lodges, and is clad worse than a day laborer in England. (§ 41)

Locke explains that while a king in America (or anywhere that property and commerce are unknown or despised) might be relatively better off than his compatriots, he is much less well off than an ordinary workman in England, a country that has accrued the benefits of property and commerce. An ordinary worker in England will have better food, shelter, and clothing than a king in America. This is not to deny that the monarch in England will have even tremendously better food, clothing, and shelter than his or her subjects, a fact about which Locke was surely aware. Locke implicitly acknowledges that the *relative* gap between a king and commoner in England will be much greater than between king and commoner in America. But in *absolute* terms the commoner in England is better off materially than even the king in America. Here we have both the fundamental achievement of and complaint against commerce. A detractor of capitalism must acknowledge its raising of living standards in absolute terms even if he wants to condemn the unequal heights to which some people are lifted in the commercial order. (He might also note capitalism's indifference to concerns of the spirit or a sense of harmony with the earth that the American Indians and others may have possessed.) A defender of capitalism must recognize its unequal distribution of goods, even while pointing out how everyone is better off in absolute terms.

The second benefit of property and commerce according to Locke is that it promotes and protects freedom. For Locke the fundamental limits on property acquisition are overturned by the invention of money. Once goods can be converted into cash, hoarding is sensible for a self-interested agent and relative inequality can increase so much such that there are no more of some goods left for others. At this moment property is delegitimized and a state of war breaks out (§ 47–50). Government is instituted to end these wars, and civil law henceforth determines the legitimacy and proper distribution of property, so the inequality of the pre-political condition can be limited or remedied by politics.[16] More than any other philosopher, Locke equates the purpose of government with the protection of property—indeed, he writes, "Government has no other end but the preservation of Property" (§ 94)—but Locke defines property in both narrow and broad terms. In its narrow sense, Locke means what we mean by property, our things, or what he calls our "estate." In the broader sense, Locke includes our "Lives, Liberties, and Estates, which I call by the general Name, *Property*" (§123). The goal of government for Locke is the protection of property in the broad sense (§124), and this leads him to two arguments on how property promotes liberty. First, Locke makes an argument of self-interest from the point of view of the rulers:

> This [i.e., the benefits of labor] shews, how much numbers of men are to be preferred to largenesse of dominions, and that the increase of lands and the right imploying of them is the great art of government. And that [a] Prince . . . shall

> be . . . so wise and godlike as by establish[ing] laws of liberty to secure protection and incouragement to the honest industry of mankind. (§ 42)

This argument about the "godlike" prince is an inexplicit version of the Machiavellian calculus: rulers should do what is good for themselves, but in wisely pursuing their own interests the society as a whole benefits, too. Rulers require wealth to thrive, so it is in their interest to give their citizens liberty to address their own material needs. As each individual prospers, so does the power and wealth of the society as a whole. This is essential to securing both the narrow interests of the rulers (as they tax wealth) and to securing the freedom of the city from external conquest. Not only does political freedom thus require economic freedom, but economic freedom also protects political freedom in another way as well. Locke conceives life, liberty, and estate as concentric circles around the core of the self. If the self is not alive, it cannot be free, and freedom is the greatest guarantee that a self can defend itself. Similarly, while liberty is the natural condition for securing one's estate, one's estate serves as a kind of "fence" around one's liberty (§§ 93, 226, and see also 18). If someone is unjustly trying to steal your goods, you should assume your liberty and life are in danger also (§ 18). Thus, economic freedom is not only a prerequisite for a strong, thriving state, it is also the first guard against tyranny. In short, in John Locke, we get the first two systematic philosophical arguments in favor of the benefits of property and commerce: they increase wealth and promote and protect freedom.

Private Vices, Public Benefits: Mandeville's Account of Modern Commerce

The self-interested (dare one say Machiavellian?) psychological underpinnings of Locke's view of commerce were humorously and cynically laid bare by the great poet Bernard de Mandeville (1670–1733), and this view emerged as the dominant psychology of the Enlightenment. Mandeville's witty allegorical poem "The Fable of the Bees" tells the story of a prosperous beehive that represents a well-to-do human polity. The secret to its wealth and happiness is its huge population whose workers are employed in all sorts of vain, wicked, and useless projects even as others are employed to negate their harms and mitigate their evils:

> Vast Numbers throng'd the fruitful Hive;
> Yet those vast Numbers made 'em thrive;
> Millions endeavoring to supply
> Each other's Lust and Vanity;
> While other millions were employ'd,
> To see their Handy-Works destroy'd. (18)[17]

Mandeville's point, which he thinks should be learned by all moralistic politicians, is that the self-interested pursuit of "Lust and Vanity" creates jobs and happiness: "every part was full of Vice/ Yet the whole Mass a Paradise" (24). As the poem's subtitle, "Private Vices, Publick Benefits," makes clear, the hive has full employment not because of some planned government program but because of the selfish and foolish calculations of ambitious, self-interested private individuals:

> Luxury employ'd a Million of the Poor,
> And odious Pride a million more:
> Envy itself, and Vanity,
> Were Ministers of Industry;
> Their darling Folly, Fickleness
> In Diet, Furniture and Dress,
> That strange ridic'lous Vice, was made
> The Very wheel that turn'd the trade." (25)

In sum, Mandeville celebrates the vices, follies, and inanities that make the human wheel "turn." People do not work unless they get paid, and what pays is fostering the folly that is fashion and flattering the pride and vanity of the rich. Without people wanting to seem apace with or above others, there would be no exchanging perfectly good shoes with a rounded front for newer shoes that are pointy toed, or throwing away straight legged pants for flair bottoms, or trading functioning buckles for laces. Fashions are inane and foolish, but they keep the garment industry, as well as all many other industries, in business.

To further illustrate the point, Mandeville imagines the consequences of a world without commerce. He describes the unemployment and social collapse that would occur if the hive, perpetually declaiming against the very vices that keep it going, is granted its wish to eliminate vice. Without vice, the community has no need for lawyers, jailers, locksmiths, and makers of iron, doors, or keys, so they all lose their jobs. They have no need for police, doctors, importers of drugs, (most) clergy, or most politicians, so they are fired. Without luxury and vanity, they have no need for palaces, craftsmen of beautiful things, stonecutters, designers, or carvers. They stop drinking, so the taverns close. There is no vice, so the brothels close. Without fickle fashion, the spinners, weavers, sowers, and manufacturers lose their jobs. In short, virtue and simplicity reign. It is an Edenic, Rousseauian paradise—but terrible and unsustainable. Since they are not needed, the craftsmen emigrate and the hive's population declines drastically. Underpopulated, the city is vulnerable to conquest and is in fact conquered.

In a section of his poem entitled "The Moral," Mandeville clearly states the paradoxical moral of his immoral tale:

> Then leave Complaints: Fools only strive
> To Make a great and Honest Hive
> T' enjoy the World's Conveniencies,
> Be fam'd in War, yet live in Ease
> Without Great vices, is a Vain
> Eutopia seated in the Brain.
> Fraud, Luxury, and Pride must live,
> While we the benefits receive. (36)

Humans have a diseased desire for a perfect "Eutopia" without realizing how truly horrible such a place would be. The Christian and Platonic visions of perfection are not only unattainable, they are destructive: "How Vain is mortal happiness!/ Had they but known the Bounds of Bliss/ And that perfection here below/ Is more than Gods can well bestow" (26). Commerce based on self-interest, folly, and vice supplies the good things in life that are realistically available to mankind. Dreams for supercelestial perfection lead to infernal unhappiness.

But Mandeville is also clear that vice can only exist within limits: "Vice is beneficial found/ When it's by justice lopt and bound" (37). Mandeville never specifies the exact nature of such limits; this is not his project. Instead, he illustrates how self-interest drives the world. Private vices produce public goods—and commerce is the bridge between them. Mandeville powerfully articulates the Machiavellian paradox that selfish motives produce virtuous actions, but whereas Machiavelli saw the necessity of a virtuous statesman acting (in part) unseen behind the scenes, Mandeville conceives of commerce as the invisible hand *avant la lettre*.

Montesquieu's Account of "*Doux*" Commerce, and Its Effect on the Regime

Like Locke and Mandeville, Montesquieu (1689–1755) argues that commerce promotes wealth and freedom—indeed, he says that commerce is incompatible with despotism—but unlike Locke, he does not make an argument for property from first principles. Montesquieu seems to take Locke's account for granted and builds from there. Part Four (of six) of *The Spirit of the Laws* is dedicated to the nature and consequences of commerce. With his characteristic brilliance, Montesquieu in this insightful and unwieldy work emphasizes the effects of commerce on the humans who practice it and commerce's consequent compatibility or incompatibility with different kinds of regimes. In contrast to both the ascetic lives of priests and the hard lives of warriors, Montesquieu describes a life of commerce as "*doux*," i.e., soft and sweet. He nicely explains how the people who practice commerce become bourgeois: "hardworking," "just," "moderate," "frugal"—and "anxious" (XX. 5, 341).[18] He explains how commerce makes individuals lose ambition for aristocratic greatness, but how it makes commercial nations "daring" and willing to take risks, because in great commercial ventures profit is to be made on the margins and the ethos of such societies must always be to go further, grander, and seek new paths to maximize profits (XX. 4, 340–41). Commerce according to Montesquieu thus fosters an ethos of innovation that is thus incompatible with traditional societies, whether based on civic virtue, honor, or fear. Moreover, Montesquieu further affirms that commerce can only exist in states under "the government by many" (XX. 4, 340), so commerce's only true home is the modern commercial republic that Montesquieu was among the first both to identify and to promote (see XI. 6).

In addition to his penetrating insight into the nature of commerce and his agreeing with Locke and Mandeville that commerce promotes wealth and freedom, Montesquieu argues that "*doux*" commerce has three interrelated additional benefits that make human interactions softer and gentler. First, he argues that "Commerce cures destructive prejudices" (XX. 1, 338). As nations interact through trade they come to appreciate that views they previously held about each other are exaggerated, caricature, or wrong. They might in time come even to appreciate their differences and the worth of customs and practices that might at first have struck them as barbarous. After all, to trade successfully, one has to know what one's partner wants and values. This is a natural spur—motivated by one's own self-interest—to understand the other, and this natural spur has the effect of counteracting and curing the "destructive prejudices" that one previously held.

The second major new benefit of commerce mentioned by Montesquieu is that it leads to gentle mores. Describing commerce and gentle mores in a reciprocally reinforcing relationship, Montesquieu writes, "It is an almost general rule that everywhere there are gentle mores, there is commerce and that everywhere there is commerce, there are gentle mores" (XX. 1, 338). The logic here of the gentle effect of commerce parallels the previous point. As one gets to know other people and perhaps even appreciate the beauty and wisdom in practices that at first seemed odd, in short, as one is cured of one's destructive prejudices, one grows gentler both toward the other and toward oneself. One is not only more tolerant toward some particular other, but reflection on the realization of one's former prejudices and mistakes is likely to make one grow less dogmatic and harsh about one's own views. Coming to see one's own views as in some sense culturally and historically determined undermines a fanatical attachment to them and leads one to a more moderate stand in the world. As Montesquieu writes, "Commerce has spread knowledge of the mores of all nations everywhere; they have been compared to each other, and good things have resulted from this" (ibid.).

The third major new benefit that Montesquieu sees in commerce is that "The natural effect of commerce is to lead to peace" (XX. 2, 338). There are two reasons why Montesquieu thinks this is so. The first reason is cultural and follows from the previous points. As one comes to understand others and grows gentler and more moderate in one's own views, one is less likely to fight over differences. The second reason is economic: "Two nations that trade with each other become reciprocally dependent" (ibid). Waging war against a trade partner disturbs one's trade benefits. A country might calculate that it is cheaper and easier (not to mention gentler and more moderate) to trade for the goods it desires than to wage war to acquire them. Indeed, for Montesquieu commerce promotes peace to the maximum extent because it fosters globalization. Arguing a point on which Raynal would later elaborate, Montesquieu declares that since all moveable goods are tradable, "all commodities belong to the whole world, which in this regard comprises but a single state of which all societies are members" (XX. 23, 352). As the globalized market interconnects not only one country with another but all countries with all others, so Montesquieu expects the "natural effect" of commerce's push toward peace to be maximized.

Montesquieu notes several moral costs that necessarily result from commerce of which two are especially noteworthy in this context: the end of moral purity and the development of a legalistic attitude toward morality. Just as commerce "polishes and softens barbarous mores" so it "corrupts pure mores, and this," Montesquieu notes, "was the subject of Plato's complaints" (XX. 1, 338). If one thinks one's mores are exactly correct and should not be altered, then one will not want commerce in one's society as commerce will necessarily relax and soften the attachment to these, as it does to all morals. Commerce thus might be said to undermine the best regime or a morally pure society. The best society or a morally pure one can only be influenced by its neighbors to make it worse. The variety and riches brought by commerce transform and expand mankind's interests and priorities: "It is the nature of commerce to make superfluous things useful and useful ones necessary" (353), and this confusion of essential goods with non-essentials and both with extraneous or distracting things, shows how commerce softly and gently undermines the pure mores of a good society. This softening might promote peace between nations by creating interdependence and mutual understanding, but it undermines a pure morality or a simple morality that promotes a particular, comprehensive view of the human good.

A second negative consequence mentioned by Montesquieu is that by promoting a culture in which each thing has its price, commerce produces what he calls a demand for "exact justice." While this might seem good, it is only qualifiedly so. Montesquieu describes this exact, or legal, justice as a mean between moral vice and moral virtue: "The spirit of commerce produces in men a certain feeling for exact justice, opposed on the one hand to banditry and on the other to those moral virtues that make it so that one does not always discuss one's own interests alone and that one can neglect them for those of others" (XX. 2, 339). In short, rather than doing the right thing for the right reason or offering aristocratic largesse, people pursue their interest within the law. They become trained to do all that the law allows and restrain themselves only from doing what the law forbids. This is good insofar as they do not break it, but it is bad insofar as they cease to do outstanding acts of moral virtue that are not legally required. For example, Montesquieu notes the old virtue of "hospitality" is "rare among commercial countries" (ibid). Apparently, they feel that everyone should pay for his own hotel.

All five of the benefits of commerce discussed by Locke, Mandeville, and Montesquieu—creating wealth and freedom, destroying prejudices, and promoting moderation and peace—are illustrated in a quintessentially Enlightenment passage by Voltaire (1694–1778) praising the civilizing effects of the London Stock Exchange:

> Go into the London Stock Exchange—a more respectable place than many a court—and you will see representatives from all nations gathered together for the utility of men. Here Jew, Mohammedan and Christian deal with each other as though they were all of the same faith, and only apply the word infidel to people who go bankrupt. Here the Presbyterian trusts the Anabaptist and the Anglican accepts a promise from the Quaker. On leaving these peaceful and free assemblies some go to the Synagogue and others for a drink, this one goes to be baptized in a great bath in the name of Father, Son, and Holy Ghost, that one has his son's foreskin cut and has some Hebrew words he doesn't understand mumbled over the child, others go to their church and await the inspiration of God with their hats on [Quakers], and everybody is happy.
>
> If there were only one religion in England there would be danger of despotism, if there were two they would cut each other's throats, but there are thirty, and they live in peace and happiness.[19]

This passage by Voltaire brilliantly encapsulates the Enlightenment position on commerce. Voltaire favorably contrasts commercial society to the medieval courts. According to him, commercial society is "more respectable" and lives in more "peace and happiness." In a commercial society "all nations" overcome their prejudices and cooperate in "peaceful and free assemblies," working together gently and moderately in pursuit of their mutual "utility."

Local and superstitious prejudices are overcome and replaced by solidarity in pursuit of wealth. As opposed to the destructive prejudices that led different religious sects to wage wars with each other—and Voltaire's passage reminds the reader both of religious wars between Jews, Christians, and Muslims as well as intramural wars between Christian factions (Presbyterian versus Anabaptist, Anglican versus Quakers)—this economic society is held together by sharing the "same faith," a worldly faith in commerce. Whether the actual London Stock Exchange worked this way or not is beside the point. Voltaire here creates an ideal that he promulgates for all of Europe, and his ideal illustrates and validates Locke's, Mandeville's, and Montesquieu's fundamental claims about commerce.

Hume's Defense of Commerce and Economic Freedom

David Hume (1711–1776) adds two new arguments to the pro-commerce camp to make commerce appealing to political rulers. Hume's essays cover many different aspects of commerce, embellishing Mandeville's psychology of commerce and repeating many of Locke's and Montesquieu's arguments on commerce. For example, echoing Locke's view of property and Mandeville's psychology, Hume writes, "Every thing in the world is purchased by labor; and our passions are the only causes of labor" ("Of Commerce," 261),[20] although Hume differs importantly from Locke insofar as he sometimes argues that property comes from custom and that labor does not create a moral claim to a thing. However this may be, Hume, following Machiavelli and Locke, applies the self-interested psychology to rulers, emphasizing how the rulers' proper pursuit of their own self-interest requires them to promote commerce in their polities, while also noting how that same commerce will make their citizens happy: "The greatness of a state, and the happiness of its subjects . . . [are] inseparable with regard to commerce; and as private men receive greater security, in the possession of their trade and riches, from the power of the public, so the public becomes powerful in proportion to the opulence and extensive commerce of private men" ("Of Commerce," 255). Hume notes the "paradox" (that we see, for example, in oil kingdoms today) of how an abundance of natural resources often leads to tyranny and poverty. Where wealth can be easily supplied there is no incentive for anyone to work hard, innovate, or improve their land, and the rulers discourage such independent activities so the citizens remain dependent on their largesse, which the natural resources enable them to provide easily. By contrast, where hard work is required to better one's condition and where the benefits can only be attained gradually over time, one insists on terms and conditions before undertaking the necessary improvements and this leads to the institution of laws. Settled laws benefit everyone and lead to industry and improvement. So Hume makes twin appeals to sovereigns to establish the rule of law and the freedoms necessary to promote commerce.

First, Hume argues that commerce is necessary for national greatness. Hume defines greatness not only in terms of power but even more in terms of civilization, of greatness in the arts and sciences. Thus he gives as a general law "That nothing is more favorable to the rise of politeness and learning, than a number of neighboring and independent states, connected together by commerce and policy" ("Of the Rise and Progress of the Arts and Sciences," 119). Commerce promotes the arts and sciences, civilization, and greatness via rivalries between nations. Driven by natural vanity or the desire for glory, each nation wants to be best. Proximity naturally fosters rivalry, and proximity is expanded beyond mere geography through commerce. Commerce thus propels nations to be greater not only than their immediate neighbors but greater than all nations and civilizations with which they have contact. Commerce is "the great spur to industry and invention," and is thus a huge and indispensible spur to national greatness ("Of Commerce," 267). Any ruler concerned with his reputation must encourage commerce to spur the global rivalry that promotes national greatness and thus the ruler's own individual glory.

Second, Hume emphasizes that in times of war the creative resources spurred by commerce can be used by the state for defense and protection. Without educated, creative, industrious citizens a nation is at great risk when new threats come along. In making this argument, Hume takes the novel view that "Trade and industry are really nothing but a stock of labour, which, in times of peace and tranquility, is employed for the ease and satisfaction of individuals; but in the exigencies of state, may, in part, be turned to public advantage" ("Of Commerce," 262). Hume shrewdly conceives of commerce as being the foundation of a state's arsenal: "manufactures increase the power of a state only as they store up so much labour, and that of a kind to which the public may lay claim, without depriving any one of the necessaries of life. The more labour, therefore, is employed beyond mere necessaries, the more powerful is any state" (262). Rather than worry that wealthy citizens might aspire to power and threaten the ruler, Hume emphasizes both the necessity of having industrious citizens vis-à-vis external attack and that the freedom and law necessary to promote commerce will mitigate the unhappiness that would lead citizens to revolt. "Thus," Hume concludes, "the greatness of the sovereign and the happiness of the state are, in great measure, united with regard to trade and manufactures" (262). Forcing people to toil on your[21] behalf will lead to resistance, but "Furnish him with manufactures and commodities, and he will do it of himself" (262). Thus, even if a ruler did not aspire to international greatness and renown and was uninterested in promoting commerce as a spur to the arts and sciences, he should nonetheless promote it so that in times of war he had a pool of creative citizens on whom he could draw to overcome new necessities. As Hume presents it, the stakes are nothing less than the survival of the state.

In conclusion, Enlightenment thinkers such as Locke, Montesquieu, Mandeville, Voltaire, and Hume radically revalued the place of commerce in human life. The Enlightenment arguments in favor of commerce are remarkably consistent with and build on each other. According to these Enlightenment thinkers, commerce is a major factor in producing and promoting most of the good things in life. Commerce creates wealth, freedom, peace, moderation, toleration, civilization, security, greatness, and power. Commerce does not bring these goods about because of high-minded idealism or because it aims to bring them about. Rather, it does so as a result of self-interest. Commerce's public benefits paradoxically result from private vices.

This emphasis on self-interest and human vices did not, however, originate in the Enlightenment. It began with early modern thinkers, such as Machiavelli, Montaigne, Bacon, and Descartes, who ushered in a deeper revolution in conceptions of human nature and what should be the aim of human moral and political life. These early modern thinkers rejected ancient and medieval otherworldly or aristocratic idealism in favor of what they deemed to be a "realistic" conception of human nature. Following Machiavelli, they aimed to take man as he is, or in Hume's dictum, "Sovereigns must take mankind as they find them" (260). What they claimed to find—and what they aimed to promote—is a worldly human being who seeks to acquire. From Machiavelli's assertion that "it is a very natural and ordinary thing to desire to acquire, and always, when men do it who can, they will be praised or not blamed"[22] to Hume's view that "Avarice, or the desire of gain, is an universal passion, which operates at all times, in all places, and upon all persons" ("Of the Rise and Progress of the Arts and Sciences,"113), modern philosophers brought about a revolution in the vision of human nature and man's place in the cosmos by emphatically rejecting ancient notions of natural perfection and the traditional Christian notions of divine perfection. Locke, Mandeville, Montesquieu, Voltaire, and Hume all share this modern framework but in contradistinction to the early modern thinkers, they were the first to revalue commerce in broad, secular, philosophic terms. Their philosophical revaluation of commerce was one of the Enlightenment's greatest innovations.[23] But other Enlightenment thinkers had a quite different point of view.

ANTI-COMMERCE ARGUMENTS OF THE ENLIGHTENMENT

While the dominant Enlightenment conception of commerce was the highly positive one just examined, the Enlightenment also contained a significant dissenting view. With its groundwork most forcefully laid by Rousseau, this critique of commerce was scientized by the Physiocrats and most influentially culminated in the ideal of the yeoman farmer in England and America. This view identified commerce as a major cause of all of the ills of the modern world.

Rousseau's Critique of Property Rights and Capitalism

Just as Locke initiated the pro-commerce arguments by firmly legitimizing the right of property, Rousseau inaugurated the anti-commerce thread by both seriously undermining the right to private property and simultaneously decrying its effects. In his "Second Discourse," Rousseau declaims property as the beginning of mankind's moral fall. He lays the blame for humanity's moral decay on "The first person who, having enclosed a plot of land, took it into his head to say *this is mine* and found people simple enough to believe him" (60).[24] "What crimes, wars, murders," Rousseau writes, "what miseries and horrors, would the human race have been spared, had someone pulled up the stakes or filled in the ditch and cried out to his fellow men: 'Do not listen to this imposter. You are lost if you forget that the fruits of the earth belong to all and the earth to no one!' " (60).

Rousseau shares Locke's assessment of how property developed and was legitimated, but he values this development antithetically to Locke. Rousseau shows that he was a good reader of Locke in acknowledging that property claims arise from nothing but "manual labor" and that "It is labor alone that . . . gives him a right" to it (66, 67), thus endorsing Locke's labor theory of value. According to Rousseau property not only leads to inequality and the formation of the state as Locke argues, but where Locke saw property also as the beginning of human progress, development, freedom, and civilization, Rousseau sees it as the beginning of the end of "natural liberty" and as an institution that "subjected the entire human race to labor, servitude and misery" (70). For Rousseau, the invention of property is perhaps the worst "revolution" in human history, followed by the invention of the state, which he envisions as nothing but a trick by the rich pulled on the poor to legitimate the rich's property (78, 69). Each of these revolutions is "arbitrary" and gradually lead the human species away from "the goodness appropriate to the pure state of nature" to a "universal desire for reputation" (78), the cultivation of the "pleasure of domination" (68), "frightful disorder" (68), and an "excess of corruption" (79) culminating in the metaphorical and perhaps literal "chains" (70) of arbitrary power, tyranny, and "despotism" (76–77, 79). In short, Rousseau sees property as the fatal step toward the moral ruin of man.

Like Locke, Montesquieu, and Hume, Rousseau also associates commerce with the arts and sciences but whereas the earlier authors consider these benefits to mankind, Rousseau decries them. According to Rousseau the consequences most directly related to commerce center on luxury, "*le luxe*," upon which he wails. The philosophical battle on the value of luxury produced by commerce was one of the fiercest of the Enlightenment. We have already seen Raynal raise questions about it and Mandeville praise it. Whereas the earlier Enlightenment writers argue that attainment of property is at the root of almost all social, economic, and political goods, Rousseau argues that it is at the root of all evil. Indeed, Rousseau's criticisms match up almost one for one with the arguments earlier Enlightenment authors presented as positives. Whereas the earlier thinkers argue that commerce promotes wealth, Rousseau in his "First Discourse" fears that luxury undermines the truly good things, especially faith and virtue: "what will become of virtue when one must become wealthy at any cost?" (12). Whereas the earlier Enlightenment thinkers argue that commerce promotes individual and national greatness, Rousseau argues that it detracts from it: "Ancient politicians spoke incessantly about mores and virtue; ours speak only of commerce and money" (12); "with money one has everything but mores and citizens" (13). Whereas Hume argues that commerce promotes civilization, Rousseau argues that luxury corrupts taste because artists lower their standards seeking applause from the crowd (13). Whereas the earlier authors argue that commerce leads to national strength and power, Rousseau argues that the lazy and luxurious mores it promotes destroy courage: "true courage is enervated, military virtue disappears" (15). Whereas the earlier thinkers argue that commerce promotes better moral behavior by promoting tolerance, gentleness, and understanding of others, Rousseau argues that it destroys morality because commerce and moneymaking put an emphasis on appearance and increase inequality. Locke acknowledges that commerce increases inequality and Montesquieu notes how commerce undermines "pure morality," but they think commerce's benefits outweighed these costs. They consciously view the worldly attachment to wealth and commerce as a superior alternative to the old aristocratic struggle for mastery. Better, they think, to let people compete for wealth, the trading of which would be mutually beneficial, than to compete for glory which was a zero sum gain. Rousseau reveals himself as a careful student of the Enlightenment philosophers' arguments about commerce and he agrees with them on the likely consequences of commerce; he radically breaks from them only in valuing the consequences differently, more in accordance with the ancient and medieval emphases on pure mores and martial valor that the Enlightenment philosophers consciously rejected.

The Physiocrats and the Agrarian Ideal

The Rousseauian fascination with nature was cultivated and scientized by a group of French thinkers who called themselves the Physiocrats. The

Physiocrats were the first to call themselves "economists" in the modern sense and they coined the term "laissez-faire," but they meant by this term something totally different from its current connotation. The Physiocrats cull from Rousseau the message that everyone who did not farm the land—and indeed commerce itself—was parasitic. While it is highly doubtful that Rousseau himself intended such a conclusion, according to the Physiocrats land alone leads to wealth, and this leads them to praise farmers not only above all else—but as the only worthy class in society. There is not much in Rousseau that supports such a deification of land and farmers, but inspired by their tame version of the noble savage, the Physiocrats use Enlightenment science to buttress their call for an agricultural entrepreneurial class. All other occupations, such as landowners and merchants, they claim, consume more than they create. The Physiocrats thus condemn every other class as sterile. According to them agriculture as a way of life not only leads to riches, but they deem it a more natural and morally superior way of living. Laissez-faire for them comes into play when people set out to maximize agriculture, which alone would maximize wealth and morality. Laissez-faire for them does not mean letting anyone do whatever they wanted, but only the agriculturalists—and this requires government to remove the obstacles to agriculture. In short, the Physiocrats, the first scientific economists in the modern sense, use Enlightenment techniques but in a limited way determined by their peculiar reading of Rousseau. They apply their Enlightenment methods only to agriculture, because they have a vision of wholesome wealth based on Rousseau's conceptions of naturalness and simplicity.[25]

In Christian agrarian thinkers such as Richard Price, the vision of the Physiocrats was turned into the ideal of the yeoman farmer: independent, self-reliant, moderate, pure, religious, and simple. The yeoman farmer avoids the twin evils of crushing poverty and corrupting luxury. They live for the simple, wholesome, basic necessities only.[26] This pious and wholesome vision is summarized by Lord Kames, the Scottish philosopher: "There seems to be but three ways for a nation to acquire wealth. The first is by war, as the Romans did, in plundering their conquered neighbors. This is robbery. The second by commerce, which is generally cheating. The third by agriculture, the only honest way . . . wrought by the hand of God in his favor, as a reward for his innocent life and his virtuous industry."[27] Thus, taking their moral passion from Rousseau, the Enlightenment's anti-commerce arguments reject the worldly, sophisticated, luxurious modernity envisioned by Montesquieu, Hume, and Mandeville in favor of a vision of rural, self-reliant simplicity.

THE CULMINATION OF THE ENLIGHTENMENT DEBATE: ADAM SMITH

The culmination of the debate on commerce in the Enlightenment takes place in the thought of Adam Smith (1723–1790). For Smith, we are by nature traders. He rejects the stay-on-the-farm agriculturalism of the anti-commerce thinkers, asserting a "propensity in human nature . . . to truck, barter, and exchange one thing for another" (I. II, 25).[28] No one speaks more beautifully about the division of labor which Smith calls the "greatest improvement" in human life. The *Wealth of Nations*, Book I, Chapter I, explains the eighteen steps in making a pin, and how instead of one person performing all eighteen steps a division of labor among a ten-man team increases productivity 240 or 4,800 fold. Smith's paean to the division of labor includes all the arguments made by Locke, Montesquieu, and Hume. Smith argues not only that commerce leads to peace and wealth, but also that the free time and wealth generated by commerce is the key to all civilization. Most strikingly, he also powerfully argues that commerce as a world force promoted equality in Europe by being the fundamental force that undermined the vestiges of the aristocratic world.[29] Whether he gets it directly from them or not, Smith in effect co-opts the Physiocrats' idea of laissez-faire, but he expands it from merely the agricultural realm (as the Physiocrats themselves narrowly applied it) to all commercial activity. Smith combines his expanded conception of laissez-faire with the self-interested psychology of Mandeville and Hume. His emphasis on self-interest, however, does not blind him to the costs paid by the laborers in commercial activity, and he both catalogues these costs and suggests remedies. But unlike the remedies suggested by the romantic, anti-commerce writers of the Enlightenment, Smith's remedies do not require a radical rejection of modern liberalism. To the contrary, like Tocqueville and Mill, Smith seeks remedies for the problems of liberal commercial republics by drawing on their own resources. In short, Smith offers the most complete account of commerce that has perhaps ever been written by a philosopher.

Like Mandeville, Hume, and the other hard-nosed liberal thinkers, Smith rejects relying on the natural goodness of man or the benevolence of virtuous fellow citizens, arguing that "it is vain" for one to expect "the help of his brethren" from "their benevolence only." Instead, Smith argues, "He will be more likely to prevail if he can interest their self-love in his favour, and shew them that it is for their own advantage to do for him what he requires of them" (I. II, 26). Smith applies this concretely as follows: "It is not from the benevolence of the butcher, the brewer, or the baker, that we expect our dinner, but from their regard to their own interest. We address ourselves, not to their humanity, but to their self-love, and never talk to them of our necessities but of their advantages"

(I. II, 26–27). Smith explicitly spells out the assumptions that were implied in the earlier pro-commerce arguments: self-interested actions promote the common good as if by an "invisible hand." As Smith famously writes, a self-interested individual is "led by an invisible hand to promote an end which was no part of his intention. By pursuing his own interest he frequently promotes that of the society more effectually than when he really intends to promote it" (IV. II, 456). Smith's extraordinary metaphor of the invisible hand encapsulates the essence of the Enlightenment's pro-commerce argument. Pursuit of self-interest as encouraged by Locke, Montesquieu, Mandeville, and Hume and as denounced by Rousseau, the Physiocrats, and the Christian agrarians is, paradoxically, the best means to most social goals.

But unlike some of its later defenders, Smith sees and admits the main problems with commerce. As much as he lauds the miracles produced by the division of labor, he openly acknowledges its costs. In passages that might have been written by Marx or Dickens, Smith laments the consequences that the rote monotony of industrial operations has on the workers who must perform them:

> The man whose whole life is spent performing a few simple operations . . . has no occasion to exert his understanding, or to exercise his invention . . . and generally becomes as stupid and ignorant as it is possible for a human creature to become. The torpor of his mind renders him, not only incapable of relishing or bearing a part in any rational conversation, but of conceiving any generous, noble, or tender sentiment. (V. I. f, 782)

> The same thing may be said of the gross ignorance and stupidity which, in a civilized society, seem so frequently to benumb the understandings of all the inferior ranks of people. A man, without the proper use of the intellectual faculties of a man, is, if possible, more contemptible than even a coward, and seems to be mutilated and deformed in a still more essential part of the character of human nature (V. I. f, 788).

Smith points out the dehumanizing drawbacks for an individual worker even while marveling over the wealth that the division of labor creates for owners, workers, and society as a whole. Indeed, like Rousseau, Smith laments how labor leads to the loss of individual, social, and martial virtues. Smith fears that the routinization of mechanical activity would routinize the mind: "The uniformity of his stationary life naturally corrupts the courage of his mind" (V. I. f, 782). Skill in one's occupation can undermine the possibility of attaining more general human virtues: "His dexterity at his own particular trade seems, in this manner, to be acquired at the expence of his intellectual, social and martial virtues" (782). Smith further claims that the economic system alone must reduce its workers to this dehumanized state: "in every improved and civilized society this is the state into which the laboring poor, that is, the great body of the people, must necessarily fall, unless government takes some pains to prevent it" (782). Unfettered capitalism will reduce not only a few but most to animals—and it will do this "necessarily . . . unless government takes some pains to prevent it."

What governmental remedies, we might ask, are necessary to reduce the dehumanizing effect of modern economic life? One of Smith's remedies for the excesses of the unfettered commercial order is public education. Unlike the romantic anti-commercial writers whose publications already announce the beginning of the end of the Enlightenment, Smith's remedy is not to return to a pre-commercial, supposed utopia; Smith also carefully details the soul-crushing poverty all too often found there. Instead, his remedy comes from within the liberal commercial republic and is consistent with liberalism's moral and political commitments. Smith aggressively promotes public education especially for society's poor: "The education of the common people requires, perhaps, in a civilized and commercial society, the attention of the publick more than that of people of some rank and fortune" (V. I. f, 784); "For a very small expense the publick can facilitate, can encourage, and can even impose upon almost the whole body of the people, the necessity of acquiring those most essential parts of education," defined as learning "to read, to write, and account" (V. I. f, 785). Indeed, not only does Smith promote education, but as Jefferson was later to propose for all Americans and as Burke proposed for Britain's slaves in the New World, Smith had a scheme for achieving it: "The publick can facilitate this acquisition by establishing in every parish or district a little school, where children may be taught for a reward so moderate, that even a common labourer may afford it" (V. I. f, 785).[30]

Like Rousseau, Smith seems to fear that the tradition of republican virtue is undermined by commercial activity, so in addition to public education, he also recommends military training. Smith agrees with Rousseau and other critics of the commercial republic that commerce makes people effete and thus vulnerable to conquest. Smith writes, "That in the progress of improvement the practice of military exercises, unless government takes proper pains to support it, goes gradually to decay, and, together with it, the martial spirit of the great body of the people, the example of modern Europe sufficiently demonstrates" (V. I. f, 786–87). Indeed, Smith goes further and advocates martial training for reasons other than mere defense: "Even though the martial spirit of the people were of no use towards the defence of society," he writes, "yet to prevent that sort of mental mutilation, deformity and wretchedness, which cowardice necessarily involves in it, from spreading themselves through the great body of the people, would still deserve the most serious attention of government; in the same manner as it would deserve its most serious attention to prevent a leprosy or any other loathsome and offensive disease, though neither mortal nor dangerous, from spreading itself among them; though, perhaps, no other publick good might result from such attention besides the prevention of so great a publick evil" (V. I. f, 787–88).

In conclusion, Smith is no atomistic individualist recklessly promoting *homo economicus*. Like all the great theorists of commerce, Smith accepts that self-interest is the world's most powerful force and the passion to be relied on. He further argues that self-interest will as if through an invisible hand realize the common good of society in a way that conscious planning for the common good can itself never realize. But Smith is also keenly aware that achieving the improvement of society through self-interested commercial motivations has individual costs. Unlike Rousseau or Marx he does not envision society as a conspiracy of the rich ruling the poor, but he is sensitive to abuses of power by the rich and powerful and to the degradation inherent in the division of labor that commerce promotes and requires. The overall benefits should be pursued but the individual degradations should be remedied. Here Smith shows that he has learned from Rousseau and his followers, but while appreciating their goals he finds more realistic remedies from within the liberal commercial republic itself.[31]

THE IDEA OF COMMERCE IN EARLY AMERICA: THE EXTRAORDINARY CASE OF ALEXANDER HAMILTON

We today often forget the important role of commerce in the events leading up to the American Revolution. The colonists' rallying cry of "no taxation without representation" was not primarily concerned with taxes on land but rather with taxes on commercial products, such as tea and sugar. We also forget the utter chaos of the commercial system in America after independence when each state had its own trade laws, tariffs, and currency. Indeed, the original authorization of the Annapolis convention of 1786 was to deal with trade issues, and because that convention failed there was a call for a constitutional convention, which was eventually held in Philadelphia in 1787. In short, commercial issues were among the core issues in both the revolutionary and constitutional periods.

Among the American Founders, one man preeminently asserted the importance of commerce to the survival of the new nation. Whereas Jefferson promoted the Physiocratic ideal of the yeoman farmer (as Madison did too after 1789), Hamilton displayed the deepest understanding of and appreciation for commerce among the great founding generation. True to his own view (but not others'), Hamilton argued, "The prosperity of commerce is now perceived and acknowledged by all enlightened statesmen to be the most useful as well as the most productive source of national wealth, and has accordingly become a primary object of their political cares."[32] Hamilton's arguments for commerce reflect the views of Locke, Montesquieu, Mandeville, Hume, and Smith. "As commerce enlarged," he told the delegates at the New York ratifying convention, "wealth and civilization increased," citing two of the long-claimed benefits of commerce.[33] Also like the pro-commerce Enlightenment authors, Hamilton argued that commerce leads to power, freedom, self-reliance, and energy, and for the same reasons: "By multiplying the means of gratification" and by promoting "human avarice and enterprise," commerce helps "vivify and invigorate all the channels of industry and to make them flow with greater activity and copiousness," because "all orders of men look forward with eager expectation and growing alacrity to this pleasing reward of their toils."[34] And following the exact logic of Smith and Hume, he saw the gradual enriching of ordinary people as a key to growing equality and freedom: as "the people began to feel their own weight and consequence," they "grew tired of their oppressions," and joined forces with monarchs and "threw off the yoke of aristocracy."[35] According to Hamilton, commerce contributed to all of these fundamental human goods. Yet, for all of his following of the Enlightenment authors, Hamilton disagreed with Montesquieu on one key point. Whereas Montesquieu argued that commerce leads to peace, Hamilton disagreed, writing, "Competitions of commerce would be another fruitful source of contention," just like every other thing that people compete over.[36] Hamilton had his own mind.

Despite disagreement on this last point, Hamilton's views of commerce reflect the general Enlightenment philosophy of "take men as they are." Like the Enlightenment philosophers, Hamilton argues that people are governed by their passions and their interests, and according to Hamilton the chief passion was ambition. Like Machiavelli, Mandeville, and Smith, Hamilton sought to channel self-interested passions and ambition toward the common good. He accepted that politicians and citizens would not be virtuous and pure after the old visions of Plato and Christianity or the newer models of Rousseau and Jefferson.

In the immediate practical task of building America, Hamilton did not apply theory in a doctrinaire or dogmatic way. Rather, he aimed to prudently apply theory to the existing realities in America. At the beginning of his highly technical but brilliant "Report on Manufactures," Hamilton distances himself from both the Physiocrats on the one side and the pure theory of Smith on the other. His rejection of the Physiocrats' position is unsurprising in itself, although it may testify to the power its adherents in America had such that Hamilton felt compelled to attack it. "It has been maintained that Agriculture is, not only, the most productive, but the only productive, species of industry," Hamilton wrote, immediately proceeding to dismiss this fancy: "The reality of this suggestion in either aspect, has, however, not been verified by any accurate detail of facts and calculations; and the general arguments, which are adduced to prove it, are rather subtile and paradoxical, than solid and convincing."[37] More surprisingly, Hamilton acknowledges that while Adam Smith was right in general, he declares that every rule has its exceptions. Arguing against Smith's anti-protectionism and in favor of protectionist measures for "infant industries" necessary to the national defense and well-being, Hamilton describes Smith's view as "founded upon facts and principles, which have certainly respectable pretensions." But he continues to say: "Most general theories, however, admit numerous exceptions, and there are few, if any, of the political kind, which do not blend a considerable portion of error, with the truths they inculcate."[38] While there are aspects of Smith's thought that support Hamilton's position (and it is likely that Hamilton knows this), Hamilton is attacking the American adherents of both philosophical extremes in order to articulate a prudent policy for America given its particular situation. As Darren Staloff has aptly described this position, "Hamilton was no fan of laissez-faire. Commercial expansion and rapid industrialization were vital American goals, and Hamilton sought to achieve them through a powerful, activist federal government. . . . Commercial and industrial development would be imposed from above by a strong centralized state."[39] But Hamilton did not want a large activist state for the same reasons that Progressives later wanted such a state. Hamilton and the Progressives envisioned different ends for the state. As a rule, Hamilton did not want to increase the role of government; he desired to increase the private sphere. Hamilton thought that given the practical realities of the American situation the government had to play a role in the beginning, then step aside after the infrastructure was in place.

Hamilton wanted America to grow into an industrial powerhouse. In his "Report on Manufactures" Hamilton argued for this on many grounds. He wanted to promote internal improvements, to reduce sectionalism by knitting the country together, and he envisioned industry as leading to massive employment, especially for women and children. But the main reason he wanted the nation to industrialize was to be powerful in war. Hamilton's vision was fought against by rural interests and rejected by those who, on a Rousseauian and Physiocratic model, wanted to avoid building dirty, sickly, corrupt cities in America. Madison and Jefferson, for example, both promoted the yeoman ideal and hoped to postpone industrialization for 100 years.[40] If they had their way, and they largely did, American industry would have to develop at a more leisurely pace. However, after a mere 800 British troops burned D.C. to the ground in 1812, Henry Clay and John Calhoun noticed their young nation's national weakness. America had to be strong, and this led to Clay's Whig Platform, "The American System," that was a plan for industrialization, but sectionalism prevented any major implementation of it. Lincoln and the Republican Party campaigned on the same thing, but only after the Civil War—after the destruction of the South and the powers of sectionalism—did it get implemented. After the war, the national government launched campaigns to build massive railroad systems, communications infrastructure, and buildings, all of which came at the price of a huge expansion of the federal government. Hamilton could not have conceived his system without the Enlightenment Philosophers' radically new views of commerce. Within thirty years of its implementation, the United States was an economic powerhouse of global proportions.

CONCLUSION

The Abbé Raynal asked if commerce was a benefit or harm to mankind. The Enlightenment philosophers answered with a resounding affirmation of it, and the prosperity and power of the American republic supports their view. Rousseau's rejection of commerce places him at the beginning of the end of the Enlightenment. All of its other major philosophers argued that commerce promotes wealth, power, freedom, peace, and toleration. According to them commerce unleashes the power of self-interest for the common good. Through the motives of self-interest, it achieves what the best intended governments with the highest motives of altruism could never accomplish. Like today's arguments for commerce, the Enlightenment arguments are rooted in the moral rights of private individuals, but they also offer an array of worldly arguments to support it based on practical wisdom, prudence, and real politik. A supporter of commerce might learn the lesson from these Enlightenment arguments that it is more persuasive to argue for commerce by appealing to one's interlocutor's interests rather than one's own rights—but that is a prudential question of effectiveness.

On a deeper level, however, one might wonder whether human self-interest is as fully beneficial to society as these Enlightenment arguments make it out to be. Indeed, all of the thinkers discussed above, even Mandeville, recognize the need for political institutions to curtail it, and one wonders if the political institutions in America, Europe, and elsewhere that have insured commerce's worldly success do not themselves rest on some prior, non-selfish foundation of virtue. Can a polity exist based solely on enlightened self-interest or is some supplemental foundation also necessary? As Raynal's vision of globalization is increasingly coming to fruition, we shall find out—for better or worse.

NOTES

I am indebted to Thomas W. Merrill and Richard Boyd for their generous comments and suggestions on an earlier draft of this chapter. An early version was presented at St. Thomas University in Houston, Texas, and I thank Daryl Koehn for the opportunity and her questioning. Darren Staloff was most helpful in formulating the section on Hamilton.

1. Abbé Raynal, *Histoire philosophique et politique des éstablissements et du commerce des Européens dans les deux Indes* (Amsterdam, 1770). Citations are to the J.O. Justamond English translation, *A Philosophical and Political History of the Settlements and Trade of the Europeans in the East and West Indies* (London: A. Strahan and T. Cadell, 1788). Diderot wrote approximately a third of this book. For more on this book and the nature of the Raynal-Diderot collaboration, see Michèle Duchet, *Diderot et l'Histoire des deux Indes ou l'écriture fragmentaire* (Paris: A.-G. Nizet, 1978); Gilles Bancarel and Gianluigi Goggi, eds., *Raynal: De la Polémique à l'histoire*. Studies on Voltaire and the Eighteenth Century (2000:12); and Guillaume Ansart, "From Voltaire to Raynal and Diderot's *Histoire de deux Indes*: The French *Philosophes* and Colonial America" in *America Through European Eyes*, eds. Aurelian Craiutu and Jeffrey C. Isaac (University Park, PA.: Penn State University Press, 2009), pp. 71–89.
2. Raynal, *Philosophical and Political History*, Book I, p. 1.
3. Raynal, *Philosophical and Political History*, Book I, pp. 1–2.
4. Raynal, *Philosophical and Political History*, Book I, p. 2.
5. Joseph Schumpeter, *Capitalism, Socialism and Democracy* (New York: Harper, 1975), p. 83. Cf: pp. 82–85. Originally published 1924.
6. Robert Nozick, *Anarchy, State, and Utopia* (New York: Basic Books, 1974), pp. 33–35. For a helpful commentary of the difficulties of Nozick's position, see Clifford Orwin and James R. Stoner, Jr., "Neoconstitutionalism? Rawls, Dworkin, and Nozick," in *Confronting the Constitution*, ed. Allan Bloom with the assistance of Steven J. Kautz (Washington, DC: AEI Press, 1990), pp. 437–70.
7. For Plato's account of the differences between desire, reason, and *thymos*, see *Republic* 436a–441c.
8. See Herbert Deane, *The Political and Social Ideas of St. Augustine* (New York: Columbia University Press, 1963), pp. 44–56.
9. For two classic Enlightenment accounts of ancient republics, see David Hume, "Of the Populousness of Ancient Nations" in his *Essays: Moral, Political, and Literary* (Indianapolis, IN: Liberty Fund, 1985), pp. 377–464, and Benjamin Constant, "The Liberty of the Ancients Compared with that of the Moderns" in Constant, *Political*

Writings, ed. Biancamaria Fontana (Cambridge: Cambridge University Press, 1988), pp. 307–28. For two excellent scholarly accounts, see Paul Rahe, *Republics, Ancient and Modern* (Chapel Hill, N.C.: University of North Caroline Press, 1992) and J. G. A. Pocock, *The Machiavellian Moment* (Princeton: Princeton University Press, 1975).

10. Machiavelli, *The Prince*, tr. Harvey Mansfield (Chicago: University of Chicago Press, 1985), chapter 3, p. 14.

11. See the classic statements on this topic by Max Weber, *The Protestant Ethic and the Spirit of Capitalism* and R. H. Tawney, *Religion and the Rise of Capitalism.* See also Benjamin Nelson, *The Idea of Usury* (Oxford: Oxford University Press, 1949) and Ernst Troeltsch, *Protestantism and Progress: A Historical Study of the Relation of Protestantism to the Modern World*, trans. W. Montgomery (New York: G. P. Putnam's Sons, 1912).

12. The Puritan writer Nicholas Barbon in his *A Discourse of Trade* (1690), published shortly after Locke's *Two Treatises of Government*, is often seen as a bridge between the religious and secular arguments for commerce.

13. Assumed in this is that we own our labor because we own ourselves, but this claim is itself new and controversial. Previously it was believed that we are all the property of our maker, God, and indeed Locke once states that we are all God's property. "Men being all the Workmanship of one Omnipotent, and infinitely wise Maker," he writes, "they are his property" (§ 6). Locke's view on the question of human ownership—ourselves or God—is much discussed in the scholarly literature and beyond our scope to resolve here. Suffice it to say that Locke initially emphasizes that we are all God's creation to establish his claim that no one has a right over another, but as Locke's argument proceeds, he ceases to emphasize God's place at the origin of this chain and instead makes a more anthropocentric argument that we each own ourselves. Some scholars find a contradiction here where others find a shrewd evolution and Locke consciously changing from a Christian worldview to a secular one.

14. All references are to John Locke, *Second Treatise of Government.* The paragraph number is cited in the text.

15. Locke never argues for total equality of persons in the state of nature. Although he does describe it as a state of "perfect freedom" (§ 4), he does not describe it as perfect equality. Instead, he distinguishes the "Industrious & Rational" from the "Quarrelsome and Contentious" (§ 34), arguing that the former qualities make their possessors better off than those dominated by the latter.

16. There are many interpretations of Locke that hinge on the transition from the state of nature to civil society. Recently a wave of scholars such as Ashcraft, Tully, Grant, and Sreenivasian have emphasized the almost majoritarian moment in Locke to articulate the possibility of a communitarianism based on redistribution of property to correct the inequalities of the pre-political order. It is of course true that civil law determines property arrangements for Locke after the institution of government, but civil law must somehow always be bound by the minimal requirements of natural law, otherwise there would be no right to resist tyrannical government in Locke. A full exploration of this literature on Locke is beyond the scope of this paper. I here emphasize Locke's prudential arguments.

17. Bernard Mandeville, *The Fable of the Bees: Or, Private Vices, Publick Benefits* (Indianapolis, IN: Liberty Fund, 1988), a reprint of ed. F. B. Kaye (Oxford: Oxford University Press, 1924). Page numbers are cited in the text.

18. Unless otherwise noted, citations are to Montesquieu, *The Spirit of the Laws*, trans. Anne Cohler, Basia Miller, and Harold Stone (Cambridge: Cambridge University Press, 1989). Textual references include the Book and Chapter numbers followed by the page number in this edition. The word I translate here as "anxious" is not in this edition, but is the literal translation of the French word *inquietude* (XX. 4, 340). See Paul Rahe, *Montesquieu and The Logic of Liberty* (New Haven, CT: Yale University Press, 2009) and *Soft Despotism, Democracy's Drift* (New Haven, CT: Yale University Press, 2009) for a penetrating explanation of *inquietude* in Montesquieu and beyond.

19. Voltaire, *Letters on England*, trans. Leonard Tancock (New York: Penguin, 1980), Letter 6, p. 41.

20. David Hume, *Essays: Moral, Political, and Literary* (Indianapolis, IN: Liberty Fund, 1987). Essays and page numbers are cited in the text.

21. Throughout this section Hume, as did Machiavelli when speaking directly to rulers or potential rulers about their naked self-interest, switches voices and speaks to the ruler as "you": "Afterwards you will find it easy to seize some part of his superfluous labour, and employ it in the public service, without giving him his wonted return. Being accustomed to industry, he will think this less grievous, than if, at once, you obliged him to an augmentation of labour without any reward" ("Of Commerce," 262).

22. Machiavelli, *The Prince*, chapter 3, p. 14.

23. For an excellent account of these arguments that parallels mine but draws different conclusions, see Albert O. Hirschman, *The Passions and the Interests: Political Arguments for Capitalism before Its Triumph* (Princeton: Princeton University Press, 1977).

24. Page citations are to Jean-Jacques Rousseau, *The Basic Political Writings*, ed. and trans. Donald Cress (Indianapolis, IN: Hackett, 1987).

25. On the Physiocrats, see Ronald L Meek, *The Economics of Physiocracy: Essays and Translations* (Cambridge: Harvard University Press, 1963); Elizabeth Fox-Genovese, *The Origins of Physiocracy: Economic Revolution and Social Order in Eighteenth-Century France* (Ithaca, NY: Cornell University Press, 1976); and Forrest McDonald, *Novus Ordo Seclorum: The Intellectual Origins of the Constitution* (Lawrence, KS: University of Kansas Press, 1985), ch. 4.

26. See Richard Price, "Observations on the Importance of the American Revolution," in ed. D. O. Thomas, *Richard Price: Political Writings* (Cambridge: Cambridge University Press, 1991), p. 145; and Price, "Observations on the Nature of Civil Liberty, the Principles of Government, and the Justice and Policy of the War with America" in Bernard Peach, ed., *Richard Price and the Ethical Foundations of the American Revolution* (Durham, NC: Duke University Press, 1979), 102.

27. Cited in McDonald, *Novus Ordo Seclorum*, p. 108.

28. Adam Smith, *An Inquiry Into the Nature and Causes of the Wealth of Nations*, ed. W. B. Todd (Indianapolis, IN: Liberty Fund, 1981). Citations are to the book number, chapter number, and page number.

29. See *Wealth of Nations*, Book III. Hume makes a similar argument in his *History of England.*

30. Compare Smith's remedy to Jefferson's various plans for public education and Burke's "Sketch of the Negro Code" (1780/1792), the latter of which calls for all slaves to be provided with a basic education and for the best students to receive more and more education. Burke's educational plan was an indispensible part of his scheme to eradicate slavery from all British territories.

31. For Smith's overall response to Rousseau, see Dennis Rasmussen, *The Problems and Promise of Commercial Society: Adam Smith's Response to Rousseau* (University Park, PA: Penn State University Press, 2008).

32. Alexander Hamilton, James Madison, and John Jay, *The Federalist Papers*, ed. Clinton Rossiter (New York: Signet, 2003), #12, 86.

33. Cited in Darren Staloff, *Hamilton, Adams, Jefferson: The Politics of Enlightenment and the American Founding* (New York: Hill and Wang, 2005), p. 80.

34. *Federalist*, pp. 12, 86.

35. Cited in Staloff, *Hamilton, Adams, Jefferson*, p. 80.

36. *Federalist*, pp. 7, 57.

37. Hamilton, "Report on Manufactures," in Jacob E. Cooke, ed., *The Reports of Alexander Hamilton* (New York: Harper & Row, 1964), p. 119.

38. Hamilton, "Report on Manufactures," p. 118. On the similarities between the unnamed position that Hamilton articulates and Smith's views, see Cooke, *The Reports of Alexander Hamilton*, pp. 117–18n3.

39. Staloff, *Hamilton, Adams, Jefferson*, p. 89.

40. Madison detested Hamilton's plan for building America, especially Hamilton's call for a national bank, which Madison considered an abuse of the federal government's limited powers. This led to their famous split in 1789. Jefferson similarly hated Hamilton's plan, condemning it as "a machine for the corruption of the legislature" whose insidious "engine" was the national bank. For a full account of Hamilton's three-pronged plan, see Staloff, *Hamilton, Adams, Jefferson*, pp. 89–102, and Peter McNamara, "Hamilton and Jefferson: Two Visions of Democratic Capitalism," chapter 8 in the present volume.

4

Understanding Friedrich Engels (and Marx) and Adam Smith on Economic Organization and the Price Mechanism

Samuel Hollander

In an influential review of W. O. Henderson's *Life of Friedrich Engels*, the late T. W. Hutchison wrote with undisguised anger that it "would be . . . quite erroneous to suppose, because Engels and Marx for decades on end believed that the demise of capitalism, which they so desired, was only months away, that they therefore felt any intellectual or moral obligation to give some thought to the kind of economic organization which would, or could, follow. The Utopian vacuities blurted out by Engels (in his *Principles of Communism*) are as far as they got."[1] The charge is yet stronger. Engels "has the effrontery to attack, for Utopian naiveté, some of the socialist rivals of himself and Marx," especially Johann Karl Rodbertus, the nineteenth-century German economist: "What is most extraordinary is the combination of penetrating critical insight regarding the vital function of the competitive price mechanism as applied to the Utopian notions of Rodbertus together with the totally uncritical, purblind complacency regarding his own and Marx's Utopian assumptions . . ."[2]

Hutchison did well to note Engels's appreciation of the rationing and information-yielding role of the competitive pricing mechanism as revealed in his critique of Rodbertus in "Marx and Rodbertus."[3] Indeed, the evidence for such appreciation is far more extensive than Hutchison apparently realized, and the putative problem that arises correspondingly more severe. Moreover, Marx applied precisely the same market-based case against Pierre-Joseph Proudhon (the French socialist) that Engels later applied against Rodbertus, and similarly made a variety of other applications of the market mechanism.

Beyond this, there is the questionable presumption that the founding fathers had little to say regarding the features of their desired system of communist organization. In taking this line Hutchison was following what seems to be received doctrine, for one finds little detailed discussion of Marx's perception of communism, and even less of that of Engels. A brief statement by Anthony Brewer sums up what seems to be the standard position: "The organization of a future society would be determined by its people as they went along, and could not be forecast in detail."[4] J. E. King writes without qualification of "Marx's refusal to provide blueprints for a socialist economy . . ."[5] And D. K. Foley points to "the fact that Marx never wrote a systematic and detailed description of what he meant by socialism, although scattered through his writings are passing comments and references to socialist economic practice and substantial critiques of other writers' conceptions of socialism."[6]

In this chapter I shall devote most attention to Engels, merely summarizing materials appearing in my *Economics of Karl Marx*;[7] and using Hutchison's review article as my point of departure. Let me state briefly my main conclusion regarding the problem raised by Hutchison (which might have been equally addressed at Marx). The resolution, I shall suggest, lies in the very character of the Marx-Engels vision of communism—throughout I refer to the first or post-capitalist stage rather than some ultimate ideal arrangement—as a form of organization simplified to the point where there would be no need for a price mechanism, whereas competing schemes retained significant features of capitalist or private-ownership arrangement rendering a pricing mechanism essential. This is my hypothesis, without which we are left with Hutchison's attribution to Engels of gross irresponsibility, even dishonesty.

There is a second major theme to this chapter. Engels, as we shall see, rejected on orthodox price-theoretic grounds the usury laws, as an instance of ineffectual intervention in the credit market. Yet Adam Smith, of all people, had supported the usury laws. This extraordinary feature of the record requires explanation if we are to pretend to appreciate *The Wealth of Nations*. The case at hand will sharpen the contrast between the Smithian and Engels-Marx perspectives on government intervention in market systems.

COMMUNIST ORGANIZATION

A prelude to the case for public ownership and the replacement of the market, which places Engels temporally ahead of Marx in this regard,[8] is already to be found in a paper of November 1843 on "Progress of Social Reform on the Continent," where Engels (then aged 23) declares that "England, France, and Germany have all come to the conclusion, that a thorough revolution of social arrangements, based on community of property, has now become an urgent and unavoidable necessity."[9] Here we encounter an important qualification to the praise accorded François Fourier on the "necessity of association," namely that a basic "inconsistency" vitiated his socialistic scheme (the so-called *Phalanstères* or associated establishments) by retaining features of "competition" and the market.[10] Engels, unfortunately, did not follow up an intention "to give an exposition" of the Communist system he himself favored. But the following year, in *Outlines of a Critique of Political Economy*, he opts for the replacement of "competition" by planning: "In a world worthy of mankind . . . [t]he community will have to calculate what it can produce with the means at its disposal; and in accordance with the relationship of this productive power to the mass of consumers it will determine how far it has to raise or lower production, how far it has to give way to, or curtail, luxury."[11]

The passage just referred to alludes apparently to planning decisions regarding aggregate investment and aggregate consumption, and does not bear upon the selection of individual consumer goods. As for this issue, Engels appears to disallow consumer sovereignty since he further maintained in the *Outlines* that the supersession of private property implied reliance on communal decision-making regarding production based upon a comparison of costs relative to the "inherent utility of the object independent of the parties concerned [in an exchange]," that is, independent of personal judgment and the "freedom of those who exchange."[12] Accordingly, the "practical application of the concept of value will then be increasingly confined to the decision about production, and that is its proper sphere." We arrive at the same conclusion when we recall that ignorance of the pattern of consumption was seen as the source of "periodic upheavals" under capitalism, in contrast to the communist solution: "If the producers as such knew how much the consumers required, if they were to organise production, if they were to share it out amongst themselves, then the fluctuations of competition and its tendency to crisis would be impossible."[13]

A further noteworthy feature of Engels's *Outlines* is the inclusion in the planning task of shadow calculations relating to interest and rent based on the productivity contributions of land and capital.[14] Costs are not restricted to direct labor alone. Indeed costs would include an allowance for "science," since "in a rational order which has gone beyond the division of interests as it is found with the economist, the mental element certainly belongs among the elements of production and will find its place, too, in economics among the costs of production."[15]

Taking leave of the *Outlines*, we note that the replacement of the market mechanism by central planning is briefly suggested in Marx-Engels's joint work *The German Ideology*: ". . . with the abolition of . . . private property, with the communist regulation of production . . . the power of the relation of supply and demand is dissolved into nothing . . ."[16] But it is more fully indicated in Engels's *Principles of Communism*.

The central features of the "new social order" are specified in the *Principles* thus: "Above all, it will have to take the running of industry and all branches of production in general out of the hands of separate individuals competing with each other and instead will have to ensure that all these branches of production are run by society as a whole, i.e., for the social good, according to a social plan and with the participation of all members of society. It will therefore do away with competition and replace it by association."[17] There is also mention of the abolition of money.[18]

These features are elaborated years later in *Anti-Dühring*, read and approved by Marx. In the first place, the notion of a central plan is made explicit in the course of observations regarding industry location: "Only a society which makes it possible for its productive forces to dovetail harmoniously into each other on the basis of one single vast plan can allow industry to be distributed over the whole country in the way best adapted to its own development, and to the maintenance and development of the other elements of production."[19]

Secondly, it is clarified that in communist society excluding money and markets, direct procedures suffice to arrive at labor embodiments. The indirect procedures of capitalism involving reference to money prices are avoided by "direct social production and direct distribution [which] preclude all exchange of commodities, therefore also the transformation of the products into commodities (at any rate within the community), and consequently also their transformation into *values*."[20] The entire notion of value in fact becomes irrelevant. All this—fully in line with Marx[21]—is confirmed by further reference to direct calculation by "society" of the labor time required in the production of, say, "a steam-engine . . . or a hundred square yards of cloth of a certain quality" without reference to any "third product" acting as some sort of measure of value.

Fully to appreciate the position in *Anti-Dühring* we must keep in mind a concern that to permit money to circulate would inevitably lead to a reemergence of capitalist organization. For example, Dühring's money did not act as "a mere labour certificate"—as did Marx's—but fulfilled a genuine "monetary" function as far as concerns private saving with potentially devastating consequences for his communal proposals.[22] The retention of money as means of purchase and payment in international trade would further encourage the private motive to accumulate and, with it, the demise of the entire communal enterprise.[23]

A third feature of Engels's proposed communist system as it emerges in *Anti-Dühring* relates to consumer demand. As mentioned, direct calculation of requisite inputs is fundamental to the central-planning process envisaged, although this, it is explained, takes for granted "the useful effects of the various articles of consumption":

> It is true that even then it will still be necessary for society to know how much labour each article of consumption requires for its production. It will have to arrange its plan of production in accordance with its means of production, which include, in particular, its labour-powers. The useful effects of the various articles of consumption, compared with one another and with the quantities of labour required for their production, will in the end determine the plan. People will be able to manage everything very simply, without the intervention of much-vaunted "value."[24]

But who calculates the "useful effects"? That Engels had in mind freedom of consumer choice is unlikely, as we concluded with respect to the *Outlines*.[25] For a little earlier in the text, he had expatiated on the anarchical character of capitalist production due in part to producers' ignorance of markets: "No one knows how much of his particular article is coming on the market, nor how much of it will be wanted. No one knows whether his individual product will meet an actual demand, whether he will be able to make good his costs of production or even to sell his commodity at all."[26] The solution to the enormous waste of resources under capitalism, with an eye to cyclical instability in particular, lay precisely in proper implementation, by means of the control system, of the "social character" not only of "the means of production" but also of "the products"[27] (266). As Dusan Pokorni expressed the matter in discussing Marx: "what will be on the shelves . . . is the prerogative of planning as an administrative command."[28] But apart from this, it is difficult to conceive how, in the absence of money and markets, consumers' preferences could be expressed—recall that labor tickets would not circulate. Rather, it is the central planners who rank social utilities in deciding on the basket.[29]

The character of Engels's control system as it applied to agriculture is indicated by a document entitled "American Food and the Land Question," composed at about the same time as *Anti-Dühring*. Here is described the American "revolution in farming, together with the revolutionised means of transport as invented by the Americans" which exported wheat to Europe "at such low prices that no European farmer can compete with it—at least not while he is expected to pay rent."[30] The "upshot of all this," Engels predicts, "will and must be that it will force upon us the nationalisation of the land and its cultivation by co-operative societies under national control. Then, and then alone, it will again pay both the cultivators and the nation to work it, whatever the price of American or any other corn and meat may be."[31] Engels thus envisaged an autarkic agricultural régime, with agriculture organized by "co-operatives" under "national control" apparently precluding inter-cooperative competition, as was also Marx's position in a reference extending beyond agriculture.[32] What this implies more generally, particularly whether autarky would also apply to industrial activity, is unclear; indeed, it is far from certain that Engels had thought this matter through.[33]

In a later letter to August Bebel, Engels writes more generally of cooperative organization as only "transitionally" acceptable, and even so subject to the same qualification regarding national control: "Nor have Marx and I ever doubted that, in the course of transition to a wholly communist economy, widespread use would have to be made of cooperative management as an intermediate stage. Only it will mean so organising things that society, i.e. initially the State, retains ownership of the means of production and thus prevents the particular interests of the cooperatives from taking precedence over those of society as a whole."[34] Since national control is insisted upon, the question of the role of cooperatives is less significant than in the case of J. S. Mill; even cooperatives could be incorporated within Engels's "one single vast plan."[35] We note, finally, that in the 1891 Introduction to Marx's *The Civil War in France* the option of decentralized decision making by "associations" or cooperatives is explicitly excluded.[36]

COMMUNIST DISTRIBUTION

In the Marxian vision of the "higher" phase of communism, the distributive rule "from each according to his abilities to each according to his needs" would apply.[37] But Marx insisted on wage differentials as a necessary feature not only of capitalist arrangement but also of the first stage of communism: "But one man is superior to another physically or mentally and so supplies more labour in the same time, or can work for a longer time"; thus while "class distinctions" are abolished "because everyone is only a worker like everyone else . . . the unequal individual endowment and thus productive capacity of the workers as natural privileges" is recognized.[38] Dühring condemned Marx for adopting a typically bourgeois perspective regarding the related matter of "compound labor": "In his lucubrations on value . . . Herr Marx never rids himself of the ghost of a skilled labour-time which lurks in the background. He was unable to effect a thoroughgoing change here because he was hampered by the traditional mode of thought of the educated classes, to whom it necessarily appears monstrous to recognize the labour-time of a porter and that of an architect as of absolutely equal value from the standpoint of economics."[39] Engels leaped to Marx's defense, insisting on wage-scale differentials under capitalism—the "higher wages paid for compound labour"—on the grounds that "[i]n a society of private producers, private individuals or their families pay the cost of training the qualified worker."[40] He remarked how fortunate it was for Dühring "that fate did not make him a manufacturer, and thus saved him from fixing the value of his commodities on the basis of this new rule [of treating all labour equally] and thereby running infallibly into the arms of bankruptcy."[41] But the complaint is extended. Dühring applied his rule to his future commune "entailing the pure heavenly air of equality and justice." By contrast, under Engels's vision, the planners would ascribe "greater values" to productions of compound labor, though pay differentials would not be recognized: "In a socialistically organised society, these costs [of training] are borne by society, and to it therefore belong the fruits, the greater values produced by compound labour. The worker himself has no claim to extra pay." There is no conflict with Marx, who insisted on the recognition of "unequal individual endowment and thus productive capacity of the workers as natural privileges," since Marx intended specifically recognition of differentials reflecting "natural" characteristics, while Engels had in mind acquired characteristics involving publicly funded training.

THE PRICE MECHANISM, AND OBJECTIONS TO RODBERTUS'S "UTOPIANISM"

It must be appreciated that Engels's championship of full-fledged communism in no way implies a failure to appreciate the information-yielding and allocative functions of the competitive price mechanism as it operates, or should be allowed to operate, in a private-property based system. We shall illustrate.

In the important work "The Housing Question" (1872, 1887), Engels approached the working-class housing transaction as a "quite ordinary commodity transaction" subject to "the economic laws which govern the sale of commodities in general . . ."[42] Engels sets out from the orthodox demand-based rule that "[a]ny investment of capital which satisfies an existing need is profitable if conducted rationally."[43] What required explanation was "precisely, why the housing question continues to exist *all the same*, why the capitalists do not provide sufficient healthy dwellings for the workers . . ." It was unproductive to blame—as did so many socialist critics—"the propertied, higher social classes . . . because they do not make it their business to provide a sufficient supply of good housing."[44] More specifically, on-going adoption of labor-displacing "machinery" and the pattern of regular trade cycles depressed average wages and employment and thus workers' purchasing power, rendering unprofitable the private provision of rental accomodation for workers relative to alternative higher-class categories.[45] By contrast, "bourgeois socialist" writers had no other explanation to offer for the housing shortage than to represent it as "the result of the wickedness of man," as "original sin, so to speak."[46] In brief, Engels insisted on an objective price-analytic diagnosis to explain the housing shortage, in contrast with the vacuity of subjective appeals for increased provision based on "justice" and "right."

Engels's critique of protectionist policies is equally revealing. His "Protection and Free Trade" makes it very clear indeed that the Infant Industry case, which he had justified on standard developmental grounds in America, must be temporary (no more than say twenty-five years), and that protection was "by now becoming a nuisance."[47] His objections to protection are in line with those of Marx against price control: "Protection is at best an endless screw, and you never know when you have done with it. By protecting one industry, you directly or indirectly hurt all others, and have therefore to protect them too. By so doing you again damage the industry that you first protected, and have to compensate it; but this compensation reacts, as before, on all other trades, and entitles them to redress, and so on *in infinitum*."[48] Beyond this, technical progress was so rapid and revolutionary "that what may have been yesterday a fairly balanced protective tariff is no longer so to-day," engendering inter-industrial and political conflicts to assure the necessary modifications.[49] But "the worst of protection" is that "when you once have got it you cannot easily get rid of it. Difficult as is the process of adjustment to an equitable tariff, the return to Free Trade is universally more difficult."[50] For "[t]he legislature, by adopting the protective plan, has created vast interests, for which it is responsible. And not every one of these interests—the various branches of industry—is equally ready, at a given moment, to face open competition. Some will be lagging behind, while others have no longer need of protective nursing. This difference of position will give rise to the usual lobby-plotting . . ."[51]

Engels objected to contemporary recommendations for government intervention in the credit market—as by Proudhon who sought to reduce the interest rate to 1 percent and ultimately to zero. Engels rejected the presumption that the interest rate can be effectively regulated by legislation, due to the operation of competitive market forces which establish the return on loanable funds, with some redirection to take account of the risk of penalty in the event of state intervention in the market: "The rate of interest will continue to be governed by the economic laws to which it is subject today, all decrees notwithstanding. Persons possessing credit will continue to borrow money at two, three, four and more per cent, according to circumstances, just as before, and the only difference will be that rentiers will be very careful to advance money only to persons with whom no litigation is to be expected. Moreover, this great plan to deprive capital of its 'productivity' is as old as . . . the *usury laws*

. . . which aim at nothing else but limiting the rate of interest, and which have since been abolished everywhere because in practice they were continually broken or circumvented, and the state was compelled to admit its impotence against the laws of social production."[52]

Here is a paradoxical situation if ever there was one. Marx and Engels—who so often focus on the market as destabilizing and who opted for Communism—yet read like von Hayek and von Mises in their approach to intervention in the market system.[53] And, compounding the apparent confusion, it is Engels who, unlike Smith, condemns the usury laws on price-theoretic grounds. We shall return to this seemingly extraordinary contrast in the final section of this chapter.

Appreciation of the allocative function of markets emerges most impressively in "Marx and Rodbertus," as Hutchison appreciated. Here he attacks Karl Rodbertus's version of labor money (in Rodbertus, *Zur Erkenntniss unsrer staatswirthschaftlichen Zustande*, 1842) precisely because it neglected the competitive allocation mechanism while retaining central features of the market system. Engels was here, in effect, repeating the same sort of complaint addressed against Fourier in 1843, and against Dühring in 1878, that they contaminated their schemes with elements of a market economy. Indeed, the retention of "exploitation" is the very core of Engels's reading of Rodbertus: "Wage labour and its exploitation remain"; and "rent and profit are . . . to continue undiminished. For the landowners and industrial capitalists also exercise certain socially useful or even necessary functions, even if economically unproductive ones, and they receive in the shape of rent and profit a sort of pay on that account . . ."[54] The sole novelty is that the state requires that exchanges "at least for a part of the products"—referring to consumer goods—must occur to reflect relative labor input.[55]

Rodbertus maintained that all markets would clear, whereas for Engels this outcome was inconceivable, the deliberate preclusion of "competition" with its characteristic price signaling to determine the appropriate mix of goods rendering inefficient resource allocation inevitable. In Engels's own words, Rodbertus had "adopted the usual utopian disdain of economic laws . . . Only through the undervaluation or overvaluation of products is it forcibly brought home to the individual commodity producers what society requires or does not require and in what amounts. But it is precisely this sole regulator that the utopia advocated by Rodbertus among others wishes to abolish." In brief, there was no guarantee "that [the] necessary quantity and not more of each product will be produced, that we shall not go hungry in regard to corn and meat while we are choked in beet sugar and drowned in potato spirit . . ."[56]

How, Hutchison protested,[57] could Engels possibly have contrived to condemn Rodbertus on the foregoing price-theoretic grounds while neglecting to raise the same objection against his own "vacuous" conception of communist organization?[58] Hutchison was, I believe, excessively harsh. Engels's position, as it has emerged above, is that Rodbertus rejected the competitive pricing mechanism while at the same time he retained significant elements of a market system. This to Engels was an unacceptable halfway house.[59] Like Marx, he perceived of a system excluding money and markets, one involving centralized decisions on investment, output, and pay, and (we have seen) precluding consumer sovereignty, the wages-goods basket allocated according to workers' claims based on their labor contributions, account taken of natural-skill differentials. In this scheme entailing central control of quantities demanded as well as quantities supplied there would be no need for an allocative mechanism to assure balance.

There is, it may appear, a "compartmentalization" or "duality" in the works of Marx and Engels since in the context of the cycle (particularly the crisis), the focus is on the chaotic character of markets, whereas the basic Marxian model and the applications discussed above assume the market process to be equilibrating in the orthodox fashion. Yet this contrast must not be pushed too far, if we keep in mind a further dimension to Engels's objection to Rodbertus. Rodbertus's preclusion of a "competitive" process, Engels observed, undermined his aim to solve the problem of crises, and in fact worsened the problem. For however defective the signaling mechanism provided by competitive prices might be, Rodbertus's alternative was far worse—particularly in an international environment—for individual producers would then be operating "completely blindfolded":

> As soon as the production of commodities has assumed world market dimensions, the evening-out between the individual producers who produce for private account and the market for which they produce, which in respect of quantity and quality of demand is more or less unknown to them, is established by means of a storm on the world market, by a commercial crisis. If now competition is to be forbidden to make the individual producers aware, by a rise or fall in prices, how the world market stands, then they are completely blindfolded . . . [T]he producers can no longer learn anything about the state of the market for which they are producing . . .[60]

MARXIAN POLITICAL ECONOMY: THE PRICE-THEORETIC COMPONENT

Lionel Robbins famously insisted on a sharp distinction between value-free economic analysis, and necessarily value-laden prescription.[61] He pointed out that the two were treated by Adam Smith and the nineteenth-century Classicals as falling within a single designation "Political Economy," to describe not only "how the economic system actually worked, or could work, but also how, according to the assumptions of the author, it ought to be made, or allowed, to work"; modern practice, by contrast, designates the analysis and description of economic phenomena as "Economics," reserving the term "Political Economy" to "the discussion of what is desirable in the way of policy as a distinct, though related, speculative area."[62] In either case, the link turns on the fact that "to prescribe what is desirable" requires "knowledge of what is possible—of what effects are likely to follow from what specific types of individual or political action," so that "discussion of the problems of what is practically desirable . . . should be conducted against a background of relevant scientific knowledge," in the sense of "a collection of value-free generalizations about the way in which the economic system works."[63]

Several of the texts discussed above justify the contention that Engels (like Marx) subscribed to the foregoing perspective taken by Robbins, regarding both value-free analysis and description and the necessity for prescriptive political economy to take what is relevant into account. Particularly indicative is the objection on price-theoretic grounds to Rodbertus's reform proposals which entail the imposition by the state of labor values, notwithstanding retention of elements of capitalist organization in a halfway house arrangement (wholly in line with Marx's criticisms of Proudhon's reform proposals). Rodbertus is charged with "utopianism" precisely because he "adopted the usual utopian disdain of economic laws."[64] The successful imposition by authority of labor-based prices in the mixed economy envisaged by Rodbertus, Engels protested, could not be assured considering the preclusion of a market mechanism and signaling device to equilibrate quantities supplied and demanded. This objection reflects not only the requirement to base policy prescription upon analysis, that is to take account of the "laws" of political economy, but the objective character attributed to those laws, in this case the competitive pricing mechanism, since the ends acceptable to Engels and Marx differ entirely from those of orthodox economists applying the identical pricing model. Thus while it is certainly true that their opposition to state intervention was doubtless in part politically motivated, the case was made scientifically in terms of the operation of the price mechanism rather than by appeal to morality and justice or by mere assertion.

We also recall the strong opposition on the part of both Engels and Marx to approaching income distribution in terms of justice, and their insistence—under communist no less than under capitalist arrangement—on the economic necessity for "inequality" with respect to wage differentials in all systems.[65] All of this indicates a value-free orientation with regard to analysis and the requirement to take account of such analysis when evaluating economic organization. Relevant too is the "Austrian" quality of their analyses emerging in objections to interventionist proposals on the grounds that such proposals neglected interdependencies between industries that generate unsuspected further interventions required to support the initial step.[66]

To the extent that our case is well made out, the celebrated Marxian designation of 1830 as marking a transition from "scientific" to "apologetic" economics must strictly be understood as referring to the use made of analysis, rather than the analysis as such.[67] But the above account is not intended to represent the alpha and omega of Marxian Political Economy, but rather to take under consideration a price-theoretic component that is conspicuously absent from secondary expositions of Marx and Engels. The account must be extended to include the more familiar macro-economic components, noting here that Engels frequently adopted strong versions of various theoretical structures for purposes of effect and propaganda, undermining to this extent the "value-free" character of analysis.[68] More generally, peculiar to Marxian Political Economy is its perception of the theoretical organon as predictive device, generating forecasts of falling real-wage and profit rates in the growth context, in contrast with classical or neoclassical practice which make no such pretension to historical prediction.[69] Prediction regarding welfare prospects under capitalism is a further major theme of Marxian Political Economy; conspicuous here is the dramatic reversal in later years of the early presumption, accorded the status almost of doctrinal principle, that social reform under capitalism was inconceivable.[70] More generally, a Marxian evolutionary dimension describing and accounting for the transition from competitive to monopoly capitalism, and ultimately to the first stage of communism, entails prediction with a vengeance. Relevant too is the related issue of Historical Materialism, and late modifications by Engels to the doctrine.[71] There are, of course, broader perspectives than ours, such as that by Arun Bose perceiving "capital as coercive social power" as "the key idea of the Marxian Political Economy."[72] All this must certainly be taken into account in a comprehensive view. But it is all the more remarkable that the competitive price mechanism should have been accorded so central a place in the approach to contemporary policy issues and proposals for reform.

* * *

We may further elaborate our conclusion by reference to the familiar quest by George Stigler for the "cause of professional conservatism," which he found to reside in the economist's scientific training:

> He is drilled in the problems of *all* economic systems and in the methods by which a price system solves these problems. It becomes impossible for the

trained economist to believe that a small group of selfish capitalists dictates the main outlines of the allocation of resources and the determination of outputs. It becomes impossible for him to believe that men of good will can by their individual actions stem inflation, or that it is possible to impose changes in any one market or industry without causing problems in other markets or industries. He cannot unblushingly repeat slogans such as "production for use rather than for profit." He cannot believe that a change in the *form* of social organization will eliminate basic economic problems.[73]

This sort of training was acquired by Engels and Marx through the study of the classical literature, and applied in a wholly "conservative" manner in campaigning against both socialist schemes of social reform and various proposals for government intervention in the market. From this point of view both emerge, however paradoxical it may appear, as defenders of the *status quo*, rejecting anything short of full-fledged communism. It will doubtless be objected that since at no time were Marx or Engels swayed from an absolute commitment to central control in place of the market they can scarcely be classified as "conservatives" in Stigler's sense. But while the distinctively contrasting ends must obviously never be lost from sight, such an objection is nonetheless invalid. As pointed out, their "conservatism" is manifest in the rejection of halfway house or compromise arrangements entailing what we would call today a "mixed economy."[74] As for Stigler's final point, that no economist can "believe that a change in the *form* of social organization will eliminate basic economic problems," our argument has been that it is precisely awareness of this fact that led to the case for a central-control system that would, it was imagined, resolve the allocation problem by means alternative to the price mechanism.

It is, in fact, instructive to perceive the Marx-Engels communist scheme as one entailing several features of a "war economy," in the sense of the term adopted by Robbins, as an alternative to the price mechanism:

There can be no question that, in a situation such as a major war, a centrally planned economy whose output has some rational significance is both conceivable and practically possible. The aim is simple: to win the war. The essential problem is therefore to produce for domestic consumption in terms of food, clothing and so on the minimum means necessary to sustain morale and health for the non-military population—quantities which to some extent can be *technically* estimated—leaving all the rest of the productive potential for the war effort. Doubtless there are profound problems arising from scarcities of materials and services even here; and the use of markets and prices in special sectors may be desirable. But the nature of the aims and the urgencies of the situation make the very idea of running a major war by the price mechanism alone a little ridiculous.[75]

While the parallel does not hold good in all respects, it does apply to the positing of a highly simplified régime avoiding markets and a pricing mechanism, to the treatment of final consumption as a residual after social ends have been met, and to the allocation of rights to a specific basket of goods decided upon centrally rather than by free consumer choice. The primary difference is this, that Marx and Engels were, in effect, proposing a "war economy" not for an emergency situation but permanently, or at least into the foreseeable future once their scheme had been put in place.

ADAM SMITH VS. ENGELS ON THE USURY LAWS

We have seen that Engels applied a price-theoretic argument against measures designed to control the interest rate and specifically against the usury laws. In this section we address the striking fact—inexplicable to commentators from Jeremy Bentham to the present day—that Adam Smith argued in favor of the contemporary 5 percent legal maximum on interest.[76] The episode is of high importance in its own right but also because it offers a clear contrast between the Smith and the Marx-Engels perspectives on government intervention in the market.

The main point to note regarding Smith's case for the usury laws is its firm basis, despite first appearance, on market principles. Smith commended the historical sequence of statutory regulations lowering the legal maximum to the ruling 5 percent, which are said "to have been made with great propriety" in that they followed downward movements in, while always remaining marginally higher than, "the rate at which people of good credit usually borrowed."[77] Elsewhere, he writes, "In a country, such as Great Britain where money is lent to government at 3%, and to private people upon good security at 4 and 4.5%, the present legal rate, 5% is, perhaps, as proper as any"; for the legal rate "though it ought to be somewhat above, ought not to be much above the lowest rate."[78]

The justification for a maximum which somewhat exceeds the range of rates appropriate for private borrowers with high credit ratings (our "prime rates") is made out carefully. Firstly, a legal maximum set too low would be unsustainable: "If this legal rate should be fixed below the lowest market rate, the effects of this fixation must be nearly the same as those of a total prohibition of interest," and proscribing interest altogether "instead of preventing, has been found from experience to increase the evil of usury; the debtor being obliged to pay, not only for the use of the money, but for the risk which his creditor runs by accepting a compensation for that use. He is obliged, if we may say so, to insure his creditor from the penalties of usury."[79] Smith further explains, "When the law prohibits interest altogether, it does not prevent it. Many people must borrow, and nobody will lend without a consideration for the use of their money as is suitable, not only to what can be made by the use of it, but to the difficulty and danger of evading the law."[80] When loans at interest are legal but a limit is set below prime the result is similar, since "[t]he creditor will not lend his money for less than the use of it is worth, and the debtor must pay him for the risk which he [the creditor] runs by accepting the full value of that use."[81] The limiting case in this regard is a maximum "fixed precisely at the lowest market price"; this too is unsustainable since "it ruins with honest people, who respect the laws of their country, the credit of all those who cannot give the very best security, and obliges them to have recourse to exorbitant usurers."[82]

Smith thus intended to preclude only transactions involving borrowers of relatively poor credit rating who would be prepared to pay interest much exceeding 5 percent. The market for "safe" loans would operate free of control, a feature that would justify Keynes's designation of Smith as "extremely moderate in his attitude to the usury laws . . . he defended [their] moderate application."[83]

Secondly, where interest rates greatly exceeding the "lowest market rate" are legally available, Smith attributed to lenders a *bias* favoring high-risk loans rather than a roughly equal distribution of preference across the spectrum of opportunities; in brief, he denied that, when faced with such opportunities, lenders would impose control over purely speculative ventures, since lenders are *prejudiced* in favor of riskiness, the majority preferring to engage in high-risk lending should the opportunity present itself: "If the legal rate of interest in Great Britain, for example, was fixed so high as eight or ten per cent, the greater part of the money which was to be lent, would be lent to prodigals and projectors, who alone would be willing to give this high interest. Sober people, who will give for the use of money no more than a part of what they are likely to make by the use of it, would not venture into the competition. A great part of the capital of the country would thus be kept out of the hands which were most likely to make a profitable and advantageous use of it, and thrown into those which were most likely to waste and destroy it."[84] The bias is, however, reversed at a legal maximum rate of interest "fixed but a very little above the lowest market rate," for then "sober people are universally preferred, as borrowers, to prodigals and projectors. The person who lends money gets nearly as much interest from the former as he dares to take from the latter, and his money is much safer in the hands of the one set of people, than in those of the other." Smith presumes here that only prodigals are prepared to offer high illegal rates, and that lenders are loath to accept such inducements, while small inducements are insufficient to compensate the risk of non-repayment. "A great part of the capital of the country," he concludes, "is thus thrown into the hands in which it is most likely to be employed with advantage."

The lack of concern with the emergence of a black credit market at an appropriate legal maximum contrasts sharply with the assumed inevitability of such an outcome in the event of a total prohibition of loans at interest. The essence of the matter is the argument that the 5 percent maximum is effective, in the sense of sustainable, since lenders engage in an effective rationing process whereby "prodigals and projectors" are excluded in favor of "sober" borrowers, thereby containing excess-demand pressures.

The contrast between the behavior of lenders who at the 5 percent maximum seek out "sober" borrowers and the overwhelming bias toward high-risk loans should the legal maximum be set too high (or, by extension, where high interest rates are freely available), requires explanation. Smith's portrayal can be accounted for in terms of his general preoccupation with irresponsibility engendered by the promise of *excessive* returns. Thus, he writes, "The high rate of profit seems everywhere to destroy that parsimony which in other circumstances is natural to the character of the merchant. When profits are high, that sober virtue seems to be superfluous, and expensive luxury to suit better the affluence of his situation."[85] Furthermore, "[w]hen the profits of trade happen to be greater than ordinary, over-trading becomes a general error both among great and small traders."[86] Where profits are high, agricultural employers are prone to adopt inefficient methods: "The planting of sugar and tobacco, can afford the expence of [inefficient] slave cultivation."[87] Of the highest interest from today's perspective is Smith's skepticism regarding government loans to rescue monopolies in danger of bankruptcy, on the grounds that they are all the more likely to repeat their sorry performance with state-provided funds. Thus "[t]he great increase of their fortune"—referring to the United Company of Merchants, a joint-stock operation protected by law from competition—"had, it seems, only served to furnish their servants with a pretext for greater profusion, and a cover for greater malversation, than in proportion even to their increase of fortune"; and "if the company were bad stewards . . . when the whole of their nett revenue and profits belonged to themselves, they were surely not likely to be better, when three-fourths of them were to belong to other people . . ."[88]

The principle is applied broadly. Regarding "the situation" of the great landowner in pre-commercial society, he writes that "it naturally disposes him to attend rather to ornament which pleases his fancy, than to profit for which he has so little occasion."[89] Smith points to typically careless consumption behavior when items absorb only a small fraction of the budget.[90] And most generally, "in publick, as well as in private expences, great wealth may, perhaps, frequently be admitted as an apology for great folly."[91] A corresponding carelessness is ascribed to the labor market in cases where individuals work part-time so that their salary constitutes a fraction of total earnings.[92]

We may summarize the case thus: Preferences with respect to commodities, bonds and labor are not independent of budget and price configurations. In our specific case, Smith rejected universally applicable behavioral assumptions, all depending on the range of opportunities open to investors, the usury laws constraining the range of available opportunities within which lenders *could* be relied upon to offer finance prudently. In particular, to allow a high interest is unacceptable to Smith because it unleashes avarice to the social disadvantage—very much an Aristotelian preoccupation. But though relatively tight markets tend to engender careful calculation, there are limits. For legal interest rates set too low entail excess demand pressures even on the part of "sober" borrowers that cannot be contained. In any event, the standard complaint that Smith neglected the potential emergence of black credit markets does not hold water, for he explains why potential excess demand at the appropriately set maximum is contained, in contrast with the illegal trades that would emerge at an inappropriately low maximum.

This is the main story emerging in the context of the usury laws. But the matter is rather more complex. Smith's apparent confidence in the effectiveness of rationing imposed by lenders at the appropriate rate must be qualified in the light of concerns raised by local banking experience. The Scottish banks were, it seemed, unable to calculate objectively the risk-worthiness of their clients, and accordingly engaged in the finance of inadvisable projects at the legal maximum. Not only that, but their incompetence was such that they themselves borrowed at effective rates far exceeding 5 percent, allowance made for compounding and costly commissions of different sorts; the practice of "drawing and re-drawing [bills of exchange]" might entail effective rates as high as 13 to 14 percent.[93] We are dealing with a failure of self-interest: "Had every particular banking company always understood its own particular interest"—and avoided inappropriate discounting of long-term investment projects—"the circulation never could have been overstocked with paper money" with dire consequences for the banks.[94] The banks were not even aware of the nature of their loans, the "bold projectors" having disguised their operations: "It was a capital which those projectors had very artfully contrived to draw from those banks, not only without their knowledge or deliberate consent, but for some time, perhaps, without their having the most distant suspicion that they had really advanced it."[95] The hoped-for control by lenders had thus not materialized, at least as far as concerned some bank accommodation. One solution envisaged by Smith was the so-called real-bills policy.[96] Another was regulation of paper-money banking by imposing a limitation upon the denomination of bank notes to a £5 minimum—admittedly a "violation" of the "natural liberty of a few individuals," but justified in the interest of the "security of the whole society."[97]

CONCLUSION

Adam Smith justified government intervention in the credit market as a means to assure a framework within which the private-property and free-market arrangement can operate to the social good. Indeed, the Usury Laws—by counteracting the finance of irresponsible "projection"—had contributed toward assuring some three centuries of progress. His commendation is not, strictly speaking, an exception to the general rule of non-intervention, since particular sectors or industries are not targeted, and there is no state "direction" of economic activity. The Usury Laws belong rather to a class of "neutral" intervention, and may fairly be seen as setting the stage for the proper functioning of, not as conflicting with, the System of Natural Liberty. Similarly, while the intervention in the credit market is also seen as discouraging the finance of luxury consumption, there is a valid contrast to be made between such measures, and prohibitions relating to the purchase of particular goods (as by Sumptuary Laws) or restrictions on the importation of specific goods. We also recall that the full technical case for "moderate" interest-rate controls entails a sophisticated appeal to the market mechanism itself,[98] rather than a crude neglect of the potential for the emergence of black markets such as has been the charge since Bentham's day.

Adam Smith's justification of the contemporary usury laws reflects his concern with what he perceived to be unjustifiable risk-tolerance, such that in a wholly free credit market lenders' prejudice toward high-risk projects would predominate to the social detriment. The relevance of this evaluation of creditors' behavior for our present-day financial crisis seems to me self-evident.[99] Relevant too are Smith's observations on the incompetence of the Scottish bankers, and the "artful" dodges of their clients. And it is not difficult to imagine what Smith would have thought of excessive bonuses to bank executives considering his objections to excessive returns in general.

A broader methodological lesson to be learned from the Smith texts is the inadvisability of seeking supposedly universally applicable behavioral axioms, a lesson reiterated by several later classical writers, J. S. Mill of course, but also Ricardo. And quite apart from this, attention to qualification and exception is likely to restrain the propensity to parody doctrine for ideological purposes.

Unlike Smith, Marx and Engels—rejecting the private-property system—had no motive to see its worst features eliminated as a means to assure its continued operation. Nonetheless, they argued on objective price-theoretic grounds that price-control and protectionist measures introduced into a capitalist-exchange system must fail in their purpose. As for the mixed systems proposed by socialist reformers, they feared their degeneration into fully fledged capitalist forms (just as von Mises—as a sort of mirror image—feared the fragility of mixed systems and their degeneration into control systems). What their reaction would be to current Chinese tendencies is apparent. On the other hand, the Chinese authorities might call upon Engels and Marx should they seek to justify wage inequality, at least differentials reflecting "natural" ability.[100] (This, of course, stands in contrast with the Enlightenment position of Adam Smith identifying the street porter and the philosopher in their natural capacities.)

There remains one final consideration. Some explanation is called for to account for the failure of Marx and Engels to provide a concerted, fully-fledged, exposition of their vision of a communist organization, so that one is obliged to draw upon a wide variety of statements frequently criticizing the schemes of others. I am able to offer no more than a tentative suggestion.

The "naiveté" of the scheme for the first stage of communism, the stage which is supposed to emerge from the final stages of (monopoly) capitalism, renders it patently inappropriate for major economies such as England, France, Germany, and the United States, especially if international trade between them is taken for granted. In brief, there is—this much must certainly be allowed to Hutchison—much of the "utopian" to the plan, akin to numerous early nineteenth-century schemes relating to small-scale and geographically constrained operations. Is it possible that awareness of this deficiency encouraged the strategy of reticence, our heroes not totally convinced by the prospective relevance of their own scheme?

NOTES

1. T. W. Hutchison, "Friedrich Engels and Marxist Economic Theory," *Journal of Political Economy* 86, no. 2 (April 1978): 315.
2. Hutchison, "Friedrich Engels and Marxist Economic Theory," 316.
3. Engels, "Marx and Rodbertus," preface to the First German Edition of *The Poverty of Philosophy* by Karl Marx, reprinted in *Marx-Engels Collected Works*, 50 vols. (1884; Lawrence and Wishart, London; International Publishers, New York; and Progress Publishers and the Institute of Marxism-Leninism [subsequently the Russian Independent Institute of Social and National Problems], Moscow, 1975–2004), 26: 278–292. Subsequent references will be to *MECW*, followed by volume and page

number. The specific items written by Marx-Engels referred to in this chapter are indicated within the text.

4. Anthony Brewer, *A Guide to Marx's* Capital (Cambridge: Cambridge University Press, 1984), 3.

5. J. E. King, "Nimitz's *Marx and Engels: Their Contribution to the democratic Breakthrough*," *Research in the History of Economic Thought and Methodology* 20 (2002): 221.

6. D. K. Foley, *Understanding Capital: Marx's Economic Theory* (Cambridge, MA: Harvard University Press, 1986), 158.

7. Samuel Hollander, *The Economics of Karl Marx: Analysis and Application* (New York: Cambridge University Press, 2008).

8. See H. Maler, "An apocryphal testament: 'Socialism, Utopian and Scientific,'" *Science and Society* 62 (1998): 48.

9. Friedrich Engels, "Progress of Social Reform on the Continent" (1845), in *MECW* 3: 392.

10. Engels, "Progress of Social Reform on the Continent," in *MECW* 3: 395.

11. Engels, *Outlines of a Critique of Political Economy* (1844), in *MECW* 3: 435.

12. Engels, *Outlines*, in *MECW* 3: 426.

13. Engels, *Outlines*, in *MECW* 3: 434.

14. Engels, *Outlines*, in *MECW* 3: 430–431. These observations raise obvious questions relating to the proposed productivity calculations. Marx, with respect to rent, shortly thereafter pointed out that "fertility is not so natural a quality as might be thought" (1847; *MECW* 6: 204). On the other hand, the preclusion of demand uncertainties by the control system would ease the task of calculating productivities.

15. Engels, *Outlines*, in *MECW* 3: 428.

16. Marx and Engels, *The German Ideology* (1845–1846), in *MECW* 5: 48.

17. Engels, *Principles of Communism* (1847), in *MECW* 6: 348.

18. Engels, *Principles of Communism*, in *MECW* 6: 351.

19. Engels, *Anti-Dühring* (1877–1878), in *MECW* 25: 282.

20. Engels, *Anti-Dühring*, in *MECW* 25: 294. The qualification regarding international trade is no small matter. It suggests that Engels was uncertain how far to generalize his case for autarky formulated in the case of agriculture (see notes 30 and 31 and accompanying text, below).

21. The absence of markets and exchange in the scheme envisaged, and thus of money and "exchange value"—the indirect measure of labor embodied—figures large in Marx's document *Grundrisse* (1857–1858; *MECW* 28: 92–96).

22. Engels, *Anti-Dühring*, in *MECW* 25: 289–290. See, for example, a passage in *Capital*, vol. 2: "The producers may, for all it matters, receive paper vouchers entitling them to withdraw from the social supplies of consumer goods a quantity corresponding to their labour time. These vouchers are not money. They do not circulate" (1867; *MECW* 36: 356).

23. Engels, *Anti-Dühring*, in *MECW* 25: 290.

24. Engels, *Anti-Dühring*, in *MECW* 25: 294–295.

25. Much of the discussion in the later document repeats and reinforces what had already appeared in the *Outlines* of 1844. The link is remarked upon by Engels him-

self, in *Anti-Dühring*, where he refers readers back to the former work. "As long ago as 1844 I stated that the . . . balancing of useful effects and expenditure of labour on making decisions concerning production was all that would be left, in a communist society, of the politico-economic concept of value . . ." (*MECW* 25: 295n). Engels refers evidently here to *MECW* 3: 426 (cited above, n.11).

26. Engels, *Anti-Dühring*, in *MECW* 25: 259.

27. Engels, *Anti-Dühring*, in *MECW* 25: 266.

28. Dusan Pokorni, *Efficiency and Justice in the Industrial World,* vol. 1, *The Failure of the Soviet Experiment* (Armonk, NY: M. E. Sharpe, 1993), 29. Oskar Lange, however, seems to attribute free consumer choice to the *Anti-Dühring* text in question, and indeed even asserts that "[w]ith some benevolent interpretation this statement of Engels may be regarded, indeed, as containing all the essentials of the modern solution," whereby "the production of each commodity has to be carried so far as to make the ratio of the marginal amount of labor used in producing the different commodities equal to the ratio of the marginal utilities (and of the prices) of those commodities." Oskar Lange, *On the Economic Theory of Socialism* (Minneapolis: University of Minnesota Press, 1938), 133n. Maurice Dobb, pointing to Marx's justification of wage differentials in the "lower" stage of communism (on which see below), maintained that "as a logical corollary of this there would naturally be a free consumers' market where such money incomes could be spent." Maurice Dobb, *Political Economy and Capitalism* (London: Routledge and Kegan Paul, 1940), 300. This seems to me unconvincing, since workers might have differential claims to a basket of goods selected by the central planners.

29. On the other hand, how the planners make the comparison between costs and social utilities is also not self-evident.

30. Engels, "American Food and the Land Question," *The Labour Standard*, July 2, 1881, in *MECW* 24: 398.

31. Engels, "American Food and the Land Question," in *MECW* 24: 399.

32. When touching in *The Civil War in France* on "the obtrusive and full-mouthed apostles of co-operative production" Marx is careful to specify that it is not competing cooperatives (upon which, as is well known, J. S. Mill insisted) that would be appropriate but some form of cooperation subject to "a common plan": "If co-operative production is not to remain a sham and a snare; if it is to supersede the Capitalist system; if united co-operative societies are to regulate national production upon a common plan, thus taking it under their own control, and putting an end to the constant anarchy and periodic convulsions which are the fatality of Capitalist production—what else, gentlemen, would it be but Communism . . ." Marx, *The Civil War in France* (1871), in *MECW* 22: 335.

33. See note 20, above.

34. Engels to August Bebel, 20–23 January 1886, in *MECW* 47: 389.

35. See note 19 and accompanying text, above.

36. Engels, introduction to Marx's *The Civil War in France* (1891), in *MECW* 27: 188.

37. Marx, "Critique of the Gotha Program" (1875), in *MECW* 24: 87.

38. Marx, "Critique of the Gotha Program," in *MECW* 24: 86.

39. Cited in Engels, *Anti-Dühring*, in *MECW* 25: 183.
40. Engels, *Anti-Dühring*, in *MECW* 25: 187.
41. Engels, *Anti-Dühring*, in *MECW* 25: 185.
42. Engels, "The Housing Question" (1872, 1887), in *MECW* 23: 320, also 375.
43. Engels, "The Housing Question," in *MECW* 23: 355.
44. Cited in Engels, "The Housing Question," in *MECW* 23: 341.
45. Engels, "The Housing Question," in *MECW* 23: 340–341.
46. Engels, "The Housing Question," in *MECW* 23: 341.
47. Engels, "Protection and Free Trade" (1888), in *MECW* 26: 526.
48. Engels, "Protection and Free Trade," in *MECW* 26: 526–527. A striking instance of Marx's respect for the market is provided by his objections to Napoleon III's plan to regulate French bread prices. See Marx, 13 December 1858, in *MECW* 16: 110–114. His objection turns on the array of further interventions that would be required to enforce the controls. He draws on the experience of Paris which had instituted them locally, and where "the experiment proved a complete failure, the price of bread rising above the official maximum during the bad seasons, from 1855–1857 . . ." Ibid., 111. His forecast regarding the extension to France as a whole in the case of "good years," and the maintenance of a price *floor*, emphasizes the unthought-of consequences of the proposed "artificial demand to be created through the means of three months' reserve." For "[i]mmense buildings for public granaries will become necessary over the whole of France; and what a fresh field they will open for jobs and plunder. An unexpected turn is also given to the trade in breadstuffs. What profits to be pocketed by the Crédit Mobilier and the other gambling companions of his Imperial Majesty! At all events, we may be sure that the Imperial Socialist will prove no more successful in raising the price of bread than he has been in attempts to reduce it." Ibid., 114.
49. Engels, "Protection and Free Trade," in *MECW* 26: 527.
50. Engels, "Protection and Free Trade," in *MECW* 26: 528.
51. Engels, "Protection and Free Trade," in *MECW* 26: 535.
52. Engels, "The Housing Question," in *MECW* 23: 332–333, 388.
53. See further Hollander, "Economic Organization, Distribution and the Equality Issue: The Marx-Engels Perspective," *Review of Austrian Economics* 17, no. 1 (2004): 5–39; Hollander, *The Economics of Karl Marx*, 401–406.
54. Engels, "Marx and Rodbertus," in *MECW* 26: 289. This formulation reflects strikingly the Marx-Engels evaluation of capitalists' activities in general.
55. Engels, "Marx and Rodbertus," in *MECW* 26: 285. That only part of the national income is allocated to private consumption refers to the deductions made by the "public authority" for public goods and the like, a feature also shared with Engels and Marx.
56. Engels, "Marx and Rodbertus," in *MECW* 26: 287.
57. See above, notes 1–2 and accompanying text.
58. Hutchison might have raised the same complaint against Marx who directed an orthodox, price-theoretic objection against the labor-based price scheme proposed by Proudhon: "Products will in future be exchanged in the exact ratio of the labour time they have cost. Whatever may be the proportion of supply to demand, the exchange

of commodities will always be made as if they had been produced proportionately to the demand. Let M. Proudhon take it upon himself to formulate and lay down such a law, and we shall relieve him of the necessity of giving proofs. If, on the other hand, he insists on justifying his theory, not as a legislator, but as an economist, he will have to prove that the *time* needed to create a commodity indicates exactly the degree of its *utility* and marks its proportional relation to the demand, and in consequence, to the total amount of wealth." Marx, "Poverty of Philosophy" (1847), in *MECW* 6: 132. In brief, Proudhon would have to show that labor values correspond to market-clearing or equilibrium prices, implying corresponding equilibrium output shares in the total product, and this he could not do: "since the labour time necessary for the production of an article is not the expression of its degree of utility, the exchange value of this same article, determined beforehand by the labour time embodied in it, can never regulate the correct relation of supply to demand . . ." Ibid., 134.

59. But see note 74, below, for two qualifications to the opposition to "halfway" compromise solutions.

60. Engels, "Marx and Rodbertus," in *MECW* 26: 288.

61. Lionel Robbins, *An Essay on the Nature and Significance of Economic Science* (1932; London: Macmillan, 1935); Robbins, *Political Economy: Past and Present. A review of leading theories of economic policy* (London: Macmillan, 1976).

62. Robbins, *Political Economy: Past and Present*, 1–2.

63. Robbins, *Political Economy: Past and Present*, 2–3.

64. See note 56, above, and corresponding text.

65. There are also essential deductions from national product for capital maintenance and accumulation and for social services to be satisfied before consumption allowances can be allowed by the planners (see also note 55). For an excellent account of some of the vagaries of Marx's position—and these would be no less pertinent in that of Engels—particularly with regard to the relevant time horizon to be adopted by the planning authority in arriving at investment vs. consumption decisions, and to the determination of what constitutes "social needs" or legitimate consumption, see Dusan Pokorni, *Efficiency and Justice in the Industrial World,* vol. 1, 30–31.

66. See above, notes 48–51, and accompanying text.

67. On the relevance of 1830, see Hollander, "David Ricardo: Economics and Ideology," *Literature of Liberty: A Review of Contemporary Liberal Thought* 2, no. 3 (July/Sept. 1979): 5–35.

68. See Hollander, *Friedrich Engels and Marxian Political Economy* (New York: Cambridge University Press, 2011), chapter 7.

69. On Ricardo and historical prediction, with special reference to the Corn Law debate, see Hollander, *The Economics of David Ricardo* (Toronto: University of Toronto Press, 1979), 509–642. See further on Engels and prediction, Hollander, *Friedrich Engels and Marxian Political Economy*, chapter 6.

70. See Hollander, *Friedrich Engels and Marxian Political Economy*, chapter 5.

71. See Hollander, *Friedrich Engels and Marxian Political Economy*, chapter 7.

72. Arun Bose, "Modern Marxian Political Economy," in *What is Political Economy? Eight Perspectives*, ed. David K. Whynes (Oxford: Basil Blackwell, 1984), 90–115.

73. George Stigler, "The Politics of Political Economists," in *Essays in the History of Economics* (1959; Chicago: University of Chicago Press, 1965), 59–60.

74. We should enter two qualifications to the Marx-Engels rejection of compromise arrangements. Firstly, the course of events forced upon them: recognition of a transition to monopoly capitalism and, correspondingly, the increasing effectiveness of welfare reform, a tendency that would be temporary only considering the imminent collapse of the system. Secondly, even a "dictatorship of the proletariat" might be obliged to tolerate a capitalist sector (and engage in tax reform and the like, namely undertake some of the measures recommended in the *Communist Manifesto*), but again this would be no more than a temporary allowance.

75. Lionel Robbins, *Political Economy: Past and Present*, 144.

76. For a fuller elaboration of Smith's position, see Hollander, "Jeremy Bentham and Adam Smith on the Usury Laws," *European Journal of the History of Economic Thought* 6 (1999): 523–551.

77. Adam Smith, *The Wealth of Nations* (1776; Oxford: Oxford University Press, 1976), 106.

78. Adam Smith, *The Wealth of Nations*, 357.

79. Adam Smith, *The Wealth of Nations*, 356.

80. Adam Smith, *The Wealth of Nations*, 112.

81. Adam Smith, *The Wealth of Nations*, 356–357.

82. Adam Smith, *The Wealth of Nations*, 357.

83. John Maynard Keynes, *The General Theory Employment, Interest and Money* (London: Macmillan, 1936), 352.

84. Adam Smith, *The Wealth of Nations*, 357.

85. Adam Smith, *The Wealth of Nations*, 612.

86. Adam Smith, *The Wealth of Nations*, 438.

87. Adam Smith, *The Wealth of Nations*, 388.

88. Adam Smith, *The Wealth of Nations,* 751–753.

89. Adam Smith, *The Wealth of Nations*, 385.

90. Adam Smith, *The Wealth of Nations*, 74.

91. Adam Smith, *The Wealth of Nations*, 523 (added in 1784 edition).

92. Adam Smith, *The Wealth of Nations,* 131.

93. Adam Smith, *The Wealth of Nations*, 308.

94. Adam Smith, *The Wealth of Nations*, 302.

95. Adam Smith, *The Wealth of Nations,* 311.

96. Adam Smith, *The Wealth of Nations,* 304.

97. Adam Smith, *The Wealth of Nations,* 324. Smith maintained that the proposed control of paper-money banking would not aggravate instability by excluding emergency lending.

98. See notes 77–84 and accompanying text, above.

99. A decade ago, Walter Eltis pointed out to me that by his concern with high-risk lending Smith, in effect, "condemned what are nowadays described as junk bonds. And who can say he was wrong in view of the financial destruction they have often created?" (communication with the author, 25 June 1998).

100. See notes 38–41 and accompanying text.

5

Ten (Mostly) Austrian Insights for These Trying Times

Bruce Caldwell

I will begin by defending the approach I am taking in this chapter, namely a historical approach in which I try to glean insights from great writers of the past that may be of relevance to today. It is significant that I should feel the necessity to defend such an approach, but I am, after all, an economist, and economists typically do not have much patience for the history of economic thought. Economics is a discipline in which cumulative progress is expected and, by the naive among us, to be the norm. The median attitude is probably well-represented by the old adage that all one really needs to know is what is in the latest working paper. (One is tempted to add: If such people have ever read Thomas Kuhn, they must have done so with their eyes closed.) My approach assumes, to the contrary, that there is much to be learned from the ideas of the past.[1]

Another observation, one commonplace among historians, should also be stressed: history provides no magic bullet. What it provides is perspective. It shows what sorts of ideas our predecessors entertained, the sorts of policies that their ideas led them to, and what transpired as a result. It also allows us to see that our times are not unique,[2] and that as bad as things sometimes seem, there have always been worse times. Think, for example, of what Friedrich Hayek lived through: two world wars, hyperinflation, the creation of the Soviet Union, the Great Depression, and the creation of the welfare state. That we might learn something from the writings of someone who experienced and responded to such events should be evident.

I mention Hayek because I am a Hayek scholar, so many of my reflections will draw on his ideas and writings. But many others could as easily have been cited, not only those who directly participated in the Austrian tradition, like Ludwig von Mises or the "German Austrian" Ludwig Lachmann, or the

Austrians who were more on the periphery, like Fritz Machlup or Gottfried Haberler, or even non-Austrians like James Buchanan, Ronald Coase, Douglass North, or Vernon Smith. I see such scholars as all contributing to a broad tradition that challenges the scientistic pretensions of economics and offers an alternative view of the way that the world works. They are all, I would submit, advocates of basic economic reasoning, the sound core of ideas that economics contains and which we forget only at our peril.

I will close these preliminary statements by noting that Hayek generally kept to the general level of ideas. He was no policy wonk. Instead, by using his knowledge of intellectual history he tried to spotlight that complex of mistaken ideas—constructivist rationalism, scientism, socialism, "the engineering mentality"—that was leading the West down the road to serfdom, and to propose in its place a return to a revitalized liberalism, one that he described and defended in such works as *The Constitution of Liberty* and *Law, Legislation and Liberty*.

In what follows I will identify ten key themes to be found in the writings of Hayek and others in the tradition to which he belonged that may provide some insights into how we might respond to the current dilemmas that we face. Some, but not all, might be described as Austrian: hence the awkward but descriptively accurate title of this chapter.

1. THE BUSINESS CYCLE IS A NECESSARY AND UNAVOIDABLE CONCOMITANT OF A MONEY-USING MARKET ECONOMY

It is perhaps an exaggeration, but sometimes it seems that people today are surprised to find out that business cycles can still happen. Hayek, whose first book was titled *Monetary Theory and the Trade Cycle*, certainly recognized the problem, as did his rival on this issue, John Maynard Keynes.

"Money-using" is a key phrase in the statement above. As introductory economics textbooks remind us, money performs many essential functions, among them to provide a unit of account and a store of value. Its most important function, though, is to facilitate trade, thereby making specialization and the division of labor profitable, and thereby establishing key pre-conditions for economic growth. Money, then, is essential. But as Hayek argued in his first book, *money is also the loose joint* in a free market system.[3] It will be intimately involved in crises.

We need not detain ourselves with a full description of the Austrian theory of the cycle here, other than to note that it offers a pretty good description of at least part of what happened in the latest meltdown, especially in terms of the Fed's interest rate policy and its effects on the housing sector. In Hayek's theory, problems start when the *market rate of interest is held too low* for too long. This always politically popular policy leads to *malinvestment*—too many investment projects get started that cannot ultimately be sustained. When people realize what has happened, investment spending collapses and a recession begins. The danger of a prolonged low interest rate regime in distorting (what the Austrians call) the structure of production is something to take away from the theory, especially given the political popularity of such a policy.

If the Austrian theory of the cycle scores pretty well for explaining the origins of at least certain cycles, it is perhaps less useful in telling us what to do when a recession is under way. Hayek talked (at least for a time) during the Great Depression about stabilizing the nominal flow of spending, and he also spoke about providing firms with more information about potential dangers. But his chief message was that, once begun, *the downturn is painful but necessary medicine for restoring equilibrium to the economic system.* This suggests that the best policy is to do nothing, to let the economy adjust.

One can understand the reasoning, for it is clear that at least some attempts to stimulate the economy can simply *perpetuate the problem.* If the chief problem is that (as the Austrians would put it) the current structure of production does not accurately reflect the true demand for goods in the economy, you certainly do not want to undertake a policy that serves to preserve that structure of production. Two examples from the recent crisis illustrate well Hayek's position. They involve the automotive and house-building industries, two that in the course of the crisis were frequently in the news. In late December 2008 GMAC, the lending arm of General Motors, was given a 6 billion dollar bailout by the Bush administration. What did they do with it? Within a day the radio and television were filled with ads saying that GMAC was now providing zero interest loans and lowering its minimum required credit scores from 700 to 621. For perspective, note that the "sub-prime" designation applies to loan applicants with credit scores of 660 and below. So to stimulate the economy and revitalize the automobile industry, a policy was adopted that essentially made it easier for people with bad credit to afford to purchase a car.

The other example is the tax credit carrying a maximum value of $8000 offered by the federal government in 2009 for first-time home buyers. The idea, I suppose, was that this would help reduce the inventory of existing homes. Unfortunately it led to a mini-boom (which began showing up in the June 2010 housing statistics) in the construction of new single-family homes. In other words, this policy further increased the supply of housing at a time when the evident problem was an excess supply of housing. These are paradigmatic examples of how targeted attempts to stimulate demand can perpetuate an initial malinvestment.

Another reason that the Austrians reject discretionary counter-cyclical policy is that it raises the *threat of inflation,* or other ills, down the road (more on which soon).

The reason that the Austrian message has been almost wholly ignored in the current debate is that it is very dour. It is also politically infeasible, for it counsels politicians to do nothing at a time when all their instincts are to show voters that the government is doing something.

This does not mean, however, that there are no Austrian policies with regard to the business cycle. Most of these have to do with tightening up the loose joint of money—that is, with institutional reforms aiming at preventing a money-induced cycle from getting started in the first place. Over the course of his long career, Hayek offered a variety of proposals for how to do this. These ranged from committing a central bank to the task of stabilizing the "total money stream," or later an index of wholesale prices, to having the international gold standard operate more automatically, to allowing individuals to have freedom of choice among currencies, to avoiding a government monopoly by allowing the competitive issue of private currency.[4] Various alternative monetary regimes, all designed to make money less of a problem, have been advocated by present-day Austrian economists, and such ideas need to be more widely disseminated and debated.[5] Given that a change in institutional structure is a radical proposal that few will ever be willing even to consider, rather than arguing directly for it, perhaps a better first step is to show the dangers of current policy. In this case, this means warning about the dangers of the revival in interest in Keynesian sorts of remedies.

2. THE 1970s: WHY KEYNESIAN ECONOMICS WAS REJECTED

Indeed, it was the experience with Keynesian policies in the 1970s that got Hayek writing about macroeconomics again. It provided for him the quintessential example of the dangers of scientism. Thus in the introduction to his Nobel lecture, aptly titled "The Pretence of Knowledge" (Hayek 1978, p. 23), he said, "economists are at this moment called upon to say how to extricate the free world from the serious threat of accelerating inflation which, it must be admitted, has been brought about by policies which the majority of economists recommended and even urged governments to pursue. We have indeed at the moment little cause for pride: as a profession we have made a mess of things."

There were good reasons why Keynesianism went into eclipse in the 1970s. Though the theory had entered academia decades earlier, the first real experiment with Keynesian demand management policy was the Kennedy-

Johnson tax cut, and it worked like a charm. Economists began to talk about "fine-tuning" the economy, a wonderful metaphor, conjuring up the images of a skilled technician working on a finely tuned machine, and also perhaps the "fine-tuning" of FM radio, the latter appealing to the innate good taste of the intelligentsia.

The heyday did not last long. When inflation began to appear in the late 1960s due to the monetization of LBJ's deficits, a precisely calibrated income tax surcharge designed to tamp down demand was imposed. But because it was viewed as temporary, it had no effect, and inflation continued to rise. This was the first signal that the machine metaphor might have been the wrong one.

Things got much worse in the 1970s, as inflation turned into stagflation. The main lesson of the 1970s was that once inflation gets started, it is very difficult to get rid of. To fight it the government has to tighten up on the economy, which induces unemployment; and because the effect on inflation is not immediate, for a time both the unemployment rate and the inflation rate go up together. This politically disastrous outcome led to all sorts of bizarre policy experiments: wage-price controls under Nixon; WIN buttons under Ford; and Jimmy Carter's sad little malaise speech (which, when people started spending again, he had to follow shortly thereafter with a "just kidding, don't spend so much" admonition). The basic problem was that, until Paul Volcker came along, policy-makers in the 1970s would start to restimulate the economy before inflation was fully driven out of the system, leading to a stop-go policy that was exacerbated by oil shocks and structural changes in the labor market (the entry of young people and women into the labor force). Stagflation was the end result, and it was not wrung out of the system until Volcker induced a very long and real recession—the worst one since the Great Depression and the one that our current downturn should be compared to. In short, *the worst recession since the Great Depression 1) was consciously policy-induced, and 2) was made necessary by the failed attempts at activist discretionary counter-cyclical policy during the previous decade and a half.* This history needs to be recounted! It is hard to imagine a more vivid cautionary tale, and explains why Keynesian demand management policy went so rapidly into eclipse three decades ago.

Am I forecasting that stagflation will reoccur? No, because the economy is too complex to make any such prediction, another Hayekian insight (more on which anon).[6] But it is clear that if one at the same time puts record amounts of money into the financial system (as the Fed has done to provide liquidity) and at the same time the federal government runs record-breaking deficits which promise to exist far into the future, the chances of any plausible exit strategy working without some sort of problem emerging becomes quite remote. As Clive Crook of the *Financial Times* put it in July 2009, "What the stimulus gives, the debt projections take away."[7]

3. SOME REGULATION IS NECESSARY, BUT . . .

How can we avoid such problems in the future? The answer that many would give is that we need more regulation: as Mark Calabria (2009, p. 1) of the Cato Institute has put it, "the growing narrative in Washington is that a decades-long unraveling of the regulatory system allowed and encouraged Wall Street to excess . . . "[8]

Hayek faced an analogous dilemma in 1930s. Free market capitalism had apparently collapsed, and the favored solution to the problems of the depression was again more regulation, which then went under the rubric of "planning." Indeed, his friend Lionel Robbins described planning as "the grand panacea of our age."[9] The problem was, then as now, that the word "planning," like the word "regulation," can mean just about anything.

Hayek's strategy was not to deny the necessity of planning. We all plan, after all. It was rather to show, first, how a certain type of planning, namely central planning of the economy, if fully implemented, would lead to disastrous economic results and ultimately to restrictions on political and personal freedoms. He made this argument in his 1939 pamphlet "Freedom and the Economic System" and developed it further in his most famous work, *The Road to Serfdom*.[10]

In these works, as well as other writings of his in the 1930s and 40s, Hayek made it clear that he was not advocating as an alternative a system of pure laissez-faire. The sort of planning that Hayek favored was a general system of rules, one that would best *enable individuals to carry out their own plans.* He put it this way,

> We can "plan" a system of general rules, equally applicable to all people and intended to be permanent (even if subject to revision with the growth of knowledge), which provides an institutional framework within which the decisions as to what to do and how to earn a living are left up to the individuals. In other words, we can plan a system in which individual initiative is given the widest possible scope and the best opportunity to bring about effective coordination of individual effort.[11]

Now, as I warned at the outset, Hayek is talking here (as was his wont) at a very general level. In *The Constitution of Liberty* and other writings he would provide a little more detail, laying out the set of social institutions that he thought would best enable individuals to utilize their own knowledge to carry out their own plans. These institutions included a market system, in a democratic polity, with a system of well-defined, enforced, and exchangeable property rights, protected by a strong constitution, and operating under the rule of law, in which laws are stable, predictable, and equally applied.

Hayek's goal was to enunciate a framework for the creation of a new form of liberalism, one appropriate for the twentieth century and beyond.

But what he came up with was still very general.[12] Even so, Hayek's contribution here was to stress the importance of the institutional setting, and in that regard he was way ahead of his time. For markets to work effectively they must be *embedded in a set of complementary social institutions.* The new institutional economics associated with the work of Douglass North, Ronald Coase, and Oliver Williamson, as well as the experimental work of Vernon Smith, all take off from this basic insight.

Those institutions seem well secured in most of the developed world. But it is also true that they can be brought to ruin virtually overnight by a dictator. The experience of Zimbabwe under Robert Mugabe should be carefully examined by every student of development on the planet. It is a case study in how to dismantle a society, and each step that was taken there can be well described as a negation of one of the principles articulated in Hayek's general vision for a liberal society.

4. A LOT OF REGULATION, WHAT HAYEK CALLED "LEGISLATION," IS FRAUGHT WITH PROBLEMS AND CAN MAKE MATTERS WORSE

Hayek was less diffident when it came to pointing out the problems with socialist planning, and many of his warnings are applicable with very little tweaking to the current scene.

Hayek thought that a planned system with prices set by the government would always be playing catch-up with the rapid price adjustments that occur in a free market system. In a like manner, regulation cannot keep up with market innovation. New sets of regulations always target problems that arose in the *last* crisis. This does little to address the problems of the next crisis, and indeed sometimes the new regulations make things worse. An example of this is the "mark to market" accounting rule that was put into effect in 1993 following the savings and loan debacle. As noted by Paul Davies of the *Financial Times*, recent research supports the commonsensical notion that a mark to market requirement tends to accelerate and exacerbate the effects of a downturn, making the collapse of a number of financial institutions inevitable.[13] If there is a period during which there is no market for certain assets held on their books, banks are required to declare them as worth zero. Needless to say, that takes quite a toll on a balance sheet. The basic Austrian insight here is that *entrepreneurs* (including those who realize that there is money to be made from devising ways of getting around regulations) *are always forward-looking, while regulators are almost of necessity backward-looking.*

Regulation also inserts *uncertainty,* or as Hayek put it, ". . . the more the state 'plans,' the more difficult planning becomes for the individual."[14] There was plentiful evidence of the adverse effects of regime uncertainty in the recent downturn. In the fall of 2008, each announcement by the Fed and Treasury, meant to reassure the markets, produced more and more panic. It also froze people into inaction. One could imagine the decision-making process that took place in many people's minds. Should I hold onto my house that is underwater, in the hopes of a government bailout? Should I buy a car now that the prices are low, or wait for some government program that will cause them to fall even lower? A stimulus plan is coming, and I don't know what it will look like; probably best to delay all decision-making for now, to wait and see. Over and over again we encounter examples of people basing their decisions on trying to guess what the government is going to do.[15] Contrast this with what happens in well-functioning markets, where people make their decisions principally by looking at changes in market prices, prices that reflect underlying scarcities.

A third problem is the tendency for even the most well-intentioned legislation to be *hijacked by strong special interests* who are able to bend it to meet their needs. The examples of this are so everywhere evident (think of the subsidization of ethanol, or the explosion in the use of earmarks) that further comment seems unnecessary.

Certain types of legislation, often justified as helping those in need, simply encourage bad behavior, causing *increased moral hazard and misaligned incentives.* Bailing out those who took large risks, be they homeowners, firms, or banks, are the standard recent example, as is the "too big to fail" philosophy more generally. About the latter, Hayek, writing in the latter half of the 1970s, had this to say:

> We must finally mention another instance in which it is undeniable that the mere fact of bigness creates a highly undesirable position: namely where, because of the consequences of what happens to a big enterprise, government cannot afford to let such an enterprise fail.[16]

He goes on to recommend that the best policy would be to deprive government of the power to provide such protection. At the time his words anticipated the federal government's bailout of Chrysler. It is telling and pathetic, but perhaps predictable, that the very same arguments about being too big to fail were being made about the very same American industry some thirty years later.

Another problem with legislation is captured in Juvenal's question: *Who is to watch the regulators?* The most notorious example here is probably still the inglorious episode of the Keating Five. The Austrians would note that the market provides its own very effective regulators: they go by the names of profit and loss.[17]

Finally, and most basically, *legislation endangers liberty*. Hayek argued passionately in the 1930s and 1940s that the nation's uncritical enthusiasm for planning put at risk not only the successful operation of a market economy, but democracy and freedom as well. It is no less true today. He found it appropriate then to quote Benjamin Franklin, who said "Those who would give up essential liberty to purchase a little temporary safety deserve neither liberty nor safety."[18] We might add, and are likely to get neither.

Hayek knew well that the urge to regulate is always with us. He attributed this in his early work to the hubris of reason, and traced its origins to the planning mentality and scientistic pretensions of his age.[19] But as he pointed out in his 1933 address, the power of markets to organize human activity was in the past most dramatically revealed when we witnessed the ill effects of attempts to regulate them. This has been the experience of centuries, and is another reason why the study of history is an essential component of a proper education.

5. THE ECONOMY IS AN EXAMPLE OF AN ESSENTIALLY COMPLEX PHENOMENON, FOR WHICH PRECISE FORECASTING (ON WHICH THE CONSTRUCTION OF RATIONAL POLICY DEPENDS) IS RULED OUT

Earlier I refrained from forecasting the likely outcome of the injection of unprecedented amounts of money into the financial system together with a massive fiscal stimulus program. I did so because we simply do not know what will happen. It is hard enough even to assess past events. Starting in fall 2008, the U.S. unemployment rate rose much faster than had originally been predicted, and indeed exceeded forecasts of what it would have been *absent* any stimulus package (so much for forecasts). Paul Krugman's response to this was that we needed a larger stimulus package. The response of most Republicans was that it showed that a stimulus program that depended a lot on increased spending simply does not work, and recommended in its place tax cuts, arguing that they would work more quickly. Larry Summers, playing the role of the baby bear, said that it was just right.[20] The point is, no one really knows; each position is consistent with the evidence, and indeed, other reasonable explanations are possible. (For example, another plausible scenario is that the announcements that were made in fall 2008 concerning the dire shape of the financial sector, whose purpose was to get the TARP bailout passed, in fact caused the ensuing recession to be much worse than it would have been, because it scared everyone so much that spending ground to a virtual standstill.) But the point is that we just cannot know.

This knowledge problem is a huge obstacle to rational policy-making. When it is joined with other political and economic obstacles, the hope of getting rational policy out of Washington becomes very dim. We know, for example, that there is a lag between the time a problem in the economy is recognized and a policy response is developed, and another between the introduction of a policy and its actually taking effect. We have plentiful evidence that the political process sometimes subordinates the stabilization goal to other government policy goals, or simply to the self-interested goals of congressmen and senators. We know that tax cuts (despite Republican rhetoric) sometimes get saved rather than spent, so they have little stimulative impact. We know that lower interest rates will not accomplish much if banks are fearful of lending or firms are fearful of borrowing: as it used to be put, you can't push on a string. In sum, the things that we actually do know all concern limitations on our knowledge and on our ability to formulate and carry out rational policy.

It is important to be clear: this does not mean that policy-makers cannot get things right when it comes to managing the economy as a whole. It is just that sometimes stabilization policy stabilizes the economy, and sometimes it destabilizes it, and we usually cannot tell in advance, and sometimes not even in retrospect, which scenario is unfolding or has unfolded.

6. THE TWO SIDES OF UNINTENDED CONSEQUENCES WHEN DEALING WITH COMPLEX ORDERS

Hayek talked a lot about the unintended consequences of intentional human action. Following Menger, the founder of the Austrian School, he pointed out that many *beneficial social institutions have emerged gradually and spontaneously throughout human history.*[21] No one, for example, *invented* language, perhaps the most useful and universal of human institutions, and indeed conscious attempts to construct a non-natural language—think of Esperanto—have been miserable failures. Other such institutions include money, the division of labor, trade, and the moral traditions (David Hume's three "fundamental laws of nature," namely "the stability of possession, of its transference by consent, and of the performance of promises," come to mind[22]) that support a market system. These institutions have created social cooperation on a global scale, leading to enormous increases in material wealth, even though that outcome was not the intent of any individual participant. Indeed, each individual participant has only a tiny bit of knowledge that they bring to the whole process. I know how to wait tables, you know how to raise chickpeas, someone else is a skilled worker in a linen factory, and from these people's efforts and those of hundreds of thousands of others, every day, Paris gets fed, though it was no one's plan, goal, intention, or desire to feed Paris. From Frédéric Bastiat to Leonard Read, many have marveled at this unintended miracle.[23] And indeed, Hayek often used the word "marvel" to describe the workings of the market mechanism.[24]

The bad side of unintended consequences is that *many attempts to impose our will on the complex adaptive system that is the economy cause things to happen that were no part of our original intention.* For example, as everyone recognizes, a market system does not satisfy our longings for "social justice."[25] In response, well-intentioned people (or those with interests who can play on the sentiments of the well intentioned) naturally seek to make adjustments in a market system so as to produce more desirable results. Unfortunately, time and again history has demonstrated that when aiming at certain ends, particularly when their achievement involves interfering with the workings of the price mechanism, all sorts of pernicious effects will occur that were no part of the original intention. Some of these patterns are so well-established that they have worked their way into our basic economic reasoning (more on which in a moment).

Hayek was not opposed to experimentation and change, which indeed is one of the driving forces in both the competitive market process and cultural evolution. He thought, though, that piecemeal change is always preferable to wholesale attempts to remake society anew, quoting to make his point Adam Smith's wonderful lines from *The Theory of Moral Sentiments* on the dangers of "the man of system."

> The man of system . . . seems to imagine that he can arrange the different members of a great society with as much ease as the hand arranges the different pieces upon a chessboard. He does not consider that the pieces upon the chessboard have no other principle of motion besides that which the hand impresses upon them; but that, in the great chessboard of human society, every single piece has a principle of motion of its own, altogether different from that which the legislature might choose to impress upon it.[26]

When the man of system is also a man of genius, someone popular and well-trusted by the public, who "declaims and insists, not only that the special improvement is a good thing in itself, but the best of all things, and the root of all other good things," the situation becomes especially dire.[27]

7. BASIC ECONOMIC REASONING CAPTURES WHAT WE CAN KNOW AND SAY ABOUT THE ESSENTIALLY COMPLEX PHENOMENON THAT WE CALL THE ECONOMY

Hayek argued that, when dealing with spontaneous orders or other complex adaptive systems, often the best that we can do is to make pattern predictions, or to offer explanations of the principle by which a phenomenon may work.[28] His examples were usually drawn from areas other than economics. Thus he explained that we all can understand the principle by which footpaths are formed, even if we never observed one being created.[29] He noted that the theory of evolution allows us to understand how speciation works, and to rule out certain evolutionary changes, but it does not allow us to predict specific changes that will occur.[30] What might constitute equivalent sorts of explanations or predictions in the domain of economics?

In my view, *the basic sorts of insights about the workings of a market order that economists teach in their introductory classes*, what I have elsewhere called basic economic reasoning,[31] *is what Hayek was talking about when he discussed "explanations of the principle" and "pattern predictions."* These insights have evolved slowly, emerging in the writings of the great economists of the past three centuries or so, and are now captured in such everyday classroom constructions as supply and demand curves and production possibility frontiers. These tools allow us to talk about the fundamental fact of scarcity, the choices that scarcity makes necessary, the costs of choice, and of ways to push back against scarcity, at which point the notions of the division of labor, specialization, comparative advantage, the productivity of capital, and the gains from trade are introduced. If one adds to these the concepts of elasticity of demand and supply, and some basic intuitions about market structures, one can explain an awful lot about the world, as anyone who has ever taught an introductory economics course knows.

I say "basic intuitions" above to emphasize that this does not have to be complicated; there is a reason why the introductory course is often labeled "Principles of Economics." I once had a conversation with a colleague about cartels. The person was a technically well-trained game theorist, and game theory is custom-made to analyze things like cartel behavior. I mentioned to her in passing the three conditions that must be met for a cartel to be able to continue to keep prices high through time (a large share of total output, no close substitutes for the product, and the ability to catch and sanction those who cheat on the collusive agreement) and said that I didn't worry too much about cartels because it is difficult to maintain all three conditions. This insight emerged in the 1940s and 1950s, before game theory had swept the profession, and is something that is easily explained with a few supply and demand curves to first- and second-year college students. Sadly, from the look on her face it was clear that she had never heard of the three conditions.

The principles course, if well-taught, is probably the most important course that anyone who wants to understand how a market system works can take. It shows how markets work, and also how they sometimes fail to work. It also helps one to identify which policy problems are real ones, and which are pseudo-problems. For those, for example, who are worried about the world running out of a natural resource like oil, it shows how the unhindered market very effectively deals with such shortages (the price of oil rises, which encourages conservation on the demand side, and makes profitable the search for new supplies of oil, as well as for substitutes, on the supply side).

Many of the most compelling examples in a principles class, however, have to do with bad policy responses, and most of these involve some form of price-fixing. Case studies that look at the effects of minimum wage laws, of agricultural price supports, of rent controls, of comparable worth policies, of price ceilings on gasoline or natural gas, of laws prohibiting the resale of concert tickets, all drive home the very predictable adverse effects of these policies. It is ironic that in a field in which forecasting is so difficult, the one area where it is relatively easy to predict results is when some form of price-fixing is involved. Indeed, in the case of price ceilings, the effects are so predictable that economists have come up with generic categories (e.g., the emergence of black markets, deterioration in product quality, and the emergence of non-price mechanisms for the allocation of the good) to describe the effects of the intervention.[32]

A good economics course will help to identify more appropriate policy responses, responses that utilize markets rather than fixing prices or trying to legislate specific outcomes. The entire field of "free market environmentalism," with its emphasis on the establishment of property rights and on the design of institutions that make the best use of market mechanisms, is a case in point.

Last but not least, a good principles of economics class can serve as a counterweight to some of the widely held myths that pass as facts within the popular culture.[33] Take the critique of "neo-liberalism," as recently articulated by Naomi Klein in her book *The Shock Doctrine*.[34] According to Klein, neo-liberals embrace the shock doctrine, the idea that multi-national corporations should enlist the power of national states during times of crisis (sometimes crises that they are complicit in fomenting) to impose a worldwide regime of free trade, thereby ensuring a steady supply of resources from less developed countries, a steady market for their goods worldwide, and a steady flow of profits to their owners. Klein's book should be widely read. Half of it could have been written by Murray Rothbard: I refer here to the places where she talks about the dangers to our liberties and economic freedoms when big states and big corporations collude, or where she documents in sickening detail case after case of states trampling on the civil liberties of its citizens, from Chile and Argentina to Russia and China. A good libertarian could take the facts documented in the book and construct a devastating case about the dangers of untrammeled state power. Unfortunately, Naomi Klein was raised by socialist parents in Canada and apparently never had an economics course, so that is not the argument that she offers her reader. Rather, she makes the fantastical accusation that economists from the University of Chicago, and in particular Milton Friedman, developed the doctrine to support the power of corporations and their owners. She is exactly wrong, of course, about Friedman's position. He supported free trade for a number of reasons, but a principle one was that it serves to *limit* the power of corporations.

Rather than an extended argument, I will only offer here an anecdote to illuminate Friedman's position.[35] When I was in graduate school I was fascinated about the question of oligopolies. Markets work well when they are competitive, but what happens when an industry, like the U.S. automobile industry in the 1960s and 1970s (this was before it was evident that the oil embargo and the subsequent increase in the price of gasoline would bring the American automobile industry to its knees, and to Washington, to beg for protection), grows too powerful? How could such powerful firms be constrained? I got my answer one day when Milton Friedman came to speak at a nearby university. I chanced to run into him as he was leaving the auditorium after his talk, so I asked him his opinion on the matter. He turned to me, put his hand on my shoulder (he had to reach up to do that, a unique experience for me, because I am not tall), and asked, "Now given your knowledge of economics, what one policy could we implement that would limit the power of the automobile industry?" "Open up our markets to foreign competition?" I ventured. He smiled, patted me on the shoulder as if to say, "Good boy," and went on his way.

Sadly, this basic insight, that international trade is a way of constraining the power of large domestic firms, has little traction among the oceans of protesters who show up at every trade meeting. They do not realize that the policies that they favor would, by granting them protection from foreign competition, make American corporations more powerful.

8. BUT WHAT ABOUT SOCIAL JUSTICE?

As noted above, Hayek recognized that a market system of necessity results in an unequal distribution of income. And he knew that humans, whose ancestors for hundreds of millennia lived in hunter-gatherer tribes, had developed norms of fairness that would resist the presence of such inequalities. Indeed, many critics of markets cite disparities in income as prima facie evidence of lack of fairness. Of course, the causes of income inequality are many, from differences in everything from initial endowments to effort to intelligence to luck. We usually do not think it unfair when someone who works hard succeeds, and only the most curmudgeonly among us would begrudge someone who has experienced a run of good luck, if only because we all wish it for ourselves. Still, the wide disparities in income that a market system naturally generates inevitably fuels calls for reform, for some sort of "social justice." How might one respond? Must those who favor markets argue for social *injustice*?

Hayek viewed the cry for social justice as both misguided and dangerous, and offered a number of arguments why. His first claim was that it was wrong even to apply the concept of "justice" to something like an impersonal market process. For Hayek, justice is an attribute of human conduct. As such, a person's or an organization's actions may be deemed just or unjust. The market process generates a specific income distribution, but because that distribution was not the result of anyone's design, it is wrong to speak of it as just or unjust, just as it would be wrong to speak of, say, a misfortune (contracting a disease, or losing a loved one) as just or unjust.[36]

A second argument invokes the rule of law, the notion that all people should be treated equally under the law. If we accept this principle, equal treatment of all, and then add the observation that people differ in their attributes, we are led naturally to the result that different people will experience different outcomes. Conversely, the only way to get similar outcomes for different people is to treat them differently. Egalitarianism of this sort goes against the rule of law, and more generally, against the idea that, if we set up a game in which the procedural rules are viewed as fair, a particular outcome might be viewed as unfortunate, but it cannot rightly be judged to be unfair.[37]

A third argument is that, even were one to accept the general desirability of some form of redistribution of income, the principles by which it might be made to work are unclear, and often presume that we possess knowledge which we can never possess. Take, for example, the notion that we should reward people according to "merit." Hayek points out that merit typically is

> not a matter of the objective outcome but of subjective effort. The attempt to achieve a valuable result may be highly meritorious but a complete failure, and full success may be entirely the result of accident and thus without merit.[38]

It should be noted that if we set up a merit system in which we rewarded people according to their efforts, regardless of outcome, those who were least skilled and therefore had to try the hardest would get rewarded the most, and those who achieved much by little the least. This is a system that, if one is concerned with the total amount of goods produced, is as perverse a system as one can imagine.[39] But leaving that aside, the simple fact is that, because merit is a matter of subjective effort, we could never have the knowledge necessary to determine which acts are in fact meritorious.[40]

Somewhat controversially in the eyes of certain Austrians and libertarians, Hayek allowed that, for a society that had reached the general level of wealth that Britain or the United States had achieved, "there can be no doubt that some minimum of food, shelter, and clothing, sufficient to preserve health and the capacity to work, can be assured to everybody" and also that the state should "assist the individuals in providing for those common hazards of life against which, because of their uncertainty, few individuals can make adequate provision."[41] He was, in short, in favor of some form of safety net, though it should also be noted that by the 1970s he worried about coalitions of organized interests, and often well-off special interests, who would use pleas for greater social justice to advance their own ends.

Wherever one might come down on the desirability of a safety net, perhaps the strongest argument for a market system is that it has led to a better standard of living for literally billions of people worldwide. The point has been well-made by Peter Saunders in his memorable piece, "Why Capitalism Is Good for the Soul."

> The way this [capitalism] has enhanced people's capacity to lead a good life can be seen in the spectacular reduction in levels of global poverty, brought about by the spread of capitalism on a world scale. In 1820, 85% of the world's population lived on today's equivalent of less than a dollar per day. By 1950, this proportion had fallen to 50%. Today it is down to 20%. . . . In 1900, the average life expectancy in the 'less developed countries' was just thirty years. By 1960, this had risen to forty-six years. By 1998, it was sixty-five years. To put this extraordinary achievement into perspective, the average life expectancy in the poorest countries at the end of the twentieth century was fifteen years longer than the average life expectancy in the richest country in the world—Britain—at the start of the century.[42]

From this perspective, the extension of free markets, while leading to income inequality, simultaneously increases the total size of the pie to be shared, and thereby benefits mankind as a whole. There are many ways to think about "social justice." Advocates of markets would do well to emphasize benefits that extend to the world as a whole.

9. THE BASIC HAYEKIAN INSIGHT: FREELY ADJUSTING MARKET PRICES HELPS SOLVE THE KNOWLEDGE PROBLEM AND ALLOWS FOR SOCIAL COORDINATION

How has the market system (what Saunders calls capitalism) been able to accomplish so much in such a short time? For Hayek, the answer was that markets allow for the coordination of individual plans on a vast scale—in short, markets help to solve "the knowledge problem."

Hayek's best articulation of the process is contained in his classic 1945 essay "The Use of Knowledge in Society."[43] He begins there by asking a very simple question: What problem must we solve if we want to construct a rational economic order? He points out that *if* (and he italicizes the *if*) we had all the relevant information about preferences, endowments, and technology, the problem solves itself, for it is simply a question of logic. In such a world, we could put everything into the hands of a central planner, who would then allocate resources and goods to their highest valued uses.

All of the *problems* for constructing a rational economic order arise precisely because we *do not* have such information. Instead, in the real world knowledge is dispersed among millions of people. Each person has a bit of localized knowledge, or what Hayek calls "knowledge of the particular circumstances of time and place."[44] In the real world, it is also the case that some people are mistaken about what they think they know. The question that must be solved in constructing a rational economic order in such a world is: how can we use the knowledge that is dispersed among millions of fallible market agents so as to achieve some level of social coordination and cooperation?

Hayek's answer was that a market system, one with freely adjusting market-determined prices, is (when embedded within an appropriate institutional structure) a marvelous mechanism for coordinating human action. As was noted above, a free market economy is a complex system. It is also an *adaptive* complex system, which helps to explain why it works. As Hayek illustrates with his famous tin example, whenever a change occurs somewhere in the system, price adjustments immediately signal millions of market participants that something has changed, and this causes some of them (those on the margin) to adjust their behavior, which of course sends further signals out into the system, causing further adjustments, ad infinitum.[45] As Hayek put it, "The whole acts as one market, not because any of its members survey the whole field, but because their limited individual fields of vision sufficiently overlap so that through many intermediaries the relevant information is communicated to all."[46]

In a world that is filled with unpredictability, where "the man on the spot" has only his own small bit of local (and sometimes tacit) knowledge, market signals provide information on which he can base his decisions. His decisions together with those of millions of others, in their turn, feed into the system to form the prices that emerge. The actions of market participants are thereby simultaneously price-determined and price-determining. Bad decisions and mistakes are constantly made. But in a market system, errors made by some are opportunities for others, and the latter's profit-seeking actions help to correct them. The self-regulating market system, when it is functioning well, reduces some of the unpredictability that we all face in the economic arena, and helps to coordinate our actions with those of millions of others. It also allows individuals to act on their own local knowledge, and thereby allows others to make use of that knowledge, even though they do not possess the knowledge themselves.

The flip side of Hayek's insights provides a warning to those who seek to improve on markets. Two sorts of errors are possible. The first is not to recognize that for the vast coordination mechanism to work, agents must be allowed to act on their knowledge, and prices must be allowed freely to adjust. Many "reforms," of course, do just the opposite, seeking to restrict entry into markets, or keep prices from adjusting, on the grounds of protecting the consumer, or assuring the quality of a product or service, or supporting diversity or equity or balance or fairness, and so on. The second is assuming that decision-makers have more knowledge than they do. Hayek admitted that *if* we had more knowledge we could do a lot more to improve the world. But we do not.[47] And in the world we live in—a world of dispersed knowledge—much of the knowledge we actually do possess is due to the workings of the market mechanism.

10. THE BASIC PUBLIC CHOICE INSIGHT: GOVERNMENT CURES OFTEN ARE NOT ONLY WORSE THAN THE DISEASE BUT LEAD TO FURTHER DISEASE

Although some have occasionally identified public choice insights in the writings of Hayek and other Austrians (e.g., Peter Boettke[48]), I think that it is fair to say that the public choice school is a separate though complementary intellectual development. Just how complementary it is will be evident once the following list of public choice insights has been outlined.

A central claim concerns the *rationally ignorant voter.* Because learning the various candidates' positions on a host of issues is costly, and the chances of an election turning on a single voter's ballot are miniscule, many voters rationally choose not to be very informed about the issues. When one couples this with Bryan Caplan's 2007 argument that public opinion generally favors policies that make voters feel good, or moral, or more American (e.g., raising the minimum wage to fight poverty; attributing a rise in gasoline prices to the greed of oil corporations) but that also make for policy outcomes that most economists, and more-educated voters, view as pernicious (e.g., increasing the incidence of unemployment among the least skilled workers; passing "excess profit tax" legislation that reduces the supply of domestically produced oil), it is hard to feel much confidence in the policy that is generated in a democracy.[49] Politicians who seek to be re-elected rationally supply the irrational policies that voters want.

A second claim has to do with the effects of *concentrated benefits and diffused costs* on policy-making. Politicians frequently pay lip service to "the public good." But if a politician is to be successful (that is, stay in office), he or she will typically support policy that is aimed at benefiting the well-organized and informed few rather than the unorganized and uninformed many. As a result, legislation tends to favor special interests over the public good, and once a policy is in place, it is nearly impossible to get rid of it.

Public choice theorists believe that politicians, like everyone else, act in their own self-interest. If consumers maximize utility, firms maximize profits, and politicians maximize votes, what do bureaucrats maximize? The answer is troubling: *bureaucrats have an incentive to maximize the size of the bureaucracy under their control.*[50] Governments don't shrink, they grow. Never has the triumph of hope over reality been better illustrated than by the steady stream of politicians who promise to pay for new programs by "reducing waste and inefficiency" in the existing government.

In their wonderfully titled 1977 book *Democracy in Deficit,* James Buchanan and Richard Wagner made the point that *democratic politics leads naturally to deficits.*[51] Politicians typically insist that they intend to constrain the growth of government spending, but in reality they seldom are able to overcome (and given the ignorance of the electorate, seldom need to do so) the natural incentives of increasing government spending and decreasing taxes. Can anyone remember a politician who campaigned successfully with a platform of *raising taxes*?

The past thirty years have demonstrated this to be one of the few areas in which bi-partisan endorsement of a basic principle has been nearly complete. For a case study of how difficult it is for politicians to actually cut government spending, even when they have a mandate to do so, one need only consult William Greider's classic 1981 piece, "The Education of David Stockman."[52] While constantly mouthing the rhetoric of balanced budgets, Ronald Reagan offered up instead tax cuts and substantially smaller cuts in government spending, and won two terms. When George H. W. Bush tried to balance the budget by raising taxes, he was excoriated by his own party and served only one term. After that, the policy of cutting taxes but leaving government spending intact became canonized in certain Republican circles under the cynical "starve the beast" philosophy. For a while, it seemed like the only difference between the two major American parties was that the Democrats favored tax and spend, while the Republicans favored *don't* tax but spend. It seems that no one these days (except Libertarians and Ron Paul) speaks about a smaller government period.

Another central concept in the public choice literature is the notion of *rent-seeking.* Firms can successfully compete in two ways. One is directly, by producing a better product at a lower cost than their rivals. The other is by getting the government to grant them an advantage over their rivals, by the granting of subsidies, or the imposition of licensing restrictions, taxes, tariffs, or quotas on their competitors. Given an expected level of added profits from getting the government to intervene, a firm would rationally spend up to that amount in lobbying the government to do so. Such rent-seeking behavior is a waste of resources, but takes place all the time. Gordon Tullock once asked, why is the level of rent-seeking as small as it is? Perhaps it is time for him to recalculate his estimates.

We said above that the best regulator for market behavior is the *carrot of profits and the stick of losses.* No equivalent regulator exists when the government undertakes a project. Indeed, if a government program does not achieve its goals, the solution always seems to be, we just need to spend more money.

Finally, it is evident that many government programs introduce *moral hazard* into the market place, undermining initiative and the taking of responsibility for actions. From welfare programs for the poor to welfare programs for the rich (the socialization of losses under the bailout programs being the most recent example of the latter), ubiquitous government intervention makes all of us more likely to seek a handout.

The list of ills that public choice theorists have identified lead one to a general three-step principle that if followed can help to minimize the impact of government intervention.[53] In capsule form: Negotiation (as occurs in market exchange) is always preferable to adjudication. If negotiation fails, adjudication that clarifies rights is always preferable to legislation. Only if both negotiation and adjudication fail should one turn to legislation. Unfortunately, too often legislation is the first and only step.

Conclusion—the Austrian/public choice one-two punch: we usually do not have the necessary knowledge to intervene effectively, and the political process is such that, even if we did, we still likely would get bad policy, together with an ever-growing government sector. This is why Austrians and public choice theorists favor smaller government. Especially in today's environment, their insights bear repetition.

NOTES

In writing this chapter, I greatly benefited from comments from participants at Peter Boettke's Workshop in Philosophy, Politics, and Economics at George Mason University, and from additional comments from Larry White. Remaining errors are my own.

1. It is a view that Friedrich A. Hayek shared. As he put it in the closing of his essay on "Comte and Hegel," ". . . I doubt whether it is possible to overestimate the influence which ideas have in the long run. And there can be no question that it is our [meaning scholars—BC] special duty to recognize the currents of thought which still operate in public opinion, to examine their significance, and, if necessary, to refute them." Hayek, "Comte and Hegel," reprinted in *The Collected Works of F. A. Hayek*, vol. 13, *Studies on the Abuse and Decline of Reason*, ed. Bruce Caldwell (Chicago: University of Chicago Press, 2010), 309.

2. What Hayek wrote in 1933, the trough of the Great Depression, about "the recurring intellectual isolation of the economist" who is "bitterly reproached if he does not emphasize, at every stage of his analysis, how much he regrets that his insight into the order of things makes it less easy to change them whenever we please," could as easily have been written by any free market economist of today. "The Trend of Economic Thinking," reprinted in *The Collected Works of F. A. Hayek*, vol. 3, *The Trend of Economic Thinking: Essays on Political Economists and Economic History,* ed. W. W. Bartley III and Stephen Kresge (Chicago: University of Chicago Press, 1991), 18, 21.

3. See, e.g., Hayek, *Monetary Theory and the Trade Cycle* (1933; New York: Kelley, 1966), 189: "So long as we make use of bank credit as a means of furthering economic development we shall have to put up with the resulting trade cycles"; p. 185: ". . . fluctuations caused by monetary factors are unavoidable"; p. 188: "no measure which can be conceived of in practice would be able entirely to suppress these fluctuations." It was in *The Pure Theory of Capital* that Hayek described money as "a kind of loose joint in the otherwise self-equilibriating apparatus of the price mechanism. . . ." See Hayek, *The Pure Theory of Capital*, reprinted in *The Collected Works of F. A. Hayek*, vol. 12, *The Pure Theory of Capital*, ed. Lawrence H. White (1941; Chicago: University of Chicago Press, 2007), 367.

4. See, e.g., Hayek, *Prices and Production,* 2nd ed. (London: Routledge, 1935), 131; *Monetary Nationalism and Economic Security*, reprinted in *The Collected Works of F. A. Hayek,* vol. 6, *Good Money, Part II: The Standard,* ed. Stephen Kresge (1937; Chicago: University of Chicago Press, 1999), 37–100; *The Constitution of Liberty* (Chicago: University of Chicago Press, 1960), 333–337; *Choice in Currency*, reprinted in *The Collected Works of F. A. Hayek*, vol. 6, *Good Money, Part II* (1976; University of Chicago Press, 1999); and "The Denationalization of Money," reprinted in *The*

Collected Works of F. A. Hayek, vol. 6, *Good Money, Part II* (1978; University of Chicago Press, 1999). For a critique of the consistency of certain of Hayek's proposals, see Lawrence H. White, "Hayek's Monetary Theory and Policy: A Critical Reconstruction," *Journal of Money, Credit and Banking* 31 (February 1999): 109–120.

5. See, e.g., some of the literature in the "Free Banking and Monetary Policy Links" section of Lawrence H. White's homepage, http://mason.gmu.edu/~whitell/links.html. Accessed June 5, 2011.

6. That there is a tension between Hayek's early step-by-step account of the unfolding of a typical business cycle, and his later work on complex phenomena, should be evident. I prefer his later work. I learned my lesson about forecasting firsthand in 1984, when the existence of large (by the standards of the day) federal deficits as the economy was nearing full employment led me boldly to predict to my classes that either a recession (if government borrowing to finance the deficit pushed up interest rates) or inflation (if the fed monetized the debt) was coming. I was of course wrong. The government started to sell bonds overseas, allowing us to escape the dilemma, a policy we have followed ever since. The ultimate effect of this policy may soon be revealed.

7. Clive Crook, "A Rocky Road for the Fiscal Stimulus," *Financial Times*, July 20, 2009, 7.

8. Mark Calabria, "Did Deregulation Cause the Financial Crisis?" *Cato Policy Report* (July–August 2009), 1, 6–9.

9. Lionel Robbins, *Economic Planning and Economic Order* (London: Macmillan, 1937), 3.

10. Hayek, "Freedom and the Economic System," reprinted in *The Collected Works of F. A. Hayek*, vol. 10, *Socialism and War: Essays, Documents, Reviews*, ed. Bruce Caldwell (1939; Chicago: University of Chicago Press, 1997), 189–211; Hayek, *The Road to Serfdom*, reprinted in *The Collected Works of F. A. Hayek*, vol. 2, *The Road to Serfdom: Texts and Documents*, ed. Bruce Caldwell (1944; Chicago: University of Chicago Press, 2007).

11. Hayek, "Freedom and the Economic System," 194.

12. One is entitled to ask: Why was Hayek so loath to fill in the details? My conjecture is that his decision was strategic: he was trying to keep a liberal coalition intact during the years in the wilderness. The various liberals who attended the Mont Pèlerin Society ranged all over the map in terms of the sorts of institutions they thought would be acceptable. On the matter of anti-trust, for example, members varied from strict laissez-faire to use of anti-trust statutes to ordo-liberalism to certain variants of social market economy under which the planning of the competitive environment became very intrusive indeed. Had Hayek provided too many details, he would perforce be taking sides.

13. Paul J. Davies, "True Impact of Mark-to-Market Accounting in the Credit Crisis," *Financial Times*, February 29, 2008.

14. Hayek, *The Road to Serfdom*, 114.

15. John Authers quotes one risk manager who put it this way: ". . . it's not just about the classic factors like equity, or default, or interest rates, or inflation or liquidity. There's also a risk factor, which is public policy. Whether we like it or not, gov-

ernment has become an integral part of markets." Authers, "Managers Seek a More Reliable Approach," *Financial Times,* October 2, 2009, 21.

16. Hayek, *Law, Legislation and Liberty,* vol. 3, *The Political Order of a Free People* (Chicago: University of Chicago Press, 1978), 82.

17. The classic citation is Ludwig von Mises, "Profit and Loss," reprinted in *Planning for Freedom* (1951; South Holland, IL: Libertarian Press, 1952), 108–149.

18. Hayek, *The Road to Serfdom*, 156.

19. In later work, e.g., Hayek, *The Fatal Conceit: The Errors of Socialism, The Collected Works of F. A. Hayek*, ed. W. W. Bartley, III (Chicago: University of Chicago Press, 1988), chapter 1, he attributed our resistance to markets to the fact that a market society satisfies neither our reason (we always think we can improve on market outcomes) nor our instinct (our hunter-gatherer heritage led to certain moral positions—distrust strangers, deal only with parties you know in face-to-face situations—that do not fit in well with market interactions).

20. Clive Crook, "A Rocky Road for the Fiscal Stimulus."

21. Carl Menger, *Principles of Economics*, trans. James Dingwall and Bert F. Hoselitz (1871; New York: New York University Press, 1976), chapter 8 on the origin of money is a classic example; see also Menger's formulation of the key question in his *Investigations into the Method of the Social Sciences with Special Reference to Economics*, 146: "*How can it be that institutions which serve the common welfare and are extremely significant for its development come into being without a* ***common will*** *directed toward establishing them?*" (Emphasis in original.) Menger, *Investigations into the Method of the Social Sciences with Special Reference to Economics,* ed. Louis Schneider, trans. Francis J. Nock (1883; New York: New York University Press, 1985).

22. David Hume, *A Treatise of Human Nature,* in *The Philosophical Works,* ed. T. H. Green and T. H. Grose, new rev. ed. (1739; London: Longmans, Green and Co., 1890), vol. 2, 258, 293. Hayek frequently quoted Hume on this; see, e.g., Hayek, "The Legal and Political Philosophy of David Hume (1711–1776)," reprinted in *The Collected Works of F. A. Hayek,* vol. 3, *The Trend of Economic Thinking: Essays on Political Economists and Economic History,* 109; "The Results of Human Action but not of Human Design," *Studies in Philosophy, Politics, and Economics* (Chicago: University of Chicago Press, 1967), 99; *The Fatal Conceit,* 34.

23. The authors, respectively, of *Economic Sophisms*, ed. and trans. Arthur Goddard (1845; Irvington-on-Hudson, NY: Foundation for Economic Education, 1996), and *I, Pencil* (1958; Irvington-on-Hudson, NY: Foundation for Economic Education, 1999).

24. F. A. Hayek, "The Use of Knowledge in Society," *American Economic Review* 35, no. 4 (September 1945): 519–30, reprinted in *Individualism and the Economic Order* (Chicago: University of Chicago Press, 1948), 87: "I have deliberately used the word 'marvel' to shock the reader out of the complacency with which we often take the working of this mechanism for granted. I am convinced that if it were the result of deliberate human design, and if the people guided by the price changes understood that their decisions have significance far beyond their immediate aim, this mechanism would have been acclaimed as one of the greatest triumphs of the human mind."

25. As Hayek put it in "Individualism: True and False," "We must face the fact that the preservation of individual freedom is incompatible with a full satisfaction of our views of distributive justice." Hayek, "Individualism: True and False," reprinted in *The Collected Works of F. A. Hayek*, vol. 13, *Studies on the Abuse and Decline of Reason* (1946; Chicago: University of Chicago Press, 2010), 65. He would later come to consider the very term "social justice" to be a dangerous misuse of the language: the second volume of Hayek's *Law, Legislation and Liberty* (Chicago: University of Chicago Press, 1976) carries the provocative title *The Mirage of Social Justice.*

26. Adam Smith, *The Theory of Moral Sentiments*, reprinted in vol. 1 of *The Glasgow Edition of the Works and Correspondence of Adam Smith,* ed. D. D. Raphael and A. L. Macfie (1759; Oxford: Oxford University Press, 1976; reprinted, Indianapolis, IN: Liberty Fund, 1982), quoted in Hayek, *Law, Legislation and Liberty,* vol. 1, *Rules and Order* (Chicago: University of Chicago Press, 1973), 35.

27. Hayek, *The Constitution of Liberty,* 190. Hayek was quoting Walter Bagehot on the "man of genius," and was using it to deride Franklin Delano Roosevelt's attempt to pack the Supreme Court.

28. For more on these concepts, see Hayek, "Degrees of Explanation," reprinted in *Studies in Philosophy, Politics, and Economics* (1955; Chicago: University of Chicago Press, 1967), 3–21; and "The Theory of Complex Phenomena," reprinted in *Studies in Philosophy, Politics, and Economics* (1964; Chicago: University of Chicago Press, 1967), 22–42.

29. Hayek, "Scientism and the Study of Society," reprinted in *The Collected Works of F. A. Hayek,* vol. 13, *Studies on the Abuse and Decline of Reason* (1952; Chicago: University of Chicago Press, 2010), 283–304.

30. Hayek, "The Theory of Complex Phenomena," 31–34.

31. Bruce Caldwell, *Hayek's Challenge: An Intellectual Biography of F. A. Hayek* (Chicago: University of Chicago Press, 2004), chapter 15.

32. It is important to note that such predictions always contain a *ceteris paribus* clause. If market conditions have changed so much that, for example, a minimum wage law fixes the minimum below the going wage rather than above it, it will have no effect: it is not "binding."

33. As Henry Simons put it in his economics syllabus, "Economics is primarily useful, both to a student and to the political leader, as a prophylactic against popular fallacies." Henry C. Simons, *Simons' Syllabus,* ed. Gordon Tullock (Fairfax, VA: Center for the Study of Public Choice, 1983).

34. Naomi Klein, *The Shock Doctrine: The Rise of Disaster Capitalism* (Toronto: Alfred A. Knopf, 2007).

35. Those interested in a more detailed response to the critics of neo-liberalism should consult Bruce Caldwell, "Hayek, Chicago, and Neoliberalism," in *Building Chicago Economics: New Perspectives on the History of America's Most Powerful Economics Program*, ed. Philip Mirowski, Rob Van Horn, and Thomas Stapleford (Cambridge: Cambridge University Press, 2011).

36. Hayek, *Law, Legislation and Liberty*, vol. 2, *The Mirage of Social Justice*, 31–33.

37. Hayek, *The Constitution of Liberty,* 87: "From the fact that people are very different it follows that, if we treat them equally, the result must be inequality in their actual position, and that the only way to place them in an equal position would be to treat them differently. Equality before the law and material equality are therefore not only different but are in conflict with each other; and we can achieve either the one or the other, but not both at the same time." Not all market critics would accept, of course, that the "game" is fair.

38. Hayek, *The Constitution of Liberty*, 95.

39. In describing how a market system allocates rewards, Hayek notes: "The long and the short of it all is that men can be allowed to decide what work to do only if the remuneration they can expect to get for it corresponds to the value their services have to those of their fellows who receive them; and that *these values which their services will have to their fellows will often have no relations to their individual merits or needs.*" *Law, Legislation and Liberty*, vol. 2, *The Mirage of Social Justice*, 72 (emphasis in original).

40. Hayek explains that we can draw distinctions of merit ". . . only where we possess all the knowledge which was at the disposal of the acting person, including a knowledge of his skill and confidence, his state of mind and his feelings, his capacity for attention, his energy and persistence, etc. The possibility of a true judgment of merit thus depends on the presence of precisely those conditions whose general absence is the main argument for liberty. It is because we want people to use knowledge which we do not possess that we let them decide for themselves." Hayek, *The Constitution of Liberty*, 95.

41. Hayek, *The Road to Serfdom*, 148; cf. Hayek, *The Constitution of Liberty*, 285–286.

42. Peter Saunders, "Why Capitalism is Good for the Soul," *Policy* 23, no. 4 (Summer 2007), 5.

43. Hayek, "The Use of Knowledge in Society," *American Economic Review* 35, no. 4 (September 1945): 519–30, reprinted in *Individualism and the Economic Order* (Chicago: University of Chicago Press, 1948).

44. Hayek, "The Use of Knowledge in Society," in *Individualism and the Economic Order*, 80.

45. The ongoing nature of this process is why Austrian economists usually use terms like "market process" or "evolving market order" when speaking about how markets function rather than "market equilibrium." The last can lead one to the false image of a system making a final adjustment to a state of rest.

46. Hayek, "The Use of Knowledge in Society," in *Individualism and the Economic Order*, 86.

47. As Hayek put it in an interview: "What we can know in the field of economics is so much less than people aspire to." Hayek, "Nobel Prize-Winning Economist," ed. Armen Alchian (UCLA: Charles E. Young Research Library, Department of Special Collections, Oral History Transcript no. 300/224). Transcript of an interview conducted in 1978 under the auspices of the Oral History Program, University Library, UCLA, 1983. © Regents of the University of California, p. 258.

48. Peter Boettke, "Hayek's *The Road to Serfdom* Revisited: Government Failure in the Argument Against Socialism," *Eastern Economic Journal* 21 (Winter 1995): 7–26.

49. Bryan Caplan, *The Myth of the Rational Voter: Why Democracies Choose Bad Policies* (Princeton, NJ: Princeton University Press, 2007).

50. The classic citation is William Niskanen, *Bureaucracy and Representative Government* (Chicago: Aldine, Atherton, 1971).

51. James Buchanan and Richard Wagner, *Democracy in Deficit: The Political Legacy of Lord Keynes* (New York: Academic Press, 1977).

52. William Grieder, "The Education of David Stockman," *Atlantic* (December 1981), 28–54.

53. See Peter Boettke, "Putting the 'Political' Back into Political Economy," in *Economics Broadly Considered: Essays in Honor of Warren J. Samuels,* ed. Jeff Biddle, John Davis, and Steven Medema (London: Routledge, 2001), 207. Cf. Hayek, writing in the 1956 Foreword to the American paperback edition of *The Road to Serfdom*: "The increasing tendency to rely on administrative coercion and discrimination where a modification of the general rules of law might, perhaps more slowly, achieve the same object, and to resort to direct state controls or to the creation of monopolistic institutions where judicious use of financial inducements might evoke spontaneous efforts, is still a powerful legacy of the socialist period which is likely to influence policy for a long time to come." Hayek, *The Road to Serfdom*, 44.

Part II

POLITICAL ECONOMY AND AMERICAN ECONOMIC EXPERIENCE

6

Promoting the General Welfare

Political Economy for a Free Republic

Richard Wagner

The American republic was founded on a vision of the political economy of freedom, to borrow from the title of a collection of Warren Nutter's essays.[1] That vision combined valuation of policy options and cognition concerning the ability of policy to achieve those options into a framework of political economy. Elsewhere I describe the problem of securing good governance as a form of social agriculture.[2] With respect to real agriculture, many different plants can grow on a particular plot of land. Valuation is necessary for selecting what to grow and what not to grow, but it is not sufficient. Cognition is also necessary for successful agriculture, as represented by such scientific fields as plant genetics and soil chemistry. After all, valuation not informed by cognition may lead to efforts to grow plants that won't thrive in that soil or climate.

Like real agriculture, political economy also involves both valuation and cognition, only now applied to people rather than to plants. The American republic was founded on the normative vision that people should live together as a society of free and responsible individuals. Within this vision, public officials were servants and not masters, and government was based on consent among the governed.

But majority dominance was not equivalent to consent. The American republic was founded as a constitution of liberty. Every society has a constitution in the sense that every society exhibits regular patterns of activity that can be described by some set of rules, just as lexicographers and grammarians describe patterns that people exhibit in their use of language. Only a few societies, however, have had constitutions of liberty. For any idealized constitutional vision to be successful, it must be capable of being regenerated as time passes, as against succumbing to some process of degeneration. The

Founders recognized that continuation of the constitution of liberty they had established was up to future generations. Benjamin Franklin acknowledged this pithily when, in response to a question about what kind of government the Founders had established, he declared "A republic, if you can keep it."

Franklin's challenge points to the cognitive component of political economy. An act of valuation might commend a constitution of liberty, but maintenance of such a constitution involves the cognitive faculties in creating a constitutional architecture that will withstand some natural processes of dissipation of which the Founders were well aware. All regimes are capable of retrogressive drift because human nature carries within itself the seeds of retrogression.[3] Those seeds are of two forms: grabbing power and ceding power. Grabbing power describes what James Madison denoted as the violence of faction in Federalist #10, wherein governing coalitions impose their will on everyone else. Ceding power refers to what Alexis de Tocqueville described as a sickness of the people, wherein people sacrifice liberty for convenience. Such ceding is articulated cogently by Vincent Ostrom and is described succinctly by James Buchanan as a fear of being free.[4] It's also portrayed by Tocqueville in *Democracy in America* in his chapter on democratic despotism, where he describes how political officials can come to regard themselves as shepherds and the people as sheep to be tended.

The American Founders framed their ideas within a theory of political economy, even if they did not expressly articulate such a theory. With respect to such express articulation, James Buchanan and Gordon Tullock's *Calculus of Consent* was written to set forth a theory of political economy that would render sensible the constitutional architecture by which the American republic was constructed.[5] Similarly, Vincent Ostrom's *Political Theory of a Compound Republic*, the first edition of which was published in 1971, sought to elaborate further the logic of that complex constitutional architecture.[6] Ostrom describes the American form of the constitution of liberty as a compound republic, which he contrasts with a simple republic. With simple republics there exists a locus of final authority. This locus has been typically described as something like "the people," but in practice this reduces to some position of dominance through the arithmetic of majority rule, especially when combined with Bertrand de Jouvenal's recognition that simple republics necessarily will have an oligarchic character because genuine deliberation among large numbers of people is impossible.[7] Simple republics are monocentric: they possess a center of authority. In contrast, compound republics are polycentric: there is open and continuing competition among multiple sources of authority. In simple republics rulers govern people; in compound republics people govern themselves. This, anyway, is the idealized vision on which the American republic was founded.

In recent years, political economy has attracted strong interest within the wider community of economic scholarship, as represented by such works as those of Persson and Tabellini, Drazen, and Besley.[8] This contemporary understanding of political economy, however, has been fashioned with reference to simple republics where a single election is the instrument through which policy choices are made. This contemporary treatment of political economy is contrary to the understanding that informed the American founding, and is incapable of illuminating the political economy of a free people. The political economy of the Founders was a political economy of freedom and limited government; contemporary political economy is a political economy of unlimited government. I shall first explore these alternative frameworks for political economy, after which I shall examine the general welfare principle of the American founding in relation to these alternative visions of political economy. This examination will center on a distinction between leveling and raising as alternative orientations toward the general welfare. While the theory of polycentric political economy that informed the American founding would have embraced a program of raising, the monocentric vision of political economy that is presently in vogue leads almost inexorably to a program of leveling.

POLITICAL ECONOMY AS A FIELD OF INQUIRY

Political economy is a compound term that denotes some form of relationship between the objects we denote as polity and as economy. But what kind of form might that relationship take? What is the process by which this compound is created? Most contemporary thought proceeds in formulaic fashion as illustrated by Political Economy = Polity + Economy. This formula tells us that the compound entity is created through addition across entities, each of which has its own principles of operation. By this formulation, polity operates according to some set of constitutional principles while economy operates according to private property and freedom of contract. Furthermore, polity acts on economy to modify the activities that had been generated within the market economy. Such contemporary treatments of political economy diverge significantly from the vision of political economy that was present at the American founding. The articulation of political economy in a manner that is congruent with a constitution of liberty requires an alternative framework grounded in complexity and polycentricity, and not in simplicity and monocentricity.

Elsewhere I have described these alternative orientations toward political economy as disjunctive and conjunctive; or as separated and entangled.

While the names have changed, the ideas represented by those names remain the same. What I mean by separated political economy is illustrated by Figure 6.1. There, the squares denote the enterprises located within the polity while the circles denote the enterprises located within the economy. This separated framework entails several significant conclusions. One is that all enterprises in the polity act as a unified entity, or as an organization, as illustrated by the complete graph of connections among those enterprises. In terms of Hayek,

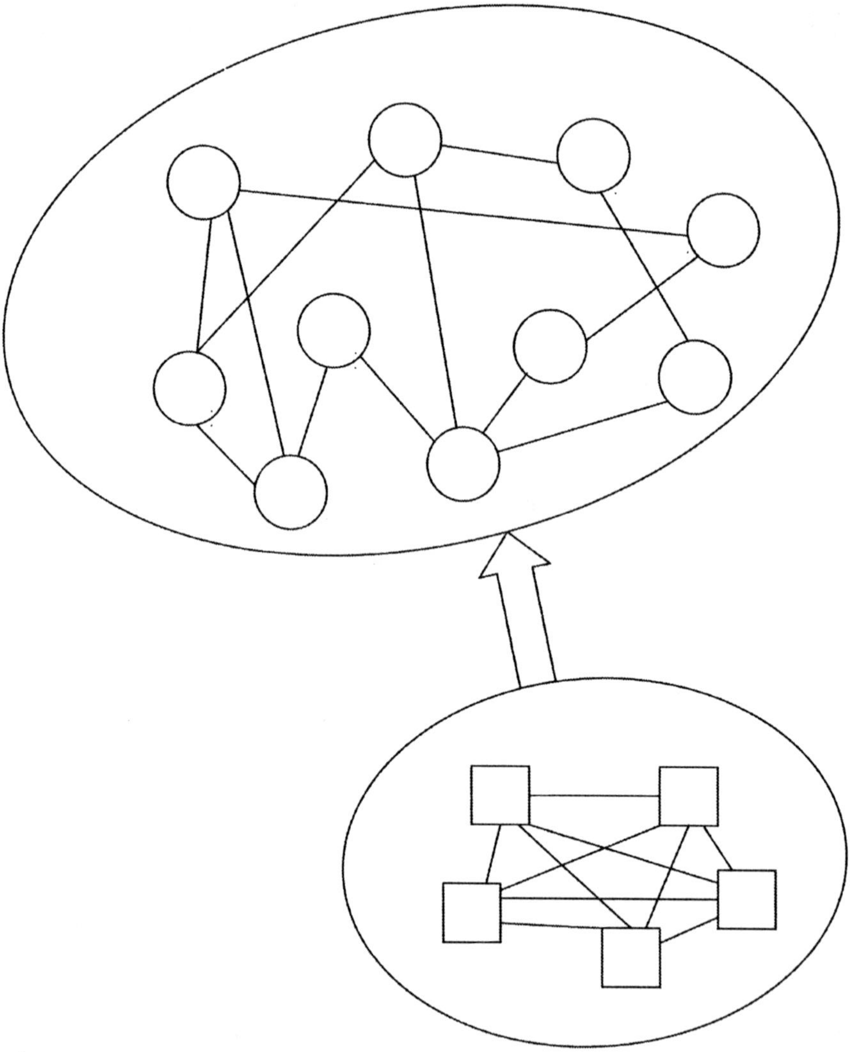

Figure 6.1. Separated Political Economy.

the polity is an organization where all participants aim at the same objective.[9] In contrast, the enterprises within the market economy form an incomplete graph, which indicates that they comprise an order and not an organization. The arrow that runs from polity to economy indicates that polity acts on economy, shifting the results of economic activity from what otherwise would have resulted. For instance, a market-generated distribution of income might subsequently be modified through politically sponsored redistribution.

The distinction between an organization and an order can be conveyed readily by comparing two familiar social configurations. One is a parade; the other is a crowd of spectators leaving a stadium. Both are orderly, in that people can conduct themselves well within either configuration. The sources of orderliness, however, are different, as befits the differing natures of those configurations. The parade is an organization. The orderliness of a parade is established by a parade marshal. The pedestrian crowd is an order. The orderliness of the crowd results through interactions and accommodation among the members as informed by morals (for instance, courtesy) and conventions (for instance, walking on the right). A political economy suitable for understanding the orderliness of crowds of spectators would be of no use for understanding parades, while an effort to treat spectator crowds as unruly parades that need to be better disciplined would be a recipe for tyranny.

The separated framework of political economy conceptualizes the establishment of market equilibrium as being followed by political intervention to change those market outcomes. Polity and economy thus denote separate entities that act independently and sequentially. Economy is the locus of activity where the first draft of the manuscript of social life is written; Polity is where that manuscript is revised and perfected, or changed in any case, for there are a good number of theorists who argue that the revision is corruption and not perfection. My interest, however, resides not in any qualitative evaluation of political action but in alternative conceptualizations of how polity and economy combine to form political economy.

The alternative, entangled framework of political economy, which reflects the vision of political economy that informed the American founding, is illustrated by Figure 6.2. As with Figure 6.1, the squares denote political enterprises and the circles market enterprises. It is still possible to distinguish polity and economy, as well as to combine them and refer to political economy. The structure of that combination differs in several respects between the two frameworks. For one thing, political entities do not form a fully connected graph among themselves. Polity is no longer an organization; instead, it comprises an order of competing organizations. Furthermore, those political entities do not act on economy as an entity but do so by acting on particular entities within the economy, as illustrated by the connections

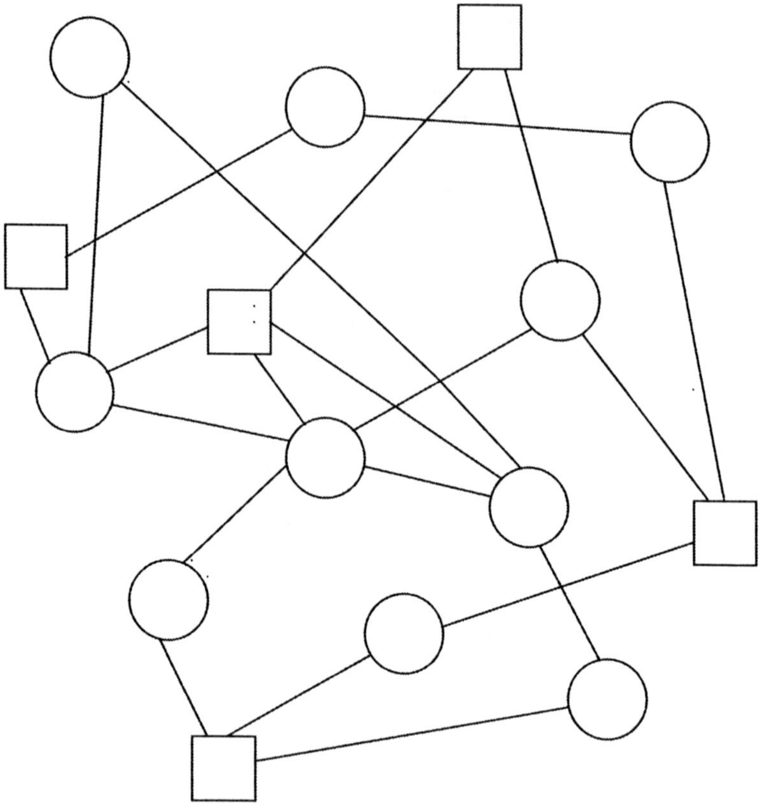

Figure 6.2. Entangled Political Economy.

between particular political entities and particular market enterprises. Still further, action occurs simultaneously in both spheres, whereas in the separated vision political action is subsequent to economic action, as it must be whenever polity is described as acting to correct or perfect market outcomes. The manuscript of societal life is composed in many venues, political and economic, but that composition occurs simultaneously in those various venues, as befits a polycentric process of free and open competition.

Figure 6.3 illustrates one further point that is significant for my analysis. It can be used to illustrate in an abstract manner a process of regime drift that I will explore more fully below. Panel A illustrates complete separation between political and commercial entities. Furthermore, it shows the political entities as encircling the economic entities. This formulation corresponds to a classically liberal vision of political economy. We should not, however, associate this pure form with some actual historical moment; Jonathan Hughes points out in his study of regulation since the Colonial period that there has

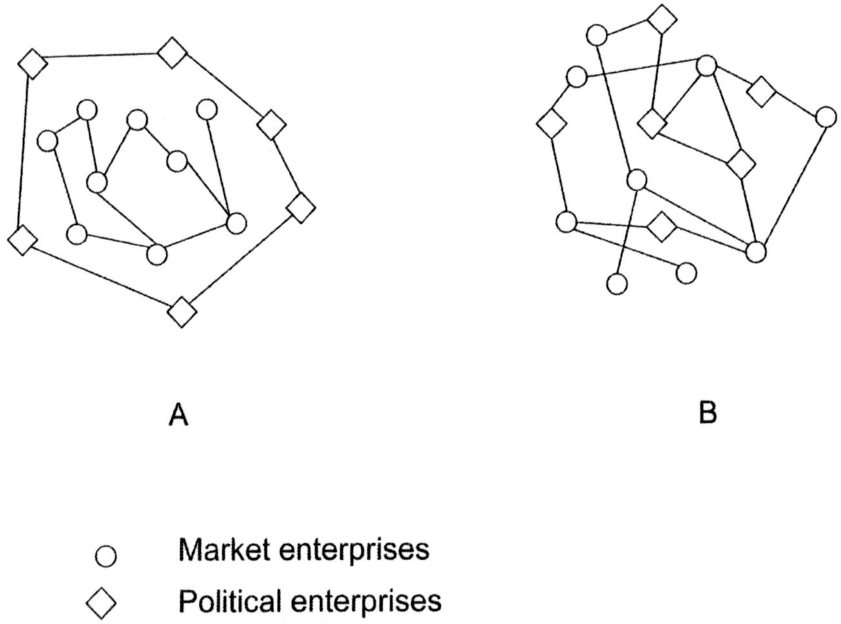

Figure 6.3. Alternative Forms of Political Economy.

always been entanglement within the American political economy.[10] At the same time, however, the extent of entanglement when political activity claims less than 10 percent of total output will be much less than when it claims more than 40 percent. Panel B is meant to illustrate an abstract rendition of a snapshot taken after entanglement had been growing for some time: Panel B represents an internally generated transformation of Panel A.

As for the transformation of Panel A into Panel B, think of the Shakespearean character Jacques's soliloquy in *As You like It*: "All the world's a stage, and the men and women on it are merely players." It is easy enough to gloss that soliloquy from the standpoint of political economy. Unlike staged drama, in the drama that is human life parts and roles are not assigned nor are scripts prepared. The drama is improvised and self-organized, though not chaotic. It's orderly and intelligible, but the order is emergent and not stipulated in advance. Within the classically liberal political economy described by Panel A, political figures are like stagehands. Their efforts are important for the human drama, even essential, but they work behind the scenes all the same. This situation was summarized aptly in the 6th century BC by the Chinese scholar Lao Tzu: "A leader is best when people barely know he exists. Not so good when people obey and acclaim him."[11] It is easy enough to understand how growing entanglement can arise within a constitution of liberty. All that is required are points of mutual attraction between political and economic entities, and with that mutual attraction pulling political entities into center stage, as seen by comparing Panel B with Panel A. A political entity can gain political advantage by forming alliances with some economic entities. Likewise, economic entities can gain competitive advantage by forming alliances with some political entities. Entanglement arises out of this process of mutual interaction.

Panels A and B are meant to illustrate two snapshots of a continuing historical process of growing entanglement between political and economic entities. Jane Jacobs distinguishes between commercial and guardian moral syndromes.[12] Her distinction does not fit completely the distinction between polity and economy, because there can be guardian activities organized within the economy just as there can be commercial activities organized within the polity. Nonetheless, her distinction fits well the ordinary distinctions people have in mind when they refer to polity or to economy, and with growing entanglement speaking to what Jacobs describes as "monstrous moral hybrids." Jacobs's treatment of such hybrids is consonant with Jonah Goldberg's analysis of the growth of liberal fascism since the Progressive era.[13] As Goldberg notes, fascism can take on various personae. Where some can be brutal, others can be gentle, much as Alexis de Tocqueville described in his chapter on democratic despotism in *Democracy in America.*

The American constitution of liberty has been under assault since the early days of the republic, and the assault became particularly strong toward the end of the 19th century. In *Congress as Santa Claus*, Charles Warren chronicled the erosion of the general welfare clause between the founding of the republic and 1932. Warren reports that 1867 was the first time money was appropriated for charitable relief, to provide seeds in response to crop failure in the south and southwest.[14] It took some time for such proposals for relief to become common items of Congressional deliberation. Not even the Chicago fire of 1872 elicited an appropriation for relief. But proposals for relief continued to gain favor in Congress, with the burden of constitutional maintenance shifting to Presidential veto, as illustrated by Grover Cleveland in 1887 when he vetoed an appropriation to aid farmers in Texas. By the end of Warren's narrative in 1932, there was no longer any recognized constitutional limit on the power to appropriate.

Warren's chronicle illustrates how the interplay between principle and practice can produce outcomes that were not part of any original intention. In saying this, I acknowledge that there is invariably some ambiguity about the intentions behind the American founding. Within any collection of people there will be multiple intentions in play. A simple comparison between the federalist supporters of the Constitution and the anti-federalist opponents will reveal some of that multiplicity. At the same time, however, what surely comes through most strongly from reading those debates is the underlying commonality in the orientations they possessed toward the place of government in the free society they were seeking to support.[15] In short, there was universal recognition that government was a necessary evil in the effort to secure good governance, and most certainly was not an instrument of unalloyed beneficence. Government represented a Faustian bargain: it involved the use of an instrument of evil, force over other people, because it was thought that the resulting good would be worth the evil, provided the instrument was used under tightly controlled circumstances. Warren chronicles the continuing weakening of those constitutional controls.

With respect to the political economy of human governance, there are really only two forms that such governance can take, though each form can take on numerous particular looks. Those forms conform to the terms liberalism and collectivism. The various liberalisms construe polities as orders that contain polycentric arrangements of political organizations. While each organization has objectives, the system itself does not, for it is an arena that accommodates peaceful interaction among the people and organizations within its precincts. People have goals and can even join their goals in corporate organizations, but society is an order of organizations and not itself a goal-focused organization. The American Founders saw this societal setting as constituted through a federal republic.

In contrast, the various collectivisms see societies as having goals, with society being an organization of organizations, as it were. The polity is thus the locus of societal articulation and action. Individual goals and actions must conform to those politically expressed priorities. A society is to be transformed from an orderly crowd of moving pedestrians, each of whom is aiming at individually chosen objectives, to a parade, each member of which is performing as directed by the parade marshal. As with any such dichotomy, there can result many variations on both the liberal and collectivist forms. Furthermore, sufficient variation in those forms could even produce the cognitive error of thinking there is a continuum of forms and not a dichotomy, and with this error abetting constitutional drift from liberalism to collectivism.[16]

To hold a liberal preference for self-governance does not guarantee that such a regime will carry the day: this is a lesson that Warren teaches trenchantly, and it is one of the lessons of the vision of political economy that informed the American founding. Liberalism can transmute into some form of collectivism even though there is no general support for this transmutation before it occurs. You cannot go from individual values to collective outcomes by simple addition across people. Recognition of this reality is treated lucidly in Thomas Schelling's recitation of several illustrations of how collective results of individual action cannot be said to reflect the preferences and valuations of the participants.[17] The situation illustrated by Panel A does not transmute into that illustrated by Panel B at one instant. That transmutation is a process that involves interaction among many people over a long duration, and with no one participant being aware of promoting such a transmutation. This is how it is with emergent processes of spontaneous ordering: individual interactions appear to occur within an invariant constitutional framework, and yet the accretion of these interactions transforms the constitutional framework.

The primary object of interest here is the ability of our conceptual frameworks to influence what we see in the first place. In a widely repeated joke, an economist is asked why he is kneeling beneath a lamppost. He responds that he is looking for his lost car keys. When asked if he was sure this was where he lost them, he responds that this was not where he lost them, but he can't look where he lost them because there is no light shining there. This joke invariably brings smiles and chuckles, which indicates some recognition of two-edged character of analytical frameworks: they allow us to see some things more clearly, including things that might not really be there, while also preventing us from seeing other things, even those that might be of particular significance. My concern is how different theories pertaining to political economy frame issues in particular ways that highlight some options while obscuring others, especially with respect to the promotion of the general welfare within a constitution of liberty. The predominant theoretical framework almost inexorably construes the task of securing the general welfare as one of the leveling of incomes within a simple republic, as illustrated by Richard Musgrave's treatment of redistribution through central authority that has shaped nearly all subsequent discourse in public finance and political economy.[18] In contrast, I explore a framework that would promote what I describe as a program of raising, and which comes into view only when it is framed within a framework of political economy that is consonant with the founding vision of the American constitution of liberty.

LEVELING AND RAISING AS ALTERNATIVE ORIENTATIONS TOWARD HUMAN WELFARE

Suppose 100 runners in a 10,000-meter race are distributed across a ten-minute interval by the time they cross the finish line. Someone might think it would be nice if the runners were more closely bunched, say within a five-minute gap. How might this desire be acted upon? There are two ways: the slower runners could be assigned head starts; alternatively, they could be induced to train harder. This distinction between receiving head starts and training harder reflects the distinction I want to make between leveling and raising as alternative approaches to promoting the general welfare. A program of leveling seeks to narrow the range of outcomes by imposing a set of head starts that would produce a closer bunching at the finish. A program of raising seeks to help the weaker runners to become stronger runners. Running is, of course, a quite different activity than participation in commercial life; moreover, people aren't forced to run but they must participate in commercial life. All the same, the distinction points in two distinct directions regarding the social organization of human welfare are flourishing. A program of raising seeks to improve bad performance; a program of leveling seeks to increase the rewards that accompany bad performance while reducing the rewards that accompany good performance.

It is well recognized that the same set of people can generate different outcomes depending on the institutional framework within which they interact. Indeed, this was the central theme of Schelling.[19] The observation surely pertains to the social organization of welfare just as it pertains elsewhere. Simple observation throughout the world shows that flourishing is not an inexorable condition of social life, but rather is a contingent feature. Some institutional frameworks are more consistent with flourishing than other frameworks. A telling illustration of this effect of institutional frameworks is a widely viewed satellite photo of the Korean peninsula at night, where the south is brightly illuminated and the north is mostly dark.

How do theories of political economy relate to leveling and raising? As I explain in a survey of this topic, contemporary political economy is based on patterns of thought that make leveling appear almost automatically as the only way to proceed.[20] Politically, the theoretical framework posits a singular locus of authority, in contrast to a constitution of liberty. Economically, the common framework presumes that observed incomes reflect the best efforts of people to transform their talents into income. People are presumed not to misuse their talents, so low income means that those well-used talents are not highly valued by other people. Poverty is thus something that cannot be addressed by individual effort and can only be addressed through systemic reform, as illustrated by a program of leveling.

Francis Edgeworth advanced the seminal formulation in this vein when he asked whether a despot could increase total utility within a society by redistributing income, and both his question and his answer have informed programs of leveling ever since. Edgeworth's baseline answer was that leveling would increase total utility in the presence of diminishing marginal utility of income.[21] Edgeworth also offered a proviso which came to inform an extensive literature on what is called optimal taxation (a literature that is surveyed in James Mirrlees' "Optimal Taxation and Government Finance"[22]). That proviso entailed recognition that leveling could also reduce the income that people generate, with this recognition operating to limit the extent of leveling.

This formulation entails the presumption that the utility from living has two separate components, consumption and effort, with consumption entering positively and effort negatively. This formulation might appear innocent enough as a blackboard exercise, but it is not so innocent when it is thought to offer insight into the goodness of societal practices and institutions. Among other things, it holds that the best life one can have is to gorge on consumption while doing absolutely nothing, perhaps as illustrated by some hugely rich playboy or playgirl.

But is the diminishing marginal utility of income a reasonable analytical construction to use in appraising institutional arrangements and societal conventions? If we apply this construction to athletic contests, we would have to conclude that games that end in ties are superior to those that have winners and losers. As compared with a tie, the pleasure gained from winning over tying is less than the humiliation suffered by losing in place of tying. That people regard ties as something to be avoided suggests the weakness of treating consumption and effort as separable (as I have elsewhere explained).[23] The alternative is to treat effort and consumption as together comprising a unit of meaningful activity. For instance, some people might enjoy a snifter of cognac together after a day of rock climbing.[24] It would be mistaken to treat rock climbing as the effort that produced the ability to consume the cognac, for this would imply that it would be better just to have the cognac without first climbing the rock. But climbing the rock and sharing the cognac form a non-separable unit of the participation in life that provides the basis of social organization. The wholeness of that participation cannot truly be separated into parts even though for some purposes it might be useful to focus attention on one thing or the other. This raises the question of how to participate effectively in the economic life of a society. If such participation is not a type of involuntary reflex like breathing but rather is something that is learned and acquired, it is reasonable to ask how different institutional arrangements promote or impede that acquisition. The extent of flourishing, or of languishing, within a society would then be mediated through those institutional arrangements.

WANTS AND ACTIVITIES IN RELATION TO LEVELING

The political economy of leveling divides a society into two sets of people: those from whom taxes are taken and those who receive transfers. This division corresponds to the commonplace distinction between "haves" and "have-nots." If one were to ask what it is that the haves have that the have-nots lack, the standard answer would be income, or perhaps wealth. This follows from the formulation which holds that people are identical in all relevant respects except their ability to convert their natural talents into income. Everyone necessarily performs to their full capacities in the conduct of their lives, but some people just have more talent for transforming effort into income.

One troubling feature of this analytical framework is the irrelevance of history to the conclusions reached about individual conduct. The orthodox presumption is that it is meaningful to compare positions people hold today without taking into account any information about how they came to attain those positions. This is hardly a sensible procedure once it is recognized that income today is a product of past actions, and that the quality with which one employs one's talents is a variable that to some extent is open to personal choice as well as subject to influence through societal institutions and public policies.

An alternative possibility, which is precluded by this standard formulation, is that the haves and have-nots can also differ in such qualities as attitudes, orientations, and activities, and with those qualities exerting a significant impact on income. Consider a variation on Henry Fawcett's tale of Robinson and Smith.[25] Each started at the same point in life in similar occupations earning similar amounts of income. Robinson spent all of his income, a good part of it on amusement. Smith saved part of his income, and put a good part of the remainder into personal improvement. As the years passed, Smith advanced into higher paying positions while Robinson stayed pretty much where he started. The incomes of the two diverged increasingly with the passing of time. If the two were compared after, say, 30 years, Smith could well be judged to be a "have" who should be taxed to support Robinson, who is a "have-not." Yet the difference between the two is only a reflection of the different choices they made over the preceding years. Robinson could have been less of a spendthrift and saved more in preceding years, as did Smith. Alternatively, Robinson might have been more energetic in his job and hence received similar advancements to what Smith received. However those comparative histories might have unfolded, an observation of comparative income positions in one particular year provides no information about how those people came to hold those positions.

It is worth noting in this respect that the theory of consumer choice, which is the typical point of departure for economic theory, starts with consumers having endowments that they apportion among objects according to their valuations and the prices of those objects. This analytical framework allows people to differ in two respects: (1) in their preferences for different items of consumption and (2) in their endowments. With such a point of analytical departure, it seems almost inevitable that analysts would probe the merits of differential endowments among people, as illustrated by the literature on optimal taxation. A program of leveling seeks to redistribute endowments that themselves exist independently of human effort.

Don Patinkin makes a vital distinction between individual experiments and market experiments.[26] There are many individual experiments that cannot be generalized into a market experiment. For instance, an individual can be faced with a higher tax rate. A society, however, cannot because it would be necessary also to take into account the use of the revenues collected by the tax. Similarly, an individual can be given an endowment, with the subsequent actions observed or theorized about. A society, however, cannot be given an endowment because there is no source to supply that endowment. For the individual experiment, the endowment can come from other people through taxation. But for a market experiment there is no source to provide an endowment. Hence, consumption cannot be an endowment for a society even though it can be an endowment for an individual. At the societal level, the standard of living is not an endowment but rather is a product of a social ecology of interacting efforts.

The political economy of leveling contains a subtext that directs the conferral of sympathy within a society toward those who have little, and with leveling transfers being a collective expression of that sympathy.[27] Having low income is a sufficient condition for receiving sympathy and transfers, as this condition is an imposition of nature and not a consequence of choice. As an individual experiment, such a direction of sympathy is probably of little consequence. This inconsequential character evaporates, however, when we move to the societal level of market experiment. If there is any sympathy to be doled out based on analytical reasoning, perhaps it should be given to those who undertake suitable efforts that contribute to societal flourishing rather than to those who act in dissipative and improvident fashion. To be sure, this might be a difficult and contentious distinction to make, for it unavoidably becomes involved with efforts to bring moral distinctions to bear on different patterns of life, as Gertrude Himmelfarb illuminates brightly.[28]

RAISING AS AN ALTERNATIVE TO LEVELING

The political economy of leveling precludes from view any possibility that the content of the moral imagination[29] can be influenced through social institutions and political programs. This analytical framework means in turn that people individually bear no responsibility for their positions in life, because the conduct of life is a natural talent that everyone possesses in equal degree in light of their genetic endowments. To claim scope for societal sources of influence is not to deny the importance of genetics. It's even possible to assign primary significance to genetics while still maintaining room for societal influence. The presumption of a blank slate[30] can be avoided without denying the ability of environmental situations to influence the content of moral imaginations. For instance, it seems to be well recognized that children, young boys in particular, who grow up without fathers present are typically less suited to market activity than other children.[31]

A program of raising would commend a different locus of sympathy and obligation than would a program of leveling. The language of obligation speaks to who owes what to whom. The political economy of leveling holds that the haves are obligated to support the have-nots. This pattern of obligation arises because the haves and have-nots are presumed to differ only in endowments that are not of their making. In contrast, the example of Robinson and Smith points to a different and more complex locus of obligation because present circumstances are a product of past choices and actions. As compared with Smith, Robinson made choices that led his standard of living increasingly to sink relative to Smith's. Rather than Smith being obligated to Robinson, it is surely reasonable to ask why Robinson is not obligated to Smith to avoid becoming a possible burden. Why doesn't the obligation run in terms of people striving to avoid becoming a have-not? A concern with raising and flourishing would surely seek to use Smith and not Robinson as an exemplar for the conduct of lives.

To be sure, the story of Robinson and Smith is only one of many that could be told. That story concerned people who at one time were in reasonably similar circumstances but who made choices concerning the conduct of their lives that led in divergent directions. Other stories could be told of different initial starting points, perhaps as illustrated by boys growing up without fathers present. Such different starting points are nonetheless consistent with the acceptance of a sense of obligation to conduct one's life in a responsible manner, which would mean in turn seeking to be a positive contributor to life in society. Difficult circumstances will always be in play, and those circumstances pretty much invariably invoke sympathetic responses through charitable activity.

Self-respect is surely a reasonable quality to find among the members of a flourishing society, and is surely something that is acquired through activity and not through consumption, as recognized by Lawrence Meade.[32] A society does not attain the quality of being flourishing independently of the actions of its members but rather attains that quality as a result of those actions. Flourishing is a product of activity and not of consumption. It is flourishing that makes consumption possible. What this suggests is the value of an inquiry into the relation between welfare and flourishing because flourishing is a product of activity and the impact of activity on character.

To speak of self-respect is to bring raising into the analytical foreground; however, raising cannot be accomplished without active participation by the person being raised. Raising requires changes in patterns of conduct, so raising involves relationships among participants that are not necessary for leveling. Raising is complex and difficult; leveling is simple and easy. The monocentric orientation that accompanies the political economy of a simple republic assimilates readily to a program of leveling. Leveling is a simple program to pursue. All that is necessary is for government to tax some people and distribute the proceeds to other people. It is obvious that governments possess the knowledge necessary to do this.

It is different with a program of raising because raising involves complex patterns of interaction. Raising is a complex quality of a system of human relationships and not a simple product of taxing and spending. Leonard Read (1958) explained that no single person knew how to make a pencil. The production of pencils is a systemic property of human interaction within an institutional framework grounded in private property and freedom of contract.[33] The social arrangements that support the production of pencils are complex, even though it would be a relatively simple matter for a government to impose a tax on the sale of pencils. While governments can tax pencils, they can't plan their production, though, of course, they could always conscript pencils from people who have produced them. A program of raising is like the production of pencils in that it requires complex patterns of social cooperation that are incapable of being duplicated by any single person or agency. Raising is a systemic property of a constitution of liberty and not something that can be systematically attained through policy planning.

INSTITUTIONAL REQUISITES FOR RAISING

It is easy enough to state the central idea behind a program of raising: it means helping people to become more effective at making their way in society. While this idea is easy enough to state, it is not easy to implement. A program of raising requires the use of knowledge that is not fully in the possession of any particular person, and involves instead institutionally structured coordination among multiple participants.[34] In such settings of complex phenomena,[35] the use of knowledge is more a matter of supporting open processes of experimentation than of assigning choice to one central source of authority. The knowledge required to level is simple and readily available, so governments are capable of pursuing a program of leveling. In contrast, the knowledge required to raise, like the knowledge required to produce a pencil, is distributed throughout a complex network of human relationships and can be put to use most effectively within a polycentric political economy of open competition among ideas and programs.

Among other things, a program of raising requires programmatic distinctions to be made between good and bad choices, and also requires a resolve to act upon that distinction. James Buchanan's articulation of the Samaritan's dilemma explains why a central authority is likely to pursue a program of leveling even if it knew how to pursue raising, which it does not.[36] While the Samaritan understands that a decision to offer aid now will lead to an increased volume of disability in the future because such aid reduces the cost of bad choices by potential recipients, the Samaritan offers aid anyway. When a position of central authority is present, that authority bears responsibility for the denial of aid and whatever might follow from that denial. It is different in a polycentric system where there are multiple authorities and not a central authority. Polycentricity reduces the force of the Samaritan's dilemma because no single denial is ever a final denial of support. This situation surely lends credibility to requirements by potential donors that potential recipients change their conduct in ways that will improve their ability to support themselves.

Monocentric governments have difficulty making credible commitments about offering or withholding aid because this form of government possesses a grantor of last resort. In contrast, a polycentric system of genuine federalism has no position of a grantor of last resort. Credible commitments with respect to offering or withholding aid are more likely within a system of genuine federalism because a rejection of support by any particular donor does not close the door on possible support elsewhere. Hence, the force of the Samaritan's dilemma is likely to be weaker.[37] One Samaritan in a system with many Samaritans will never be in the position of being the last option for a supplicant seeking aid. Since raising requires actions by the recipient as a condition of receiving support, the possible denial of support by a potential donor is a more credible possibility in a polycentric system of Samaritans than in a monocentric system where there exists a Samaritan of last resort.

The distinction between good and bad choices is easy enough to make at an abstract level: good choices are those that lead to flourishing lifestyles while bad choices lead to debilitation and destitution. But that abstract character leads to numerous difficulties at the level of practical implementation. Early in life, families are the crucible in which the moral imaginations of children are shaped. Some parents pay attention to this and do it well, other parents do not. Political processes are not adept at supervising or policing parental action, and children cannot be said to have chosen their characters or the contents of their moral imaginations. While Hillary Clinton's claim that it takes a village to raise a child raised a fair amount of controversy, it was accurate all the same.[38] What was not accurate, however, was the presumption that the ideal village operated in hierarchical fashion much like a Health and Human Services bureaucracy, in contrast to the polycentric operation of a genuine village.

If we ask whether the status of being a have-not is a natural condition or is self-inflicted, as it was for Robinson, the reasonable answer is that both sources are present and with the relative significance of those sources differing among people. Robinson became a have-not by choice. A woman who has several children while living on welfare without a father present also had choices. Her children, however, will typically face greatly restricted options regarding the mental and moral orientations they are likely to possess as they enter adolescence and adulthood.[39] As always, there are two types of errors in this situation: one error is to aid the Robinsons when they had the capacity to be like the Smiths; the other error is to fail to aid those Robinsons who had no capacity to be like the Smiths. Furthermore, it is misleading to characterize these errors simply in terms of an amount of aid, for this is the approach of leveling. The aid that accompanies a program of raising involves relationships aimed at promoting the acquisition of orientations and talents that would contribute to flourishing. There is no recipe for perfection in the face of such matters of multi-dimensional complexity.

It is here where the political economy of the compound republic comes into play.[40] A compound republic can accommodate multiple sources of experimentation, which is particularly valuable in the presence of complex phenomena.[41] The distinction between simple and complex phenomena is vital in this respect. As mentioned earlier, leveling is a simple program that can be described by just two elements: (1) a distribution of tax extractions and (2) a distribution of transfers. It is easy to implement leveling. In contrast, raising is a complex program that has numerous components that can be combined in myriad different ways. Each of these combinations represents a different approach to raising. The elements involved in raising can be combined in different ways to generate a huge number of distinct programs. This is a feature of the combinatorial arithmetic that pertains to complex phenomena. Suppose you ask how many different ways you can combine 13 cards out of a deck of 52. The answer exceeds 635 billion. If a program of raising were to involve combining 13 components out of 52, you would likewise have over 635 billion distinct programs of raising.

Raising is predicated on the presumption that those classified as have-nots differ in qualities that render them less effective in participating in the economic life of a society, in contrast to the presumption on which leveling is based, namely, that everyone invariably does the best they can with their talents, and it just so happens that some talents do not pay well. Hence a program of raising must address numerous elements, each of which speaks to the use of talents and each of which can be combined in numerous distinct ways. For instance, the treatment of fatherless boys is but one of many elements that would have to be combined to comprise a program of raising. But that element has various forks that generate still more options, as does each of the other elements. For instance, one fork might concern whether to treat fatherless boys by leaving them with their mothers or by putting them into foster care. But each of these options leads to other forks in this road of complex possibility. The branch where the boy stays with the mother, for instance, could differ depending on whether the siblings are boys or girls, and also on the numbers involved. The branch where foster care is the option likewise might differ according to whether the home is proprietary, church operated, or an intact family. In the presence of such complexity, open experimentation is the best procedure we know for generating knowledge, as explained by the essays in Bergh and Höijer.[42] Such openness of experimentation, I might add, has nothing to do with central government grants for local programs, for such grants operate to restrict rather than to promote experimentation because they specify in advance particular branches that must or cannot be explored.

In a similar vein of thought, Elinor Ostrom explains that private property is likewise a complex phenomena that is composed of several building blocks that can be combined in numerous distinct ways.[43] She identifies seven distinct types of rules that constitute private property, and with each of those rules capable of taking on numerous particular configurations. For instance, there are position rules that identify the participants in a particular situation, boundary rules that establish the connections and relationships among participants, and choice rules that establish what actions are open to the different participants. Suppose for each of these seven sets of rules there are five particular ways those rules can be structured. In this case there will be $5^7 = 78,125$ particular paths by which private property can be established.

Economists, and perhaps social scientists generally, fail to appreciate how fully it is that unarticulated practices contribute to the generation of patterns of individual action that would be denoted as beneficial. Until recently in the United States, for instance, commerce operated under the doctrine known as "hire at will," which entailed the ability of employers also to fire at will. To be sure, it is costly for firms to replace employees, so firing typically would not be an arbitrary action. Yet this doctrine surely operated in the direction of promoting generally beneficial patterns of conduct. Someone who is fired for being too often late to work might be induced to acquire some discipline by setting an alarm clock or by refusing to carouse so late into the night. Even if that person fails to acquire such discipline, other people will be induced to do so to avoid suffering a similar experience. As that doctrine has been overturned through legislation and judicial ruling, it has become more costly to dismiss employees. We may expect such rulings to weaken the forces of self-discipline by weakening the connection between actions and consequences,[44] as would the offer of higher payments for being unemployed.

Many issues turn upon whether people make bad choices or are victims of misfortune outside of any reasonable prevision, as addressed by Milton Friedman's examination of the relative roles of choice and chance in the determination of personal incomes.[45] A reasonable answer would be that both are in play and, moreover, that there is no foolproof recipe for making relevant distinctions and judgments. It is surely reasonable all the same to think that the ability to make such judgments requires particular knowledge of particular circumstances pertaining to the different potential claimants. This knowledge is more likely to be distributed throughout a polycentric system than to be possessed by some central authority. A system of free and open competition can incorporate such distributed and localized knowledge that is largely excluded from national action because such knowledge is generated through the processes of experimentation within a system based on open competition.[46]

Time preference offers a good vehicle for some of these matters pertaining to flourishing and of the impact of institutionally structured practice on the ability of people to flourish. One central feature of the conduct of life is recognition that all action is aimed at the future. That future is discerned via an act of imagination that people can project with sharper or weaker discernment. Edward Banfield argued that poverty was significantly a matter of how people projected themselves onto the future, with high time preferences representing weak projection.[47]

With respect to the story of the three little pigs, two of whom were eaten by a wolf in consequence of their weak projection, we come to a fork in the road regarding efforts to prevent such situations. One fork would be to build brick houses for those pigs. This would be a program of leveling, and would surely promote a lowering of time preferences within the society, and would likely prove impossible all the same. The other fork would rely upon sad stories about eaten pigs to induce more sober and farsighted action by the remaining pigs. This would be a program of raising. Such a program seems almost impossible within monocentric polities because the burden is too much to bear for a Samaritan of last resort. For any particular Samaritan within a polycentric set of Samaritans, however, it is imaginable that such experimental processes will operate and institutionalized practice within that society will operate more fully to promote human flourishing within the society because the talents and capacities at play among the members of that society become more congruent with the requisite conduct necessary for flourishing.

CONCLUSION

Discussions regarding the political economy of welfare are dominated by propositions about the desirable extent of leveling to be pursued collectively within a polity. Perhaps the main thing that can be said in support of a program of leveling is that it lies within the competence of governments, because the only type of competence that is involved is that of taxing and spending. A program of leveling embraces the presumption that all members of a society are inescapably doing the best they can to promote their flourishing, thereby contributing to societal flourishing. The cardinal presumption here is that the haves and the have-nots differ only with respect to the income they have, and with that income having nothing to do with previous choices they made or actions they took.

Once it is recognized that those choices and actions matter, the implications of leveling for the types of choices and actions that people make must be explored. This exploration leads into a consideration of a program of raising as an alternative to leveling. A major difficulty with raising is that there is no easy formula by which to pursue such a program. Leveling is easy to pursue; raising is a difficult and complex process that is filled with unknowns and uncertainties. While there is no simple formula by which a program of raising can be implemented, there is good reason for thinking that the openly competitive process of a polycentric system that can accommodate experimentation and variation is the best way possible for proceeding with a program of raising and flourishing.

NOTES

1. G. Warren Nutter, *Political Economy and Freedom* (Indianapolis, IN: Liberty Press, 1983).
2. Richard E. Wagner, "Complexity, Governance, and Constitutional Craftsmanship," *American Journal of Economics and Sociology* 61 (2002): 105–22.
3. See Richard Wagner, "Retrogressive Regime Drift within a Theory of Emergent Order," *Review of Austrian Economics* 19 (2006): 113–23.

4. Vincent Ostrom, *The Meaning of Democracy and the Vulnerability of Societies: A Response to Tocqueville's Challenge* (Ann Arbor: University of Michigan Press, 1997); James Buchanan, "Afraid to Be Free," *Public Choice* 124 (2005): 19–31.

5. James Buchanan and Gordon Tullock, *The Calculus of Consent: Logical Foundations of Constitutional Democracy* (Ann Arbor: University of Michigan Press, 1962).

6. Vincent Ostrom, *The Political Theory of a Compound Republic*, 2nd ed. (Lincoln: University of Nebraska Press, 1987).

7. Bertrand de Jouvenal, "The Chairman's Problem," *American Political Science Review* 55 (1961): 368–72.

8. Torsten Persson and Guido Tabellini, *Political Economics: Explaining Economic Policy* (Cambridge: MIT Press, 2000); Allan Drazen, *Political Economy in Macroeconomics* (Princeton, NJ: Princeton University Press, 2000); Timothy Besley, *Principled Agents? The Political Economy of Good Government* (Oxford: Oxford University Press, 2006).

9. Friedrich A. Hayek, *Rules and Order* (Chicago: University of Chicago Press, 1973).

10. Jonathan Hughes, *The Governmental Habit* (New York: Basic Books, 1977).

11. Quoted in Jane Jacobs, *Systems of Survival: A Dialogue on the Moral Foundations of Commerce and Politics* (New York: Random House, 1992), 157.

12. Jacobs, *Systems of Survival.*

13. Jonah Goldberg, *Liberal Fascism* (New York: Random House, 2008).

14. Charles Warren, *Congress as Santa Claus: National Donations and the General Welfare Clause of the Constitution* (Charlottesville, VA: Michie), 75.

15. See Herbert Storing, *What the Anti-Federalists Were For* (Chicago: University of Chicago Press, 1991).

16. Richard Wagner, "Retrogressive Regime Drift within a Theory of Emergent Order."

17. Thomas C. Schelling, *Micromotives and Macrobehavior* (New York: W. W. Norton, 1978).

18. Richard Musgrave, *The Theory of Public Finance* (New York: McGraw-Hill, 1959).

19. Schelling, *Micromotives and Macrobehavior.*

20. Richard Wagner, "Raising vs. Leveling in the Social Organization of Welfare," *Review of Law and Economics* 6 (2010): 421–39.

21. Francis Edgeworth, "The Pure Theory of Taxation," reprinted in *Classics in the Theory of Public Finance,* ed. Richard Musgrave and Alan T. Peacock (1897; London: Macmillan, 1958), 119–36.

22. James Mirrlees, "Optimal Taxation and Government Finance," in *Modern Public Finance,* ed. John M. Quigley and Eugene Smolensky (Cambridge: Harvard University Press, 1994), 213–31.

23. See Richard Wagner, *Fiscal Sociology and the Theory of Public Finance* (Cheltenham, UK: Edward Elgar, 2007), 189, 196.

24. George Loewenstein, "Because It Is There: The Challenge of Mountaineering . . . for Utility Theory," *Kyklos* 52 (1999): 315–43.

25. Henry Fawcett, *Pauperism: It's Casuses and Remedies* (London: Macmillan, 1871).

26. Don Pantinkin, *Money, Interest, and Prices*, 2nd ed. (New York: Harper & Row, 1965).

27. Harold M. Hochman and James D. Rodgers, "Pareto Optimal Redistribution," *American Economic Review* 59 (1969): 542–57.

28. Gertrude Himmelfarb, *The Idea of Poverty* (New York: Alfred A. Knopf, 1983); Himmelfarb, *Poverty and Compassion: The Moral Imagination of the Late Victorians* (New York: Vintage, 1992).

29. Himmelfarb, *Poverty and Compassion: The Moral Imagination of the Late Victorians.*

30. Steven Pinker, *The Blank Slate: The Modern Denial of Human Nature* (New York: Viking, 2002).

31. Kyle D. Pruett, *Fatherneed: Why Father Care Is as Essential as Mother Care for Your Child* (New York: Free Press, 2000).

32. Lawrence Meade, *Beyond Entitlement: The Social Obligations of Citizenship* (New York: Free Press, 1986).

33. Leonard Read, *I, Pencil* (Irvington, NY: Foundation for Economic Education, 1958).

34. F. A. Hayek, "The Use of Knowledge in Society," *American Economic Review* 35, no. 4 (September 1945): 19–30.

35. F. A. Hayek, "The Theory of Complex Phenomena," reprinted in *Studies in Philosophy, Politics, and Economics* (1964; Chicago: University of Chicago Press, 1967), 22–42.

36. James Buchanan, "The Samaritan's Dilemma," in *Altruism, Morality, and Economic Theory*, ed. Edmund S. Phelps (New York: Russell Sage, 1975), 71–85.

37. Richard Wagner, *To Promote the General Welfare* (San Francisco: Pacific Research Institute, 1989), 170–73.

38. Hillary Rodham Clinton, *It Takes a Village, and Other Lessons Children Teach Us* (New York: Simon & Schuster, 1996).

39. Pruett, *Fatherneed.*

40. Ostrom, *The Political Theory of a Compound Republic.*

41. F. A. Hayek, "The Theory of Complex Phenomena."

42. Andreas Bergh and Rolf Höijer, *Institutional Competition* (Cheltenham, UK: Edward Elgar, 2008).

43. Elinor Ostrom, *Understanding Institutional Diversity* (Princeton, NJ: Princeton University Press, 2005).

44. Thomas C. Schelling, *Choice and Consequence* (Cambridge, MA: Harvard University Press, 1984).

45. Milton Friedman, "Choice, Chance, and the Personal Distribution of Income," *Journal of Political Economy* 61 (1953): 277–90.

46. Martti Vihanto, "Competition between Local Governments as a Discovery Procedure," *Journal of Institutional and Theoretical Economics* 148 (1992): 411–36.

47. Edward C. Banfield, *The Moral Basis of a Backward Society* (Glencoe, IL: Free Press, 1958); Edward C. Banfield, *The Unheavenly City: The Nature and Future of Our Urban Crisis* (Boston: Little, Brown, 1970).

7

The Economic Theory of the American Founding

Thomas G. West

In light of the stark differences between the economies of the present day and the late 18th century in which the Founders lived, can we learn anything about economics by studying the principles and approach of our Founders? Perhaps surprisingly, the answer is yes. If we look to the actions they took and the rationale they offered for their actions, we will see that the Founders' approach still offers us a guide to pressing economic questions of our day.

Although there are many scholarly treatments of the Founders' understanding of economics (the production and distribution of goods and services), few present an overview of the complete package of the principles and policies upon which they agreed. Even the fact that there *was* a consensus among the Founders is often denied. Scholars who study this topic often focus on their differences rather than their agreements.

It is true that there were bitter disputes over particular policies during the Founding era, such as the paying of the national debt, the existence of a national bank, and whether to subsidize domestic manufactures, and these differences seemed tremendously important in the 1790s. But in spite of these quarrels, there was a background consensus on both principles and the main lines of economic policy that government should follow. John Nelson's verdict on the 1790s is sound: "[W]hen the causes of the slow dissolution of consensus among America's ruling elites after ratification of the Constitution are detailed, the evidence points to *specific* disagreements over programmatic issues and not fundamental schisms over the essential role of government."[1]

The danger is that by concentrating on these and other Founding-era contests, we will fail to see (as the Founders themselves often failed to see) their agreement on the three main policies that, taken together, provide the necessary protection of property rights: the legal right to own and use property in land and other goods; the right to sell or give property to others, or acquire it, on mutually agreeable terms (market freedom); and government support of sound money. Their battles were fought over the best means to those ends and over such subordinate questions as whether and how large-scale manufacturing should be encouraged.

The Founders' approach to economics, when it is discussed by public figures and intellectuals in our time, has been much criticized. One reason many on the Left reject the Founders' economic theory is that they think it encourages selfishness and leads to an unjust distribution of wealth. The prominent liberal thinker Richard Rorty believed that the "moral and social order" bequeathed to Americans by the Founders eventually became "an economic system which starves and mutilates the great majority of the population." Such is the "selfishness" of an "unreformed capitalist economy." For this reason, there is "a constant need for new laws and new bureaucratic initiatives which would redistribute the wealth produced by the capitalist system."[2]

Another common opinion is that the Founders' view of economics is obsolete. It may have been reasonable to protect property rights and free markets in a simpler time with vast tracts of available land, but these policies, we are told, cannot address the problems of today's complex industrial society. William Brennan, the Supreme Court's leading liberal during the second half of the 20th century, wrote:

> Until the end of the nineteenth century, freedom and dignity in our country found meaningful protection in the institution of real property. . . . [B]efore this century . . . a man's answer to economic oppression or difficulty was to move two hundred miles west. Now hundreds of thousands of Americans live entire lives without any real prospect of the dignity and autonomy that ownership of real property could confer.[3]

Besides this supposed problem of the closing of the frontier, many economists claim that the modern economy is subject to "market failure," or the inability of free markets to provide a fair allocation of goods and services.[4] This view assumes that current knowledge of economics and production is unquestionably superior to that of the long-dead amateurs who founded the American regime.

Even many conservative intellectuals are quick to criticize the Founders' work in establishing a free economy, arguing that market capitalism is a system which undermines morality and erodes the character of citizens. For instance, Gertrude Himmelfarb, quoting Joseph Schumpeter, argues that "Capitalism creates a critical frame of mind which, after having destroyed the moral authority of so many other institutions, in the end turns against its own."[5]

All of these criticisms—that the Founders' approach to economics is unjust, that it is too primitive to be applied today, and that it cultivates selfishness and undermines morality—are based on a misunderstanding of their actual approach to economics. As for the Founders' supposedly primitive understanding, we will see that their views were remarkably sophisticated and arguably superior to the dominant views of our day. They provide principles and policies by which even the most complex economic order can be governed. And the economic system they established, far from appealing to greed and selfishness and leading to an unjust distribution of wealth, has helped to create the wealthiest nation in human history—a nation in which even those Americans who are classified as often poor enjoy a degree of prosperity unimaginable to almost anyone a few generations ago.

THE JUSTICE—AND UTILITY—OF THE RIGHT TO PROPERTY

In the Founding era, defenses of property rights proceeded along two main lines: justice and utility. The justice approach treats property as a fundamental right that it would be morally wrong to infringe, regardless of whether it served a useful purpose. The Continental Congress declared in 1774, for example, that "by the immutable laws of nature," the people "are entitled to . . . property." In the Virginia Declaration of Rights (1776), property is an "inherent" right. Massachusetts (1780) called it a right "natural, essential, and unalienable." Four other states used similar language.[6] Viewed in this way, to deprive someone of his property is to violate a right—to commit an injustice.

Over the past two centuries, writes Greg Forster, "the moral argument for capitalism became less prominent. The case for capitalism was more often made on efficiency grounds alone." Earlier defenders of property rights—"from Aquinas to Locke to our own time—have successfully availed themselves of both approaches."[7]

The Founders' argument from justice rests ultimately on the claim that "all men are by nature equally free and independent, and have certain inherent rights," one of which is "the means of acquiring and possessing property."[8] All six of these early state declarations of rights use almost the same language. In this understanding, all are born free; that is, they own their own minds and bodies. Since all are free, all may freely use their talents to acquire property and to keep or use the property they acquire. For individuals or government to forcibly prevent someone from acquiring property, or to use coercion to transfer property from one person to another, deprives that person of the fruits of his labor. It is a violation of his liberty as well as his property. From the point of view of justice, deprivation of property rights is immoral.

Property rights were also understood and defended in terms of their usefulness to life and society, independently of the question of justice. The Founding generation argued that protecting property rights was the best way to ensure prosperity for society. Charleston, South Carolina, affirmed that without property rights, "soon would desolation frown over the uncultivated earth."[9] But property is also a means to something more than avoiding "desolation." It is necessary for liberty and happiness. There is, then, both a low (mere life) and a high (freedom and happiness) use of property. Everyone needs food, clothing, and shelter, and therefore has a right to acquire and possess these goods, for the sake of mere life and for the sake of the good life—of happiness. Government must protect that right so that people can survive and thrive.

Defenders of property rights today generally neglect the first way of treating property (as a matter of justice) and turn instead to the second way (expedience or utility). However, the utility of private property is typically described in terms of material abundance as opposed to life, freedom, and happiness. When property rights are no longer spoken of in terms of justice, and when usefulness is defined in merely materialistic terms, capitalism comes to be seen as low and ignoble. This is, of course, a widespread conviction in our time.

THE RIGHT TO POSSESS *AND ACQUIRE* PROPERTY

So far, I have spoken of "property rights" as though the meaning of that phrase is obvious. It is not. To begin, we must dispose of the most common misconception. It is a mistake to think of property rights merely in terms of possession of what one already has. Adopting this error, law professor Kenneth Karst, for example, writes that "the protection of property and economic liberty" is something that matters only "to people at the top of the heap."[10] Karst is thinking of property as something that the rich possess and the poor lack, but this is to conceive of property as static rather than dynamic, as if one person's ownership is another's deprivation. This view of property rights is summed up in the well-known cynical remark, "[T]he majestic equality of the laws . . . forbid[s] rich and poor alike to sleep under the bridges, to beg in the streets, and to steal their bread."[11]

The Founders anticipated this criticism by insisting that the right to property includes not only *possession* of what one has, but also *acquisition* of what one needs. The Virginia Declaration of Rights states that "all men . . . have certain inherent rights," including "the means of acquiring and possessing property."[12] Five other state constitutions omit "the means," but all speak of the right of "acquiring, possessing and protecting property."[13] If the right includes both *acquiring* and *possessing* property, then it is not enough to be allowed to keep what you possess. Such a right would benefit only those who already have what they need. There must be some "means of acquiring" more than one already owns so that the poor as well as the rich can benefit from property rights.

In the Founding, the right to acquire property precedes the right to possess it because the right to acquire is the foundation of the right to possess, not only because of the needs of the poor, but also because of the natural right to liberty itself. As James Madison's *Federalist* #10 explains, there is a "diversity in the faculties of men, from which the rights of property originate. . . . The protection of these faculties is the first object of government." Madison is saying that property rights originate in the fact that each person owns himself, his "faculties" (his mind, body, and talents). This is the basic premise of the Founders' natural law approach: "all men are born free" means that no one has a natural right to own anyone else. There are no natural masters or natural slaves. Therefore, the *first* object of government is not to protect the physical property acquired by the employment of our faculties, but to protect the faculties themselves. They are the means of *acquiring* property, as Madison says: "From the protection of different and unequal faculties of acquiring property, the possession . . . of property immediately results."[14]

No one would make the effort to acquire anything that would immediately be stolen. The right to acquire is primary, for possession serves acquisition. Government protects the possessions of the rich in order to guarantee the right of the non-rich to acquire what they need for their convenience and happiness.

Is There a Conflict Between Possession and Acquisition?

The existence of a natural right to acquire property leads to a surprising consequence. If everyone has a right to acquire *and* to possess property, a conflict between the haves and have-nots will be unavoidable in a condition of extreme scarcity. Unless the possessors voluntarily choose to spread their wealth around, those who are starving will have no way of getting what they need except by theft or violence.

One might argue that there is no conflict of rights here because, as John Locke writes, "it would always be a sin, in any man of estate, to let his brother perish for want of affording him relief out of his plenty."[15] But Locke supposes a state where some property owners have "plenty." What happens when the possessors do not have "plenty," but only barely enough to subsist? Then one party or the other must starve. The non-owners will have a right to acquire, and the owners will have a right to defend their possessions. It will be a war of all against all, where, as Hobbes says of the state of nature, "one *by right* invades, and the other *by right* resists."[16]

This potential and sometimes actual conflict between natural rights was also acknowledged during the Founding era. The property rights of the individual cannot always be respected when the survival of the community is at stake—for example, in a time of foreign invasion. In an 1810 letter, Jefferson recalls examples of grave but necessary government inroads on property rights during the Revolutionary War:

> When, in the battle of Germantown, General Washington's army was annoyed from Chew's house, he did not hesitate to plant his cannon against it, although the property of a citizen. When he besieged Yorktown, he leveled the suburbs, feeling that the laws of property must be postponed to the safety of the nation.[17]

Would the Founders' principles lead to the conclusion, then, that socialism or some other scheme of government redistribution of income could be the most just economic order? Using government coercion to redistribute property certainly violates the natural right to *possess* property, but what if this policy is the best way to enable everyone to exercise their right to *acquire* it? Would that not be in greater conformity with natural right than the starvation or deprivation of the poor?

That conclusion would follow only if there is no way to reconcile the right to acquire and the right to possess. The Founders' natural rights principles therefore require the analysis of an empirical question: What government policies most effectively enable property owners to keep their property while enabling everyone else to acquire property of their own? The answer requires an understanding of how wealth is produced. Economics thus becomes an indispensable part of the practical application of natural law and natural rights.

Someone might object that an analysis of the facts of economic production has nothing to do with natural law. We seem to be exceeding, and therefore exposing, the limits of the natural rights theory. But this objection misunderstands the idea of natural right. The theory provides only the basic principles of moral and political order. It does not lead self-evidently to a complete legal code. The challenges in the application of natural law to political life arise from nature itself, which gives us the goals and the broad, general rules but leaves it up to us to find out what laws and government structure best achieve those goals.

It is easy to state that there is a natural right to acquire and possess property, but it is a much more difficult task to spell out what rules will enable everyone to exercise the right to acquire property effectively. That is what we will now proceed to explain.

ELEMENTS OF ECONOMIC THEORY IN THE FOUNDING

Nowhere in the writings or laws of the Founders are the elements of their economic theory set forth with clarity and completeness. We have to reconstruct their position by gathering into a coherent whole the relevant constitutional provisions, laws, and official reports, supplemented by remarks of individual Founders when these help to explain the official documents.

The Founders did not hold the view that government's sole role in regard to property is to get out of the way.

Government has an extensive set of responsibilities that it must fulfill in order to enable people to exercise their right to acquire and possess property. There are three main Founding-era economic policy principles that make possible sufficient production, for rich and poor alike, of the goods that are needed for life and the pursuit of happiness.

The first principle is *private ownership*. Government must define who owns what, allow property to be used as each owner deems best, encourage widespread ownership among citizens, and protect property against infringements by others, including unjust infringement by government itself.

The second principle of sound policy is *market freedom*. With some exceptions, everyone must be free to sell anything to anyone at any time or place at any mutually agreeable price. Government must define and enforce contracts. Means of transportation must be available to all on the same terms.

The third principle is *reliable money*. To facilitate market transactions, there must be a medium of exchange whose value is reasonably constant and certain.

One finds the same three principles both in classical economists like Adam Smith and Jean-Baptiste Say and in some current economists. For example, the core of Anders Aslund's book on the recovery of capitalism in Eastern Europe is three chapters on each of these three topics. His fourth chapter is called "Liberalization: The Creation of a Market Economy"; the fifth, "From Hyperinflation to Financial Stability"; and Chapter 6 is "Privatization: The Establishment of Private Property Rights."[18] The first author known to have explained these three elements of a market economy is (perhaps surprisingly) Plato in his account of the "healthy city" in *The Republic*.[19] In other words, the Founders were following or anticipating competent writers on economics, ancient and modern.

The beginning of economic wisdom, for the Founders as for all serious economists, is the need for the division of labor. Hamilton, Madison, and James Wilson all mention its importance in their writings. For example, Hamilton wrote that the division of labor makes possible "[t]he greater skill and dexterity naturally resulting from a constant and undivided application to a single object." This "has the effect of augmenting the productive powers of labor, and with them, the total mass of the produce or revenue of a country."[20] The greater the division of labor, the more and the better will be produced for all.

PRIVATE PROPERTY

The first of the Founders' economic principles is private property. Several government policies adopted during the Founding era contributed to this end. Five in particular merit our attention.

Policy 1: Government Must Define with Precision What Constitutes Ownership of Property

This is often taken for granted, but government cannot protect the right to property unless it establishes clear legal rules determining who owns what. Five early state constitutions therefore specifically mention the office of register or recorder of deeds.[21] Today, all of the land in America is officially surveyed, and records of the surveys and owners are kept in a central location in each county (or equivalent). In the early days of the republic, much of the nation was uncharted wilderness, occupied sporadically. An early federal law, the Land Ordinance of 1785, provided for the surveying and recording of land in the Northwest Territory, so that clear ownership would be firmly established. The Northwest Ordinance of 1787 required these property titles to be sustained in the transition from territory to statehood: "The legislatures of those districts or new States shall never interfere with the primary disposal of the soil by the United States in Congress assembled, nor with any regulations Congress may find necessary for securing the title in such soil to the bona fide purchasers."[22] Although it is true that this concern for establishing clear title does not appear in the federal Constitution, the Northwest Ordinance has quasi-Constitutional status. It is listed in the federal code as one of the four organic laws of the United States. This Ordinance was intended to be, and became, the authoritative pattern by which future states were to be admitted.[23]

Outside of the Western nations, titles of ownership mostly do not exist. "[T]oday," writes one economist, "only about 1 percent of land in Africa is registered under the formal system."[24] Without clear title, there can be no mortgages, no title insurance, no use of property as collateral for business loans, and no confidence in the continued right of occupancy for those who improve their property. It is important to reiterate that there is a legitimate and even *necessary* role for government in this regard in order to preserve the right to acquire and possess property.

Policy 2: There Must Be Few Restrictions on the Use of Property

The owner alone—and no one else, especially not government officials claiming to be experts—is most likely to have either the necessary skill for production or a financial interest in hiring or renting to someone with skill. As Madison said, "if industry and labor are left to take their own course, they will generally be directed to those objects which are the most productive, and this in a more certain and direct manner than the wisdom of the most enlightened legislature could point out."[25]

Still, the Founders did accept the need for regulations to be placed on the use of property. They did not consider property to be an absolute right, although some scholars have contended they did.[26] They approved not only of taxation, but also of limits on the free use of property. These limits were included in what was later called government's "police power," the power to make laws protecting the public health, safety, and morals.[27] One such early regulation was an 1823 New York City law restricting the right to bury the dead in certain portions of the city. The law was challenged in court by two churches claiming abridgement of their right to free use of property. The city successfully defended itself by pointing out that cemeteries in heavily populated areas constitute a public nuisance, because of the greater prevalence of disease around burial sites. The city implied that this exception to the general rule in favor of the free use of property was necessary to protect the natural rights of all. Eric Claeys explains:

> According to [the Founders' understanding of] the law of nature, property may not be used in a manner that threatens others' rights to health or safety. . . . [S]elf-preservation takes precedence over the acquisition of property. Every owner benefits equally from a moral command barring all her neighbors from using property to inflict serious health or safety risks on their neighbors.[28]

Claeys notes that it is characteristic of this case and of many 19th-century cases that the courts routinely invoked the natural law principles of the Founding as a means to interpret both state and federal constitutions and laws.

Those whose negligent or malicious use of property led to their neighbors' harm could be sued or prosecuted. But in the Founders' approach there was a presumption in favor of freedom, in this case the freedom of the private property owner. Laws limiting the use of property were subjected to scrutiny in state courts.

As long as Americans continued to follow the Founders' understanding of natural law—until about 1900—the police power tended to be exercised in a way that was compatible with broad economic freedom. Legal historian Jeff Lewin writes, "In the early years of the twentieth century, legal positivism superseded natural rights as the dominant philosophy in American jurisprudence, particularly with respect to property rights." The legal community's Restatement of Torts in 1939 cut off nuisance law "from its natural rights origins, substituting a positivist right determined according to utilitarian criteria of cost and benefit." The positivist approach treats government limitations on the right to use one's own property "as a pure question of policy," no longer as a violation of individual rights. At that point, there are no moral limits on government regulation. Government may do whatever it finds convenient.[29] The political theory of Progressivism, followed by later 20th-century liberalism, made use of this new unbounded conception of state power to justify government encroachments on property rights previously considered sacred.

Policy 3: Government Must Encourage Widespread Ownership

This will enable property to be put to maximum productive use and hold open to the poor the greatest opportunity to acquire property. The Land Ordinance of 1785 set the example for the next century of federal land policy. This law arranged for the sale to private owners of almost all public land west of the original thirteen states.

Since about 1900, the presumption in favor of private ownership has faded. Private owners are viewed with growing suspicion as threats to the environment or exploiters of the poor. Contrary to Madison's claim, government is now presumed to know best how property is to be used. One consequence is that in the Western states, which were settled last, the federal government owns over 50 percent of the land. In the Northeast, which was settled earliest, federal land amounts to only 3 percent.[30]

Reforming inheritance laws was one aspect of the Founders' approach to encouraging widespread ownership. For instance, colonial Virginia law supported both primogeniture and entail. Primogeniture meant that the inheritance of land would pass to the oldest son only, and entail required the current owner to keep his land intact for his descendants. It could not be sold either as a whole or in part.[31] Jefferson's most urgent legal reform after the Declaration of Independence was to get rid of these two limits on property owners. These reforms would allow owners to divide, sell, or develop their property as they pleased. Property would be distributed more equally among all heirs, male and female, thus promoting widespread ownership of property. All states that had primogeniture and entail abolished them during the American Revolution.[32] Four state constitutions (Pennsylvania, Vermont, North Carolina, and Georgia) explicitly prohibited them. An anti-entail provision was also included in the Northwest Ordinance of 1787.[33]

Jefferson wrote that "The transmission of this property" through primogeniture and entail "from generation to generation in the same name raised up a distinct set of families who, being privileged in the law in the perpetuation of their wealth were thus formed into a Patrician order. . . . To annul this privilege," Jefferson continued, "was deemed essential to a well ordered republic. To effect it no violence was necessary, no deprivation of natural right, but rather an enlargement of it by a repeal of the law."[34] The "natural right" being enlarged here is the right to dispose of one's property, which was restricted by the law of entail. Jefferson's reasoning was widely shared, as can be seen in the 1784 North Carolina law abolishing entails: "entails of estates tend only to raise the wealth and importance of particular families and individuals, giving them an unequal and undue influence in a republic, and prove in manifold instances the source of great contention and injustice."[35]

Policy 4: Government, Through Civil and Criminal Law, and National Defense, Must Protect Property Owners against Harm to Property by Fellow Citizens or by Foreign Nations

Without a strong national defense and an effective criminal law, none of the measures already explained will suffice. Property cannot be secure if it is exposed to violence or theft, whether foreign or domestic. Government protects us against domestic violence by means of the criminal laws (providing for government prosecutions) and civil laws (providing for private lawsuits to recover damages). The Massachusetts Declaration of Rights explains:

> Each individual of the society has a right to be protected by it in the enjoyment of his life, liberty and property, according to standing laws. . . . Every subject of the Commonwealth ought to find a certain remedy, by having recourse to the laws, for all injuries or wrongs which he may receive in his person, property, or character.[36]

Government secures property rights against foreign violence by maintaining strong armed forces and using them to defend against those who would subordinate America to the will of another nation. In Mexico, in Russia, in most of Africa, and in some American cities, the laws do not reliably protect businesses and persons against the violence of thieves and competitors. This is an abdication of government's basic economic responsibility to protect property rights from injury by other individuals.

Policy 5: Government Must Protect Property Owners against Harm to Property by Government Itself

Government officials can deprive someone of property just as effectively as fellow citizens or foreign nations can. The Founders' remedy is to allow government to take property only by laws formally enacted and enforced with appropriate judicial procedures to protect the innocent (such as jury trial, right to examine witnesses, and right to hire a lawyer). Six state constitutions and the U.S. Constitution's Bill of Rights therefore included "due process" or "law of the land" clauses along with specifications of trial procedures.

Today, government is given a wide leeway to seize property without having to prove in court that a law has been violated. Drug laws allow government officials to seize cars and money without trial. The Internal Revenue Service freezes people's bank accounts and credit for months merely on suspicion of wrongdoing.[37] The situation is even worse in countries outside the West. In 2000, a man driving from Germany to Kyrgyzstan reported that police stopped him 120 times to pay "fines" (bribes).[38]

Sometimes government needs to take private property for such purposes as roads, public buildings, and military bases. The Fifth Amendment of the Constitution provides, "nor shall private property be taken for public use, without just compensation." Five state constitutions had similar provisions.[39] Besides the "just compensation" limit, in both the state and federal constitutions, government could take property only for "public use." Government was therefore forbidden, as one federal court stated, to "take land from one citizen, who acquired it legally, and vest it in another."[40]

Today, it is routine, as famously shown in the *Kelo* case,[41] for government to take property from one person and give it to someone else who is expected to pay more taxes, create more jobs, or build more attractive buildings. Again, the situation is far worse in other countries.

The Right to Own Property in the U.S. Constitution

Someone might ask why, if property ownership was considered so fundamental, the U.S. Constitution was silent on the subject. The answer is that although the Constitution does not explicitly mention property, it is in fact not as silent as one might think. We have already noticed the Due Process and Takings Clauses of the Fifth Amendment, which was added soon after the Constitution went into effect. Moreover, in the original Constitution, "The Citizens of each State shall be entitled to all Privileges and Immunities of Citizens in the several States."[42]

The pre–Civil War case law applying this provision generally agrees with the finding in a 1797 Maryland case, *Campbell v. Morris*, that "one of the great objects [of the clause] was the enabling [of] the citizens of the several States to acquire and hold real property in any of the States."[43] This conclusion is supported by the most important pre-Civil War case on the Privileges and Immunities clause, *Corfield v. Coryell* (1823).[44] In these ways, the U.S. Constitution affirms property rights throughout the United States. Furthermore, the Fourteenth Amendment extended federal protection to privileges and immunities to each state's own citizens.

FREE MARKETS

So far, we have discussed how government secures the rights of those who own property, but that is only the first step. In order for specialists in the various productive skills to get what they need from each other, they must have an opportunity to exchange the goods they produce for other people's products. Markets must be permitted and protected by government. James Madison sets forth the basic rationale for division of labor and free markets:

> I own myself the friend to a very free system of commerce. . . . It would be of no advantage to the shoemaker to make his own clothes to save the expense of the tailor's bill, nor of the tailor to make his own shoes. . . . [E]ach [is] capable of making particular articles in sufficient abundance to supply the other—thus all are benefitted by exchange, and the less this exchange is cramped by government, the greater are the proportions of benefit to each.[45]

The question is, how does government secure freedom of exchange? To this end, the Founders adopted three fundamental policies that were affirmed in state and federal constitutions, as well as in other official and unofficial documents of the Founding period.

Policy 1: In General, Everyone Must Be Free to Sell Anything to Anyone at Any Price

The right "to take, hold and dispose of property, either real or personal"[46] is one of the privileges of citizenship protected in the U.S. Constitution. The right of a property owner to "dispose of property" may seem obvious, but primogeniture and entail prevented fathers from dividing their land among their children.

All states that had primogeniture and entail abolished them during the Revolution. The abolition of entail had the additional effect of expanding the number of people who owned land, which was another of the Founders' property policies, as explained previously.

Monopolies are a second limitation on the right to buy and sell. The term "monopoly" must be properly understood. Today, a monopoly is often understood as a private company that dominates a particular market, such as Microsoft in computer software. In the Founding, however, a monopoly was a government grant of "exclusive advantages of commerce" to particular persons, such as an exclusive right to provide telephone service or electricity. Four state constitutions prohibited monopolies. Maryland's constitution gave this explanation: "[M]onopolies are odious, contrary to the spirit of a free government, and the principles of commerce; and ought not to be suffered."[47] The constitutions of North Carolina and Tennessee prohibited monopolies as "contrary to the genius of a free State."[48] The "genius [i.e., character] of a free state" requires, as Massachusetts says in its own prohibition of monopolies, that "No man, nor corporation, or association of men, have any other title to obtain advantages, or particular and exclusive privileges, distinct from those of the community, than what arises from the consideration of services rendered to the public."[49] Monopolies contradict "the principles of commerce" because by arbitrarily excluding some citizens from particular trades or professional pursuits, they impose a legal obstacle to the natural right to acquire property.

The U.S. Constitution permitted Congress to give authors and inventors monopolies "for limited times" to "promote the progress of science and useful arts."[50] The important phrase here is "limited times." To allow a permanent right to produce a particular kind of property is to create a permanent monopoly. It would therefore deny to many their natural right to acquire, possess, and use property. The Founders would not have approved of today's practice of indefinite protection of intellectual property rights. The Copyright Act of 1790 provided for a 28-year maximum protection of published works. The 1998 Copyright Term Extension Act, in contrast, covers publications for up to 120 years.

Today, it is customary for government to establish quasi-monopolies through licensing requirements that limit market entry in a variety of areas, from air-conditioning repair to public transportation to cosmetology. Licensing requirements that truly protect the public against harm, such as licensing of doctors, were indeed employed in the early Republic. Today, however, licensing is often used to prevent new or small businesses from competing in markets dominated by existing businesses. Carlos Slim, the world's richest man in 2010, acquired much of his wealth by means of a government-granted monopoly on telephone service in Mexico.[51]

The principles that I have sketched in this discussion of market freedom were not always observed during the Revolutionary War. Serious obstacles to free trade were imposed by state governments. Forrest McDonald explains:

"New York and Pennsylvania, through which neighboring states did most of their importing, collected sizable revenues from import duties that were ultimately paid by consumers in New Jersey, Delaware, and Connecticut."[52]

In one of the few areas where the federal government was authorized to interfere with the domestic policy of the state governments, the U.S. Constitution prohibited state taxation of imports and exports.[53] The Constitution also instructed Congress that "no preference shall be given by any regulation of commerce or revenue to the ports of one State over those of another."[54] These and similar provisions, together with Congress's power to regulate commerce among the states, were meant to establish a nationwide free market.

Policy 2: Government Must Define and Enforce Contracts

A second requirement of freedom of exchange is that there must be both clear legal definitions and impartial enforcement of contracts. That is one reason why the right "to institute and maintain actions of any kind in the courts of the state" was considered a privilege of citizenship.[55] Seven early state constitutions therefore said that everyone "ought to find a certain remedy, by having recourse to the laws, for all injuries or wrongs which he may receive in his person, property, or character" (or an equivalent phrase).[56]

A corollary to this is the provision of the U.S. Constitution providing that "No state shall . . . pass any . . . law impairing the obligation of contracts."[57] The Northwest Ordinance of 1787, anticipating this provision of the Constitution, explicitly links its contracts clause with security of property rights:

> And, in the just preservation of rights and property, it is understood and declared, that no law ought ever to be made, or have force in the said territory, that shall, in any manner whatever, interfere with or affect private contracts or engagements, bona fide, and without fraud, previously formed.[58]

In the Founding, a voluntary contract between two individuals or associations was understood as a sign of the equality between them. Each agrees to give up some of his own property in exchange for property that he values more than his present possession. In an employer–employee relation, the owner has money that he wants to exchange for labor, while the workers have, to quote Madison's article on property, "free use of their faculties, and free choice of their occupations, which . . . constitute their property in the general sense of the word."[59] Historian William Forbath writes that "abolitionists talked about the freedom of the Northern worker in terms of self-ownership, that is, simply not being a slave, being free to sell his own labor."[60]

There was one exception to the rule that everyone is legally obliged to fulfill his contractual obligations. In colonial America and even after the

Founding, when a person did not have enough property to pay, he was sometimes sent to debtors' prison. Recognizing that the inability to pay debts is not necessarily due to a moral fault, states began to allow bankruptcy. The U.S. Constitution authorizes Congress to "establish . . . uniform laws on the subject of bankruptcies throughout the United States."[61]

Freedom of contract is viewed with widespread suspicion today. Many believe that such freedom leads to exploitation and oppression of workers by employers. America now limits freedom of contract in many ways: for example, by minimum wage laws, laws allowing unions to coerce employers into bargaining and laws that deny employers the right to hire and fire as they choose ("affirmative action" and disability laws).

Policy 3: There Must Be Equal Access to Transportation

The privileges of citizenship protected in the Constitution and by the state governments included the right to travel and to have access to "common carriers" such as coaches, ships, and (later) railroads. The Northwest Ordinance explicitly guaranteed access to the public waterways and highways that were used to transport goods to market.[62]

Access to markets is made easier by better opportunities for transportation, as Hamilton pointed out (quoting Adam Smith) in his "Report on Manufactures."[63] State governments therefore promoted and often funded the building of roads and canals. This is of course a departure from the general principle that goods and services are to be provided by the market, but the difficulty of acquiring long stretches of contiguous land for a road or canal by voluntary purchase was thought to justify the exception.

STABLE MONEY

Besides private property and free markets, there is a third major requisite for the protection of property rights: money. In particular, there must be a stable and reliable measure of market value. The reason is simple: If there is no stable measure of market value, the prices of goods and services can fluctuate rapidly. Rapid fluctuation in prices means that debts and investments can be eliminated through inflation, and property can be taken by manipulating the supply of money.

Lack of money was a major difficulty that almost led to the failure of the American Revolution. Congress, lacking the power to tax, issued "bills of credit," paper money known as "Continentals." By 1780, these bills had lost almost all of their face value. Historian Forrest McDonald explains that

Congress, through this policy of degrading the value of money, in effect "engineered a massive expropriation of private property through a calculated policy of inflation."[64] James Madison later justified this dishonesty by pointing to the desperate situation of a war for national survival: "Being engaged in a necessary war without specie [gold or silver] to defray the expense, or to support paper emissions for that purpose redeemable on demand, and being at the same time unable to borrow, no recourse was left, but to emit bills of credit, to be redeemed in future."[65] Congress and the states also financed the war by borrowing money from American and European lenders. These loan certificates were eventually paid off as a consequence of Hamilton's financial policies in the 1790s, but the worthless bills of credit were never redeemed.[66]

State governments were no better. The policy of intentional inflation of the currency complemented the "stay laws" passed by states, which freed debtors from part of the obligation to pay back their loans. All this led to further economic turmoil as states passed tender laws requiring merchants and creditors to accept paper currency at face value in payment of debts. Curtis Nettels explains the situation in North Carolina: "In 1787–1788 the specie value of the paper had shrunk by more than fifty percent. Coin vanished, and since the paper had practically no value outside the state, merchants could not use it to pay debts they owed abroad; hence they suffered severe losses when they had to accept it at inflated values in the settlement of local debts."[67] Partly as a result of these gyrations in the value of money, the nation fell into a serious economic recession.

Due in large part to these difficulties and the subsequent economic turmoil caused by manipulation of money by both state and national governments during the 1780s, there was a strong demand for an end to government-issued paper money. The remedy was to be a return to the gold and silver standard. The U.S. Constitution therefore specifies that the states may not "coin money; emit bills of credit; [or] make any thing but gold and silver coin a tender in payment of debts."[68] Emitting bills of credit was not on the list of powers given to Congress. "Fiat" paper money (bills of credit), issued by the U.S. government (and every other government in the world) since the 1930s, was precisely what the Framers of the Constitution were trying to prevent.

James Madison summarized the Founders' arguments against fiat money in *Federalist* #44:

> The extension of the prohibition to bills of credit must give pleasure to every citizen in proportion to his love of justice, and his knowledge of the true springs of public prosperity. . . . [S]ince the peace, [America has suffered] from the pestilent effects of paper money on the necessary confidence between man and man; on the necessary confidence in the public councils; on the industry and morals of the people, and on the character of Republican Government.[69]

Here, importantly, Madison explained that the problems of fiat money were both moral and economic. The argument was as much about justice, character, and morality as it was about economic efficiency and prosperity.

LEGITIMATE RESTRICTIONS ON PROPERTY USE AND FREE MARKETS

An objection to the preceding analysis may be raised. Not only did all of the states engage in regulation of commerce, but Congress too was given the power to "regulate commerce with foreign nations, and among the several states."[70] Is not regulation a power of government to interfere with market freedom? Does this not demonstrate that the Founders were not as devoted to free markets as I have maintained? The answer depends on what sort of regulation we are discussing.

First, as noted earlier, some regulations, such as prohibitions of excessively loud or dangerous activities in crowded neighborhoods, benefit property owners generally. They are meant to enable every owner to enjoy the use of his property as much as possible, consistent with other owners' enjoyment of their property. Negligent use of property, such as reckless driving, can lead to fatal accidents. These are "police power" regulations that protect the public health, safety, and morals. They do not conflict with the Founders' natural law theory. In fact, they are required by it.

Second, government may intrude on private property by taxation. Since government really does provide a service to the people (securing their natural rights), the Founders viewed it in the same light as they viewed any other "producer" who asks for compensation for providing something of value to the consumer.[71] As the Massachusetts Constitution stated, everyone is obliged "to contribute his share to the expense" of government protection of the person and property of all.[72]

Third, the misuse of property can harm others in more subtle ways. In his *Lectures on Law*, James Wilson writes that

> [Nuisances are] a collection of personal injuries, which annoy the citizens generally and indiscriminately. . . . [P]ublic peace, and order, and tranquillity, and safety require them to be punished or abated. . . . To keep hogs in any city or market town is a common nuisance. Disorderly houses [brothels] are public nuisances. . . . Indecency, public and grossly scandalous, may well be considered as a species of common nuisance.[73]

In Wilson's list of nuisances, he links together things that we would think of as distinct: the stink created by hogs in a city, the use of property as a place to sell sexual favors, and public obscenity and nudity. The case of hogs is easiest to understand. Wilson's assumption is that the right to use one's property for any purpose must be limited by the principle that one should use one's own property in such a way that it does not injure another's. Vile odors can impair or destroy the use of one's property (for example, as a residence) no less than arson can.

As for brothels, when Wilson compares them to pigsties, he implies that they create what one might call a "moral stink." For the explanation of this, one would have to consider the Founders' view that the preservation of a self-governing society, including the security of property rights, presupposes a certain character in the citizens. In particular, the integrity of the family, the institution for the generation and civilizing of children, was thought to require self-restraint in sexual conduct. The public sale of sex was believed to contribute to a moral atmosphere hostile to the sexual fidelity required for stable families. The same concern informed the prohibition of public nudity and obscenity.[74]

This brings up a topic that is rarely treated as part of economic theory: the relation between the character of a people, including the integrity of the family, and the security of property rights. The Founders did not believe that property rights or any other kind of rights could be protected without some degree of self-restraint, reasonable self-assertion, and public belief in the natural law and natural rights ideas of the Founding.

OBJECTIONS AND COMPARISONS

There are two final objections that deserve at least a brief response. Ralph Lerner argues that the commercial republic produced by the Founders' natural law principles is "built on" "the common passions for private gratification and physical comfort."[75] This raises a question: Did the Founders undertake heroic labors for unheroic or even base objectives? Is there any place in the society created by the Founders for beauty, poetry, or greatness? Or is the pursuit of economic self-interest the highest thing that people strive for in a free-market society?

The Founders were wise enough to know that property is not an unambiguous good and not the highest object of human pursuit. "From the conclusion of this war," wrote Jefferson in 1781, "we will be going down hill." The people "will forget themselves, but in the sole faculty of making money."[76] John Adams worried that "without virtue, there can be no political liberty. . . . Will you tell me how to prevent riches from being the effects of temperance and industry? . . . Will you tell me how to prevent luxury from producing effeminacy, intoxication, extravagance, vice, and folly?"[77]

Hamilton wrote, "True liberty, by protecting the exertions and talents of industry, and securing to them their justly acquired fruits, tends more powerfully than any other cause to augment the mass of national wealth and to produce the mischiefs of opulence." However, after acknowledging the difficulty, Hamilton then posed this sensible question: "Shall we therefore on this account proscribe liberty also? . . . 'Tis the portion of man assigned to him by the eternal allotment of Providence that every good he enjoys shall be alloyed with ills, that every source of his bliss shall be a source of his affliction—except virtue alone."[78]

In response to these concerns, the Founders developed policies and practices that would help to sustain a society not only where public spirit and self-restraint would not be overwhelmed by the wealth and moneymaking spirit unleashed by freedom, but also where they would be encouraged by a variety of private institutions and public policies.

The 20th century forgetting of the Founders' understanding may be seen in a story told by President Dwight Eisenhower. At the end of World War II, Eisenhower commanded the armed forces of America and its Western allies, while Georgy Zhukov commanded the Soviet forces. After the war, Eisenhower toured the Soviet Union with Zhukov. Eisenhower later reported:

> [O]ne evening we had a three-hour conversation. We tried, each to explain to the other just what our systems meant, our two systems meant, to the individual, and I was very hard put to it when he insisted that their system appealed to the idealistic, and we completely to the materialistic. And I had a very tough time trying to defend our position, because he said: "You tell a person he can do as he pleases, he can act as he pleases, he can do anything. Everything that is selfish in man you appeal to."[79]

Eisenhower, who served America honorably during the war, had a "very tough time" defending America's system of self-government and free enterprise against the verbal attack of a high-ranking official in an oppressive Communist system whose leader was the mass murderer Joseph Stalin.[80] Clearly, Eisenhower no longer embraced or even understood the view of the Founders, for whom, as was often said in the Founding era, liberty "is totally different from licentiousness. Many have no other idea of liberty, but for everyone to do as he pleases—to be as honest as he pleases—to be as knavish as he pleases. . . . Such a liberty . . . ought to be done away with."[81] Capitalism, after all, requires people to keep their legally binding promises and pay their debts.

Nor would the Founders have hesitated for a moment to repudiate a claim of "idealism" raised by Zhukov, a man whom they would have regarded as a minion of a bloody tyrant. If "idealistic" policies are those that enable the poor to escape poverty and allow all to live in freedom (not licentiousness) under law, then the most idealistic economic order is one that secures the natural right to acquire and possess property.

At the end of the Declaration of Independence, the Founders pledged to each other "our lives, our fortunes, and our sacred honor." They did not think they were striving for an unworthy goal. They were prepared to give up life and property in the noble fight to establish a nation based on the true principles of justice: a nation that would secure the lives and property of their families and descendants. Such a nation was judged worthy of their devotion because they believed that justice is the purpose of civil society. If all went well, America was going to be the most just nation ever created. The opposite of life, liberty, property, and the pursuit of happiness is not some sort of transcendent political perfection. It is death, slavery, poverty, and misery—the reality of daily life under Stalin.

A second objection may be raised: Property rights will lead to inequality in the distribution of property. The Founders were aware of this. In *Federalist* #10, as noted, Madison correctly observes that "From the protection of different and unequal faculties of acquiring property, the possession of different degrees and kinds of property immediately results." People with more talent and ambition will generally acquire greater wealth. Can that be just? The Founders' answer was "yes," for two reasons.

First, no adult can justly be compelled to submit to the will of another. Whatever differences in wealth may emerge, property rights benefit all classes equally insofar as they protect the body and mind of every individual from exploitation or enslavement. Whenever government uses compulsion to redistribute wealth for the purpose of equalization, it violates the "first principle of association": the right to liberty, the right to the free exercise of one's own mind and body. Jefferson wrote:

> To take from one, because it is thought his own industry and that of his fathers has acquired too much, in order to spare to others, who, or whose fathers, have not exercised equal industry and skill, is to violate arbitrarily the first principle of association, the guarantee to everyone the free exercise of his industry and the fruits acquired by it.[82]

The Founders' second argument justifying unequal distribution of property is summarized by James Wilson: "The right of private property seems to be founded in the nature of men and of things. . . . Exclusive property multiplies the productions of the earth, and the means of subsistence. Who would cultivate the soil, and sow the grain, if he had no peculiar interests in the harvest?"[83] An economic order in which some acquire more than others is the condition of greater prosperity for all.

The Founders were aware that there will always be some who, through no fault of their own, are unable to provide for themselves. The families of children, the disabled, and the unemployed were expected to take care of them. If their families were unable or unwilling, churches, private charities, and other private associations would often step in; but if private institutions failed, government assumed the obligation to provide a "safety net" of last resort.

That safety net, however, must not be so generous that it would entice people to prefer government benefits to gainful employment. The poorhouse, where people would be required to work to the extent of their ability in exchange for room and board, came to be the preferred solution, and the administration of the "poor laws," as they were called, was to be done by local government so that the true circumstances of those claiming to be in need would be known.[84]

CONCLUSION

Government today has strayed far from the Founders' approach to economics. However, the older policies have not been altogether replaced. Some of the Founders' complex set of policies to protect property rights are still in force.

America has abandoned the Founders' views on the gold and silver standard, the prohibition of monopolies, the presumption of freedom to use property as one likes, freedom of contract, and restricting regulation to the protection of health, safety, and morals. But in other respects, America continues to offer a surprising degree of protection to property rights in the Founders' sense of that term.

NOTES

1. John R. Nelson, Jr., *Liberty and Property: Political Economy and Policymaking in the New Nation, 1789–1812* (Baltimore: Johns Hopkins University Press, 1987), 77.

2. Richard Rorty, *Achieving Our Country: Leftist Thought in Twentieth-Century America* (Cambridge: Harvard University Press, 1998), 47 (quoting with approval Herbert Croly's 1909 critique of capitalism), 76.

3. William Brennan, "To the Text and Teaching Symposium," Georgetown University, October 15, 1985, in Edwin Meese III et al., *The Great Debate: Interpreting Our Written Constitution* (Washington: The Federalist Society, 1986), 19.

4. Francis M. Bator, "The Anatomy of Market Failure," *Quarterly Journal of Economics* 72, no. 3 (August 1958): 351.

5. Gertrude Himmelfarb, *One Nation, Two Cultures* (New York: Vintage Books, 2001),12–13.

6. Declarations of Rights of Virginia, 1776, Art. 1; Pennsylvania, 1776, Art. 1; Vermont, 1777, Art. 1; Massachusetts, 1780, Art. 1; New Hampshire, 1784, Art. 2; Delaware, 1792, Preamble. In *The Federal and State Constitutions*, ed. Francis Newton Thorpe (Washington: U.S. Government Printing Office, 1909). All susequent quotations from state constitutions may be found here.

7. Greg Forster, "Sacred Enterprise," *Claremont Review of Books* 9, no. 3 (Summer 2009): 40.

8. Virginia Declaration of Rights, 1776, Art 1.

9. Resolution of Charlestown, South Carolina, June 4, 1774, in *American Archives: Fourth Series: Containing a Documentary History . . . from . . . March 7, 1774, to the Declaration of Independence*, ed. Peter Force (Washington: M. St. Clare Clarke and Peter Force, 1837–1853), 1:383–384.

10. Kenneth L. Karst, *Belonging to America: Equal Citizenship and the Constitution* (New Haven: Yale University Press, 1989), 179.

11. Anatole France, *The Red Lily*, trans. Winifred Stephens (New York: John Lane, 1910), 95.

12. Virginia Declaration of Rights, 1776, Art. 1.

13. Declarations of Rights of Pennsylvania, 1776, Art. 1; Vermont, 1777, Art. 1; Massachusetts, 1780, Art. 1; New Hampshire, 1784, Art. 2; Delaware, 1792, Preamble, has "acquiring and protecting reputation and property."

14. *Federalist* #10, in Alexander Hamilton, James Madison, and John Jay, *The Federalist Papers*, ed. Clinton Rossiter, intro. and notes by Charles R. Kesler (New York: New American Library, Signet Classic, 2003), 73.

15. John Locke, *Two Treatises of Government* (1690), ed. Peter Laslett (Cambridge: Cambridge University Press, 1960), *First Treatise*, sec. 42.

16. Thomas Hobbes, *De Cive* ("On the Citizen"), in *Opera Philosophica quae Latine Scripsit*, ed. William Molesworth (London: Bohn, 1839), 2:166, ch. 1, § 12 (my translation; the italics are in the original).

17. Jefferson to James B. Colvin, September 20, 1810, in *The Founders' Constitution*, ed. Philip B. Kurland and Ralph Lerner (Chicago: University of Chicago Press, 1987), 4:127.

18. Anders Aslund, *How Capitalism Was Built: The Transformation of Central and Eastern Europe, Russia, and Central Asia* (New York: Cambridge University Press, 2007).

19. *The Republic of Plato*, trans. Allan Bloom (New York: Free Press, 1968), 369b–372e. The absence of slavery from this part of *The Republic* reflects its free-market orientation. Everything is done by voluntary agreement.

20. Hamilton, "Report on Manufactures," 1791, in *The Papers of Alexander Hamilton*, ed. Harold C. Syrett (New York: Columbia University Press, 1961–1979), 10:255, 249.

21. Pennsylvania Constitution, 1776, ch. 2, sec. 34; New Hampshire, 1784; Vermont, 1776, sec. 31; Massachusetts, 1780, ch. 6, sec. 2; Delaware, 1776, Art. 14.

22. Northwest Ordinance, 1787, Art. 4, in *The Documentary History of the Ratification of the Constitution*, vol. 1: *Constitutional Documents and Records, 1776–1787*, ed. Merrill Jensen (Madison: State Historical Society of Wisconsin, 1976), 173.

23. Richard Cox, *Four Pillars of Constitutionalism: The Organic Laws of the United States* (Buffalo: Prometheus Books, 1998). The Declaration of Independence, Articles of Confederation, Northwest Ordinance, and U.S. Constitution were formally established as the organic laws of the nation by Congress in 1878.

24. William Easterly, "Can the West Save Africa?" National Bureau of Economic Research *Working Paper* No. 14363, September 2008, at http://www.nyu.edu/fas/institute/dri/Easterly/File/can%20the%20west%20save%20africa.pdf (September 28, 2009).

25. Madison, Speech of April 9, 1789, First Federal Congress, in *Founders' Constitution*, 2:442.

26. "[I]n their political discourse they generally described property in absolutist terms. . . . [O]ur Founders in one breath were defending the absolutism of property while also supporting legal limits on property rights." David Schultz, "Political Theory and Legal History: Conflicting Depictions of Property in the American Founding," *American Journal of Legal History* 37 (1993): 491, 493.

27. See, e.g., *Munn v. Illinois*, 94 U.S. 113 (1876), 125.

28. Eric R. Claeys, "Takings, Regulation, and Natural Property Rights," *Cornell Law Review* 88, no. 6 (Sept. 2003): 1577–78.

29. Jeff L. Lewin, "*Boomer* and the American Law of Nuisance: Past, Present, and Future," *Albany Law Review* 54 (1990): 210. See also Robert G. Bone, "Normative Theory and Legal Doctrine in American Nuisance Law: 1850 to 1920," *Southern California Law Review* 59 (1986): 1224.

30. U.S. Bureau of the Census, *Statistical Abstract of the United States: 1997* (Washington: U.S. Government Printing Office, 1997), Table 369 (Total Federally Owned Land), p. 228. A more recent *Statistical Abstract* (2008, Table 349) does not provide regional percentages of federal ownership, but the state-by-state figures have not changed much.

31. Holly Brewer, "Entailing Aristocracy in Colonial Virginia: 'Ancient Feudal Restraints' and Revolutionary Reform," *William and Mary Quarterly* 54, no. 2 (April 1997): 307–346.

32. Gordon S. Wood, *The Radicalism of the American Revolution* (New York: Knopf, 1992), 183 (explaining changes in inheritance laws in the founding era).

33. Pennsylvania Constitution, 1776, sec. 37; North Carolina, 1776, sec. 43; and Vermont, 1777, sec. 34: all said: "The future legislature of this State shall regulate entails in such manner as to prevent perpetuities." ("Perpetuities" were legal arrangements that kept the land in the same family forever.) The Georgia Constitution, 1777, Art. 51, reads: "Estates shall not be entailed; and when a person dies intestate [without making a will], his or her estate shall be divided equally among their children." Northwest Ordinance, 1787, Art. 4, in *Documentary History*, ed. Jensen, 1:168–69.

34. *Autobiography*, in Jefferson, *Writings*, ed. Merrill D. Peterson (New York: Library of America, 1984), 32–33.

35. John V. Orth, *The North Carolina State Constitution: With History and Commentary* (Durham: University of North Carolina Press, 1995), 75.

36. Massachusetts Declaration of Rights, 1780, Arts. 10 and 11.

37. For example, *United States v. $124,700 in U.S. Currency*, 8th Cir. 2006. See also Leonard W. Levy, *A License to Steal: The Forfeiture of Property* (Chapel Hill: University of North Carolina Press, 1996).

38. Aslund, *How Capitalism Was Built*, p. 244.

39. Declaration of Rights of Vermont, 1777, Art. 2, and of Massachusetts, 1780, Art. 10; Pennsylvania Constitution, 1790, Art. 9, sec. 10; Delaware Constitution, 1792, Art. 1, sec. 8; Tennessee Constitution, 1796, Art. 11, sec. 21.

40. *Vanhorne's Lessee v. Dorrance*, 2 Dall. 304, Circuit Court, District of Pennsylvania, 1795, in *Founders' Constitution*, 1:599–600.

41. *Kelo v. New London*, 545 U.S. 469 (2005).

42. U.S. Constitution, Art. IV, sec. 2.

43. Samuel Chase's opinion in *Campbell v. Morris*, 3 H. & McH. 535, 553–554 (Md. 1797), in *Founders' Constitution*, 4:490.

44. *Corfield v. Coryell*, 6 F. Cas. 546, 551–552 (C.C.E.D. Pa. 1823), in *Founders' Constitution* 4:503. David R. Upham, "*Corfield v. Coryell* and the Privileges and Immunities of American Citizenship," *Texas Law Review* 83 (2005): 1483–1534.

45. Madison, Speech of April 9, 1789, in First Federal Congress, in *Founders' Constitution*, 2:442.

46. *Corfield v. Coryell.*

47. Maryland Declaration of Rights, 1776, Art. 39; North Carolina Declaration of Rights, 1776, Art. 23; Massachusetts Declaration of Rights, 1780, Art. 6; Tennessee Constitution, 1796, Art. 11, sec. 23.

48. North Carolina Declaration of Rights, 1776, Art. 23; Tennessee Constitution, 1796, Art. 11, sec. 23.

49. Massachusetts Declaration of Rights, 1780, Art. 6.

50. U.S. Constitution, Art. I, sec. 8.

51. Matthew Miller and Luisa Kroll, "Bill Gates No Longer World's Richest Man," Forbes.com, March 10, 2010. Andres Oppenheimer, *Bordering on Chaos: Mexico's Roller-Coaster Journey Toward Prosperity* (New York: Back Bay Books, 1998), 92.

52. Forrest McDonald, *Novus Ordo Seclorum: The Intellectual Origins of the Constitution* (Lawrence: University of Kansas Press, 1985),102–106.

53. U.S. Constitution, Art. I, sec. 9.

54. Ibid.

55. *Corfield v. Coryell.*

56. Declaration of Rights of Massachusetts, 1780, Art. 12; of New Hampshire, 1792, Art. 14; of Maryland, 1776, Art. 17; Pennsylvania Constitution, 1790, Art. 9, sec. 11; Delaware Constitution, 1792, Art. I, sec. 9; Kentucky Constitution, 1792, Art. 12, sec. 13; Tennessee Constitution, 1796, Art. 11, sec. 17.

57. U.S. Constitution, Art. I, sec. 10.

58. Northwest Ordinance of 1787, Art. II.

59. James Madison, "Property," March 29, 1792, in *Founders' Constitution*, 1:598. The Founders would have rejected Ayn Rand's extreme libertarianism in regard to sex and the family (to say nothing of other topics), but they would have agreed with this assessment of market freedom: "To trade by means of money is the code of the men of goodwill. Money rests on the axiom that every man is the owner of his mind and his effort. Money allows no power to prescribe the value of your effort except the voluntary choice of the man who is willing to trade you his effort in return. Money permits you to obtain for your goods and your labor that which they are worth to the men who buy them, but no more. . . . When money ceases to be the tool by which men deal with one another, then men become the tools of men. Blood, whips and guns—or dollars. Take your choice. . . ." Ayn Rand, *Atlas Shrugged* (New York: Dutton, 1992; orig. pub. 1957), pt. 2, ch. 2, pp. 411, 415 (speech on money by Francisco D'Anconia).

60. William E. Forbath, "The Ambiguities of Free Labor: Labor and the Law in the Gilded Age," *Wisconsin Law Review* 4 (1985): 783, summarizing Eric Foner, *Politics and Ideology in the Age of the Civil War* (New York: Oxford University Press, 1980), 73.

61. U.S. Constitution, Art. I, sec. 8.

62. Northwest Ordinance of 1787, Art. IV.

63. Report on Manufactures, 1791, in *Papers of Hamilton*, ed. Syrett, 10:310–311.

64. McDonald, *Novus Ordo Seclorum*, 154.

65. James Madison, "Money," 1791, in *The Papers of James Madison*, ed. William T. Hutchinson and William M. E. Rachal (Chicago: University of Chicago Press, 1962), 1:305.

66. E. James Ferguson, *The Power of the Purse: A History of American Public Finance, 1776–1790* (Chapel Hill: University of North Carolina Press, 1961), 25–47, 57–69.

67. Curtis P. Nettels, *The Emergence of a National Economy, 1775–1815* (New York: Holt, Rinehart, and Winston, 1962), 82.

68. U.S. Constitution, Art. I, sec. 10.

69. *Federalist* #44, p. 278.

70. U.S. Constitution, Art. I, sec. 8.

71. Boston, Rights of the Colonists, 1772, in *Writings of Samuel Adams*, ed. Harry Alonzo Cushing (New York: Octagon Books, 1968; orig. pub. 1904–1908), 2:354, explicitly compares government officials to hired employees who deserve pay for their services.

72. Massachusetts Declaration of Rights, 1780, Art. 10. Similar taxation provisions are in the Declarations of Rights of Pennsylvania, 1776, Art. 8; Maryland, 1776, Art. 13; Vermont, 1777, Art. 9; and New Hampshire, 1792, Art. 12.

73. James Wilson, "Of Crimes, Affecting Several of the Natural Rights of Individuals," ch. 6 of *Lectures on Law*, 1792, in *Collected Works of James Wilson*, ed. Kermit L. Hall and Mark David Hall (Indianapolis: Liberty Fund, 2007), 2:284.

74. Thomas G. West, *Vindicating the Founders: Race, Sex, Class, and Justice in the Origins of America* (Lanham, Md.: Rowman & Littlefield, 1997), ch. 4, "Women and the Family."

75. Ralph Lerner, *The Thinking Revolutionary: Principle and Practice in the New Republic* (Ithaca: Cornell University Press, 1987), 201. In the passage quoted, Lerner is discussing European thinkers like Adam Smith and David Hume who promoted the idea of the commercial republic, but he implies later in the chapter that the Founders were broadly in agreement with their program.

76. Jefferson, *Notes on Virginia*, Query 17, in *Writings*, ed. Peterson, 287.

77. Adams to Jefferson, December 21, 1819, in *The Adams–Jefferson Letters*, ed. Lester J. Cappon (New York: Simon & Schuster, 1959), 551.

78. Alexander Hamilton, "Defense of the Funding System," July 1795, in *Papers of Hamilton*, ed. Syrett, 19:32.

79. Dwight D. Eisenhower, Presidential News Conference, July 15, 1957, The American Presidency Project, ed. John T. Woolley and Gerhard Peters, University of California at Santa Barbara, at http://www.presidency.ucsb.edu (August 7, 2008).

80. Stéphane Courtois et al., *The Black Book of Communism: Crimes, Terror, Repression* (Cambridge: Harvard University Press, 1999) (calculating the quantity of Stalin's many millions of victims).

81. "A Freeman: To the People of Connecticut," *Connecticut Courant*, December 31, 1787 (arguing for ratification of the Constitution), in *Documentary History of the Ratification of the Constitution*, ed. Jensen et al., 1976–), 3:519. The New York Constitution, 1777, Art. 38, makes the same distinction: "the liberty of conscience, hereby granted, shall not be so construed as to excuse acts of licentiousness."

82. Jefferson to Joseph Milligan, April 6, 1816, in *Founders' Constitution*, 1:573.

83. James Wilson, "History of Property," in *Collected Works*, ed. Hall and Hall, 1:305–306.

84. For more on the Founders' poor laws, see ch. 6, "Poverty and Welfare," in West, *Vindicating the Founders*.

8

Hamilton and Jefferson

Two Visions of Democratic Capitalism

Peter McNamara

The debate between Alexander Hamilton and Thomas Jefferson over the shape of democratic capitalism (they would have used the term "commercial republicanism") provides a model worthy of close study for those seeking to reintegrate the disciplines of politics and economics. This is not to suggest that there is some obvious and easy synthesis of the two visions or that one man was correct or that one view is correct now. As we will see, each man's position had and has its virtues and its vices. The value in surveying the debate is that it sets out the critical issues for any effort to take politics and economics seriously. Both Hamilton and Jefferson acknowledged and reckoned with the broader implications of their economic theories. This is particularly true in the way that each man placed his economic arguments in a constitutional framework.

Hamilton and Jefferson are famous for their titanic rivalry but before we turn to their disagreements, it is important, first, to observe certain fundamental points of agreement and, second, to indicate why it is difficult today to appreciate fully the original contours of their debate. To begin with, both men believed in the revolutionary doctrine of natural rights. Growing out of this belief, both men believed that the primary role of government is to secure rights, among which are the rights to life and liberty, to worship as one wishes, and to pursue and acquire property. A corollary to this last right to property is that individuals bear the primary responsibility for providing for themselves, rather than the government. Lastly, both men agreed on the significance and importance of a written constitution for republican government. Indeed, it was their agreement on this point that gave shape to their fierce and profound debate over economics. What Hamilton and Jefferson disagreed about was the way in which a written constitution is significant.

Two factors in particular make it difficult for us to enter easily into this debate and to discern clearly the two protagonists' distinctive visions of democratic capitalism and their relation to constitutional government. The first is our idea of economics as a science that provides precise, technical, value-neutral guidance for policy makers. It is important for economists and policy makers to recover the awareness that, among other things, economic theories are not simply value-neutral either in their conception or in their effects. The foundations of mainstream economics owe much to classical liberalism, including the idea of natural rights. Furthermore, economic theories have profound social effects. For example, the idea that markets are *always* efficient might legitimize and reinforce economic behaviors that are highly damaging for individuals and society at large. Not every economic decision, as we have recently been harshly reminded, is truly a rational one.

The other obstacle to understanding the Hamilton-Jefferson debate is the powerful legacy of the New Deal. This is so in at least two significant ways. The New Deal swept away the constitutional limits on the powers of the national government. The question of the *legitimate* ends of government tends to disappear leaving only a debate about the available means to *any* posited end. The older view, shared by Hamilton and Jefferson, that the Constitution pointed to the legitimate ends of government, was forgotten. In this respect the New Deal and its proponents had something in common with mainstream economists: policy questions are merely technical questions to be solved by experts. The second way in which the New Deal distorts our understanding of Hamilton and Jefferson is that it attempted to synthesize Hamilton and Jefferson. Roosevelt believed that Jeffersonian independence and self-government in the twentieth century required the creation of greater economic security for citizens. By using Hamiltonian *means* of activist government Roosevelt sought to accomplish the Jeffersonian *ends* of an independent, self-governing citizenry. Roosevelt's synthesis obscures both the extent to which Hamilton and Jefferson, as we have seen, agreed about ends and about the precise character of the means they advocated for achieving those ends. Moreover, it blinds us to the real virtues and vices of Hamiltonianism and Jeffersonianism. One example must suffice. Like so many policy makers and scholars in the twentieth century, Roosevelt saw democracy and capitalism as necessarily in conflict. He saw Hamilton as simply out to preserve the privileges of the financial class. From this perspective, Hamilton is the enemy of democracy and Jefferson the enemy of capitalism. Neither contention is correct. Hamilton and Jefferson had two distinct visions of democratic capitalism. Their disagreements were serious and substantial. Each man tried to leave his stamp on the early republic. Neither was completely successful. Neither was completely correct. Both deserve to be listened to today.

HAMILTON'S HERCULES

There are good reasons for judging Hamilton the greatest Secretary of the Treasury. He possessed an ability to formulate big plans, the courage to persevere in bold actions, an astonishing attention to detail, a prodigious capacity for work, and a powerful desire for real fame. He put these skills to work in establishing the financial credibility of the United States government and in putting into place the conditions for future private sector prosperity. Before assuming his position at Treasury, Hamilton had spent more than a decade studying the economic situation of the United States and its connection to the broader political situation. He read and absorbed David Hume and Adam Smith as well as the celebrated economic practitioner and French finance minister Jacques Necker's *Treatise on the Administration of the Finances of France*.[1] A simple review of Hamilton as Treasury Secretary is the best way to come to terms with the way he combined action and ideas.

Hamilton went to work with two presuppositions in his mind. First, he saw the new Constitution primarily as a major grant of new powers to the national government. These new powers were essential for the accomplishment of the basic purposes of government: national security; economic prosperity; and the establishment of the rule of law. Hamilton believed that the effective limitations on the use of these powers would come from the checks and balances within the national government, from the states, and from the people acting through the regular political process. Hamilton's second presupposition was that the greatest danger facing the new government was that it would be either too weak or too timid to govern. Hamilton feared the power of the states, he doubted the ability of any government to govern a nation of the unprecedented size of the American republic, and he worried that the democratic character of the people would make a wise administration of government impossible.

Hamilton drew a simple, clear, if difficult to hold to, inference from his two key presuppositions: the national government must exercise its new powers quickly and effectively. He believed that this kind of effective energetic government would build confidence in and support for the new government, respect for it abroad, and breathe life into the new Constitution. Hamilton's idea of government was elitist but it was not anti-republican (or anti-democratic). All governments must earn the confidence of the people; republican governments more than others. Here was the challenge: could a republican government provide good government? Jefferson saw things differently. For him the challenge was whether republicans could finally defeat their enemies and establish a pure republican system. Hamilton's work as Treasury Secretary divides roughly between his concern with money and his concern with manufactures.

Money

The immediate problem for Hamilton was that the United States had ceased to pay its debts. These debts had been incurred during the Revolutionary War. The several states were also in default on their war debts. The public debt as a whole amounted to about 40 percent of the GDP. Today this sounds like a very manageable problem but the extraordinary difficulty of Hamilton's task should be understood. Although Congress quickly passed a series of import and tonnage duties, it had no administration—Treasury officials, tax collectors, or a coast guard—to put them into effect. In other words, the national government had large debts and no revenue. Furthermore, the country lacked the financial infrastructure—a sound currency, banks, and a securities market—to facilitate the restoration of public credit. More generally still, the nation's economy was largely agricultural and reliant on barter rather than money exchanges.

Pressing as this situation was, Hamilton managed to look at the nation's financial situation in a broader and ultimately more important political context. The United States was a new, weak nation, and surrounded by enemies (Britain, Spain, and certain of the Native-American tribes; France lurked in the background still stung by the loss of its American empire). The United States was, of course, in Hamilton's evocative words, a "Hercules in the cradle" but it would take time and concerted effort for that potential to be realized.[2] When Hamilton was asked by Congress to report on ways to support public credit and to encourage manufactures, he set about these tasks looking to this broader political context. The result was a series of state papers proposing a plan to restore the public finances, establish a national bank, and recommending measures to encourage manufactures. In the course of the debates over his reports, Hamilton wrote another major state paper, his "Opinion on the Constitutionality of a National Bank," justifying a broad construction of the Constitution.[3]

Hamilton's first priority was to establish the financial credibility of the new United States government. The plan, once all its parts were laid out, was breath-taking in scope and detail. It initiated what has aptly been described as a "Financial Revolution" comparable to the financial revolution that had transformed Britain earlier in the century.[4] The key elements to Hamilton's plan were an "assumption" of the state debts, "funding" the debt, new taxes, and a national bank. His "First Report on Public Credit" recommended "funding" the debt. This meant dedicating specific revenues for the payment of the interest on the debt (but not necessarily for paying down the principal of the debt). In the present impecunious circumstances of the United States, Hamilton believed that refinancing the debt and paying the interest was all that was possible.

Hamilton gave priority to the foreign debt. He believed that it should be paid in full according to the exact terms of the loans. The domestic debt was a more complicated matter. Here his plan was truly revolutionary. First, Hamilton recommended that national government "assume" the Revolutionary war debts of the states. His reasoning on this point was complex. The state debts had been incurred in a national struggle. Like the national government's debts they were "the price of liberty."[5] In addition, placing responsibility for providing for the debt in one set of hands meant that the treatment of the public creditors would likely be more efficient and certainly more equitable. All public creditors would receive similar treatment rather than a different treatment by each of the thirteen states. (The move not only tended to equalize state tax burdens, it also greatly reduced tax burdens within the states.[6]) Lastly, the move would unite all public creditors in support of the new national government, a factor that Hamilton believed to be a critical support for any modern government.

The assumption proposal was controversial. To many, it appeared a power grab by the national government—and in a sense it surely was. But perhaps the bigger immediate sticking point was that the proposal made no allowance for the different ways, some more diligently, others less so, that the states had dealt with their debts. Hamilton was of the view that in great national matters like this one slight anomalies should be overlooked in the national interest. The issue was settled in a famous dinner bargain between Hamilton and Madison, facilitated by Jefferson. Madison, then the leader of Hamilton's opposition in the House of Representatives, would withdraw his opposition to assumption if the new national capital were situated on the banks of the Potomac River. Hamilton traded away the interests of his own state for the national interest.[7] Hamilton was an American nationalist from reasons of personal reputation and out of genuine concern for the public good. For better or for worse, he seldom if ever distinguished between the two motives.

Hamilton's second proposal was that the domestic debt be "funded." This involved a highly complex and inventive set of financial maneuvers. Even a simple funding of the debt was not possible without resorting to oppressive and counterproductive levels of taxation. Hamilton's recommendations involved raising new foreign loans at better rates than the existing loans (something he believed possible if the financial circumstances of the government continued to improve) and offering owners of the federal and state debt the option of exchanging their current "unfunded debt" for packages of securities that offered greater certainty as to the terms and, more importantly, an assurance of government support. Hamilton's plan would effectively lower the interest rate the government was paying on its domestic debt but do so in a way that appealed to the "interests" rather than the "necessities" of creditors.[8] Congress simplified Hamilton's plan by limiting the number of options creditors would have but it followed the spirit of Hamilton's recommendations.

Republicans, including Jefferson, relentlessly criticized Hamilton's failure to provide for a more rapid paying down of the debt. Hamilton's response was that he had no choice: the revenues were not there. Another Republican attack on his proposals required a more complex response. Madison, among others, objected to the idea that Hamilton's plan made no distinction ("discrimination") between the current and original holders of the debt. Hamilton planned to honor the terms of the contract with whoever owned the debt. Madison argued that this would involve an injustice to those who had sold their government debt at depreciated prices and an unjust reward to speculators who had snapped up debt at low prices (sometimes 10–15 cents on the dollar). The most important of Hamilton's responses was that it is essential for a government to honor the precise terms of contracts it makes. This was all the more the case in a new government yet to establish its credibility at home or abroad. Hamilton wrote to Washington that at such times a "peculiar strictness" in the conduct of the public finances was required.[9]

There was, nevertheless, an element of illusion mixed in with Hamilton's plan. The debt was large, funds were limited, and the people's patience far from limitless. What was necessary was that the government take such measures as would make clear to all that it had the will and the wherewithal to put its fiscal house in order. In a sense the government would be doing less than might have appeared. But it was not a misleading or harmful illusion. Hamilton believed that "opinion" is at the heart of all matters relating to credit because it necessarily involves a bet or bets about an uncertain future.[10] Having said this, it is important to be clear on Hamilton's attitude toward public debt. In a passage that is often quoted Hamilton suggests that the "proper funding of the present debt, will render it a national blessing." Hamilton believed that a proper funding of the debt would build support for the government among creditors and would benefit the entire community, because once the value of debt had stabilized it could serve the purposes of money and act as capital in a capital scarce nation. Hamilton went on to say that he did *not* subscribe to the theory that "public debts are public benefits." Such a theory invites "prodigality" and is "liable to dangerous abuse."[11] Hamilton urged that ideally when new debts were acquired the means for their extinguishment ought also to be established. His situation was, of course, far from ideal.

Hamilton's plan included new taxes. Congress had passed taxes on imports and tonnage duties that favored American shipping. Hamilton supported these laws for their revenue-generating rather than for protectionist qualities. But he did not think they could be raised much further without damaging trade, decreasing revenues, increasing smuggling, and creating tensions with trading partners. New sources of revenues were required. Hamilton proposed an excise tax on distilled spirits. This controversial measure was first rejected but later passed by Congress on March 3, 1791. Hamilton knew that Americans did not like taxes and that the British experience with excise taxes had been accompanied by bitter controversy. Hamilton responded that there was a need for revenue, a more diverse tax base, and that the alternatives such as land or head taxes were even more unpalatable. In correspondence with Washington, Hamilton gave an additional reason: if the government did not use its new powers they might become mere words on paper.[12]

The final part of Hamilton's financial plan was the establishment of a national bank to serve as the government's banker. Hamilton thought such an institution essential, and obviously so, for both the day-to-day operations of the government and as a source of loans during crises, particularly wars. In important respects the bank was the lynchpin of his whole financial program. Hamilton drew on British and American experience. The latter was extremely limited. There were just three banks in the United States at the time. Hamilton himself had drawn up the charter for one of those banks, the still-operating Bank of New York.[13] In size and organization Hamilton's national bank, the Bank of the United States, would be something quite new. It differed from the existing American banks and from the Bank of England. In terms of size, the bank would have a capitalization of $10 million, substantially more than the other three American banks combined. The government would contribute $2 million of the amount, would be represented on the Board of Directors, would incorporate the bank with a charter for twenty years, and the bank would be required to furnish reports to the government. The bank would, however, be a private bank operating largely on private sector principles. Hamilton wanted to insulate the bank from undue political pressure. He thought it better to rely on the "keen, steady, as it were, magnetic sense, of their own interest, as proprietors, in the Directors of the Bank, pointing invariably to its true pole, the prosperity of the institution," as "the only security, that can always be relied upon, for a careful and prudent administration." This kind of administration alone could establish "permanent confidence" in the bank.[14] The bank was essential for the operations of government but Hamilton believed it would also benefit the private economy. What the nation most lacked was capital and the bank's broader activities would help alleviate this key problem.

Manufactures

Hamilton's last, but in the short run least influential, great report was on the subject of encouraging manufactures. It is now recognized as a classic of its kind and as having exercised a considerable influence on American economic policy in the nineteenth century. Congress asked Hamilton to report on encouragement and promotion of such manufactures as would render the United States independent of other nations for essential (particularly military) supplies. Hamilton's report responded to this request with a series of recommendations designed to promote manufacturing. He recommended increases in tariffs on certain commodities along with subsidies ("bounties") to certain industries and rewards for new inventions. His recommended tariff increases were far short of establishing a *protective* tariff and in some cases he even recommended tariff reductions. Congress did not take up Hamilton's bounty proposals but it did, after some delay, pass a new tariff schedule in 1792 mirroring Hamilton's recommendations.[15] Hamilton's relatively modest tariff proposals reflected his distaste for a tariff as a method for encouraging manufactures. He viewed very high and, therefore, truly protective tariffs as a blunt and divisive policy instrument that rewarded inefficient domestic producers. Furthermore, Hamilton viewed the tariff primarily as a revenue measure essential to the success of his plan to restore public credit. Tariffs high enough to choke off trade would create a new fiscal crisis.

What makes the "Report on Manufactures" of enduring significance is that Hamilton couched his specific policy recommendations in the context of a sweeping theoretical consideration of the political, economic, and, to some extent, the moral advantages of manufacturing and of the best means for their encouragement. Hamilton argued that as a general rule free trade at home and abroad was the best economic policy. He aimed to create a vast free national market linked together by modern communication and financial arrangements. Furthermore, as noted, he did not favor a protective tariff. Yet, Hamilton did see that there are exceptions to the general rule of free trade. The Report notes two. First, and most gravely, the international economic order is not one of free trade. Hamilton thought that war was an ever-present possibility in international affairs and, as a result, national economies must be able to meet national emergencies. Furthermore, short of war, nations pursue their own economic interests as they think best. As Hamilton states, this is not a cause for lament or complaint; it is simply the way of the world. This state of affairs led Hamilton to the conclusion that the United States ought to develop a diverse, balanced economy that included a domestic market for its agricultural goods. Second, Hamilton believed that there were times when enlightened self-interest would not be powerful enough to overcome the accumulated force of habit. Hamilton judged that the situation of the United States in the 1790s was one such time. Both the polity and the economy were in need of transformation. Government action could play a role in promoting needed changes in the economy. Hamilton's plan to modernize the American financial system by expanding access to capital and facilitating the shift from barter to money transactions was part of this effort to change American habits. He also believed that government policies to encourage manufactures could also play a role in the transformation of American economic habits. There was a social and moral dimension as well to the transformation Hamilton envisaged. The Report notes that in a diverse economy there are greater incentives to industry and a greater scope for the utilization of natural talents. Hamilton provides a backhanded critique of the agrarian republic: it will have fewer incentives to industry and will stifle the talents of many. Hamilton saw, in a way that Madison and Jefferson did not, that a commercial life, even factory work, did not necessarily rob an individual of his or her dignity. Indeed, by providing a means for individuals to pursue their livelihood such a life contributed to human dignity. In addition, he believed a fully commercial society, because of the variety of pursuits it opens up, was more likely to provide each individual with the opportunity to find an outlet for his or her particular talents and inclinations.[16]

Hamilton's reports ignited a profound constitutional debate. The trigger was his proposal to establish a national bank. Hamilton did not feel the need to present a constitutional argument for the bank when he presented his report to Congress. But James Madison, his collaborator in writing *The Federalist*, led a constitutional challenge to the proposal in Congress. Madison argued that the power to incorporate a national bank was neither among the enumerated powers granted by the Constitution nor could it be said to be "necessary and proper" for carrying into effect an enumerated power. The necessary and proper clause, he believed, could not be used to create new "important powers" but only to authorize subordinate powers. He buttressed his reading of the Constitution by referring to the Constitutional Convention and to the State Ratifying Conventions where he claimed the idea had been rejected either explicitly or implicitly.[17] Jefferson, in an opinion submitted for Washington's consideration, went further than Madison arguing for a *strict* construction of the Constitution. He held that "necessary" meant absolutely necessary. For Jefferson, the key to understanding the Constitution was the soon to be ratified Tenth Amendment reserving powers not granted to the national government to the states or the people. Following from this, he contended that the Constitution's purpose in granting specified powers was to "lace them up straitly" within the enumerated powers.[18]

Hamilton responded to Washington's request for a constitutional defense of the bank with a *tour de force* performance. Hamilton explained to the first President of the United States that nothing short of the future of the nation (and, by implication, Washington's fame) was at stake in this controversy. If the views of Madison and Jefferson were accepted the government would be crippled in its infancy. When a government is charged with a particular task or function it must be assumed, barring some explicit limitation, that it has also been granted all means requisite for the accomplishment of the task or function. This is a basic "axiom" or first principle of government. Hamilton discounted the evidence of the Convention and the State Ratifying Conventions partly because it was debatable but mainly because the text of the Constitution itself must guide interpretation. Hamilton argued that necessary means useful or convenient rather than strictly necessary. All that it is constitutionally necessary to show is that "*politically* speaking" a national bank bears a "natural & obvious" relationship to one of the enumerated powers. Hamilton cited the powers to tax, to borrow, to raise armies and navies, to regulate trade, and to manage the government's property. The natural and obvious character of these relationships stemmed from the intrinsic connections between ends and means. In discerning these connections, Hamilton gave greater weight to the general practice of nations than "the theories of Individuals."[19]

Hamilton was able to convince Washington (and indirectly the Marshall Court) of the need for a broad construction of the national government's powers. In the "Opinion on the Constitutionality of a National Bank" and in the "Report on Manufactures" Hamilton applied his textual approach to the interpretation to the "general welfare clause" arguing that it permitted *spending* (but not regulation) in all areas even outside of the enumerated powers as long as the objects were "general" rather than "local" in nature. Hamilton believed that there were meaningful distinctions between local and general concerns and between interstate and intrastate commerce. He also believed that under the Constitution the states retained a broad and important "police power."[20] Nevertheless, it is clear that Hamilton's approach opened the door to a powerful and energetic national government.

JEFFERSON'S EXPERIMENT

Jefferson characterized his own time as being distinguished by its "experiments in government on a larger scale than has yet taken place."[21] He repeatedly referred to the American effort in self-government as an experiment. Jefferson, we will see, had in mind a grand economic experiment to accompany and support the experiment in self-government. A number of factors have tended to obscure the fact that Jefferson had thought deeply about economic matters. Jefferson's own hapless personal financial management and his occasional calculated feigning of ignorance of financial matters have contributed to the image of Jefferson as something of a novice in economics.[22] Jefferson's proneness for making extreme statements, many of which he would later qualify or abandon, is another reason. Of this ilk were his suggestions that the United States would be best off if it could follow the closed-economy policies of China and his suggestion that all public borrowing be banned.[23] Historiographical trends placing Jefferson in the so-called classical republican school have also been a factor in shaping our image of Jefferson.[24] In truth, Jefferson was far from an advocate of selfless devotion to the public good, nor was he fearful of commerce. Jefferson looked forward to all kinds of progress: moral, intellectual, political, *and* commercial. What is at issue is the quality of his ideas and his judgment.

Hamilton was not fooled by Jefferson's studied pose as a simple, honest republican. Hamilton attributed Jefferson's mistakes to his bad modern ideas rather than to his lack of ideas or his antiquated classical ideas. Jefferson's writings reveal that he read closely the Physiocrats, Hume, Smith, Say, and Destutt de Tracy who, Jefferson thought, had corrected the mistakes and synthesized the best in all his illustrious predecessors.[25] In an astute observation, Hamilton suspected that Jefferson coveted his job at Treasury.[26] Jefferson had a vision of a republican political economy starkly at odds with Hamilton's. It was a bold construct: a geographically expanding, technologically advanced, commercial, agrarian republic, based on hard (metallic) money, free of public debt, and that was gradually reshaping the international economic system.

Jefferson's understanding of the new Constitution was central to his vision. As noted earlier, Jefferson saw the Constitution as an attempt to confine the national government strictly to its enumerated powers. He was, as he wrote to Madison, no friend of "very energetic government. It is always oppressive."[27] Furthermore, Jefferson believed all governments tend toward centralization (or "consolidation," the term he generally used). Any sign of or simple opening to consolidation ought to an object of popular vigilance. War was the greatest source of consolidation. Jefferson saw consolidation as the forerunner of monarchy and it was his constant charge against Hamilton and the Federalists that their policies would introduce monarchy into the United States. The very limited role he saw for the national government in domestic politics was contrasted with the large role he saw for the states, for federalism, and for an educated republican citizenry. Jefferson sought policies to implement his economic vision that were compatible with this limited role for the national government. Jefferson's experiment in political economy might usefully be divided into his views on agriculture and his views on finance.

Agriculture

The simplest place to begin is Jefferson's classic statement on agrarianism in Query No. 19 of his *Notes on Virginia*. This starting point is also problematic for two reasons: first, Jefferson subsequently qualified it and, second, Jefferson's goal of preserving the primacy of agriculture created a host of tensions, if not outright contradictions, in his policies. These tensions and contradictions raise a number of doubts about the lasting significance of his policies.

Having been asked to comment on the state of North America, Jefferson took the opportunity in the *Notes* to explain and to defend the United States. He acknowledged that America lacked large cities and a sophisticated manufacturing sector. For Jefferson, this was a good thing. Jefferson explained that "Corruption of morals in the mass of cultivators is a phenomenon of which no age nor nation has furnished an example." The independence of the agricultural way of life itself promotes virtue. The farmer is free from direction from a superior because he is self-employed, and he is free from the caprices of the market because he is largely self-sufficient. "Those who labor in the earth," Jefferson famously contended, "are the chosen people of God, if he ever had a chosen people." In contrast, the dependence inherent in city life "begets subservience and venality, suffocates the germ of virtue, and prepares fit tools for the designs of ambition." Jefferson concluded that "While we have land to labor . . . let our workshops remain in Europe."[28] One policy implication of Jefferson's preference for agriculture was clear: geographic expansion as a means of retaining the predominance of agriculture as long as possible.

Jefferson never overcame his skepticism of commercial pursuits but even from the outset his view was qualified, and the qualifications became more extensive as the events of the early republic unfolded. In the first place it ought to be remembered that one major purpose of the *Notes* was to make clear that Americans were not in any way in a degenerative state, something which their dependence on agriculture might imply. They were, in Jefferson's estimation, in fact poised to make enormous political progress if they arranged their polity and economy correctly. Furthermore, Jefferson observes just three queries later that while commerce (here meaning international commerce) does lead nations into conflict, he accepts that Americans are successful in and habituated to international trade. In light of this situation, he outlines his view of the correct international economic policy: "Our interest will be to throw open the doors of commerce, and to knock off all its shackles, giving perfect freedom to all persons for the vent of whatever they may choose to bring into our ports, and asking the same in theirs."[29] Jefferson believed the United States could defend itself with a relatively small navy and no standing army. This task would be all the easier if the international system were reformed so as to conform to the principles of free trade and to enlightened ideas regarding the rights of neutral nations during wartime. This brings us to one of the greatest paradoxes in Jefferson's thought. If Hamilton wished to establish an energetic national government so as make a place for the United States in a frequently hostile world, Jefferson's plan for a peaceful agrarian republic involved not only constant expansion but nothing short of remaking the world order.

Jefferson regarded Great Britain as the chief obstacle to transforming the international system. Britain discriminated against American ships and goods and from the early 1790s onward interfered more and more with American ships on the high seas. France's republican revolution intensified Jefferson's belief that Britain was the problem. The question was what to do? Diplomacy had accomplished little and Jefferson thought war with Great Britain neither practical nor moral. He also thought war was to be avoided because of its centralizing political consequences. The way forward, he thought, was to use the economic power of the United States to force Great Britain to change its ways. He was optimistic that a young vigorous republic could inflict enough economic pain on a corrupt and debt-ridden monarchy that it would yield.[30] Jefferson's 1793 "Report on Commerce" called for a policy of "reciprocity." America's preference should be for free trade but where a nation did not adhere to this standard, retaliatory measures were justified. Britain, because of her policies and because of the sheer scale of her trade with the United States, was the clear target of the Report. Jefferson's approach involved a toleration of certain kinds of manufacturing. Jefferson knew that retaliatory measures would stimulate domestic manufactures but he did not object. Furthermore, he exhorted the state governments to use their local knowledge to encourage "liberally" "artists" in such manufactures as might be suitable to their states. Jefferson singled out the desirability of fostering the progress of "*household* manufacture."[31]

Later, President Jefferson put his (and Madison's) theory to the supreme test in response to depredations on American shipping by implementing an embargo on American trade, both imports and exports. The results were disastrous. The embargo brought about no change in British behavior. In the United States itself, it was terribly unpopular especially in trade-dependent New England. To enforce the embargo Jefferson had to resort to severe measures curtailing civil liberties exceeding anything the Federalists undertook during the quasi-war with France in the late 1790s. The one beneficiary of the embargo was, of course, the American manufacturing industry. The War of 1812 brought about a change of heart in Jefferson and most Republicans regarding manufactures. The war brought into the open the difficulties of relying on foreign suppliers for manufactured goods in general and especially for military supplies. It also emphasized the problem of relying solely on foreign markets as an outlet for domestic agricultural surpluses.

Many Republicans adopted a neo-Hamiltonian position that embraced a broad construction of the Constitution, the encouragement of manufactures, and a re-chartering of the national bank. Jefferson explained his new openness to manufacturing as a gradual shift. To begin with, in the *Notes on Virginia* he was speaking of the manufacturing workers and the cities of Europe, not America, he contended. American manufacturers were as moral and as intelligent as those people engaged in agriculture. As long as they had the opportunity when the situation became oppressive to leave the cities and find land to work, then their character was safe. Furthermore, the time since 1785 (the year the *Notes* was published) had made clear that great hopes for a reformed international system were, for the time being at least, premature.[32] Jefferson never, however, embraced large-scale manufacturing. He continued to speak of manufacturing in terms of small-scale or household manufacturing along the lines of the self-employed artisans in the city and his own efforts at nail-making and spinning.[33]

Money

There is one important area in which Jefferson showed no change of mind and that is the area of banking and finance. Jefferson had opposed Hamilton's bank on constitutional grounds but he also had a well-thought-out theory of banking and finance that differed from Hamilton's. Jefferson's theory might even have been one of what Hamilton referred to in his opinion on the constitutionality of the bank as "the theories of Individuals" as distinct from the general policy of nations. Jefferson's theory of public finance was framed in terms of his theory that every living generation is sovereign—"the earth belongs to the living."[34] One generation has no right to bind a succeeding one with laws or with debts. Jefferson, as we have noted, harshly criticized Hamilton for not making provision for the elimination of the public debt. When he became President he made its elimination a priority. After the War of 1812, he fretted that the public debt would be perpetual. In addition to protecting the right of subsequent generations, Jefferson had a powerful additional reason for opposing public debt. He was convinced by the experience of the Eighteenth century that allowing a government the capacity to borrow encouraged war by shifting the costs of war to the yet unborn.

A "wise and frugal Government," as he put it in his First Inaugural Address, would be the first line of defense against indebtedness.[35] In a way few Presidents ever have, Jefferson acted on his stated beliefs after coming to office. He cut expenditures and he cut taxes by doing away with various internal taxes, including Hamilton's controversial excise tax. Jefferson did not dismantle Hamilton's bank but this does not mean that it had gained his approval. Neither the experience of his own purchase of Louisiana with money borrowed from British and Dutch bankers nor the embarrassments faced by the United States in financing the War of 1812 changed Jefferson's mind on this matter. Jefferson, unlike Madison, did not support the re-charter of the national bank. When it came to necessary government borrowing he believed that the national government did not need a national bank. His solution for how to handle such situations was for the government to issue notes (with or without interest) that would later be redeemed in the form of taxes. Jefferson thought this system desirable because it would maintain the value of the circulating paper, provide for its eventual extinction, and remind voters that all borrowing comes with the sting of taxation.

Not only did Jefferson think the Bank of the United Sates unconstitutional and unnecessary, he was convinced of its hostility to his administration and to republican government. He did try to republicanize the branches of the Bank of the United States by making sure the right people were appointed to office and by directing government business to sympathetic branches, but without much hope of success.[36] Jefferson feared the Bank partly because of the enormous influence it had as the government's bank and partly because many of its shares were foreign owned, but he also feared it because it was a typical American bank that issued bank notes (credit) that circulated as money throughout the country. Jefferson's fears were twofold. By the time of the re-chartering of the Bank of the United States there were over 200 banks, all issuing banknotes. As with the Bank of the United States, there was no check on how much they could issue, save for the threat that the note would be redeemed at some point. Jefferson correctly saw that a financial crash was in the making. Rather than acting as a restraint the new Bank of the United States contributed to the mania. When it finally retrenched the Panic of 1819 ensued.

In addition to the inflationary tendency of banks, Jefferson harbored political fears as well. He worried that the banks—Jefferson referred to them as "self-constituted authorities"—were a political force in their own right and directed by persons of either low character or anti-republican views or both. Jefferson wondered whether the banks might be able to dictate policy to the government, even on matters of war and peace.[37] Jefferson saw the "bank bubble," as he called it, as a recurrence of the speculative frenzy that accompanied Hamilton's financial program.[38] More generally, he saw it as part of a general resurgence of Federalism and monarchism.

Jefferson had a two-part plan for dealing with the banks which he pressed on his contacts in Congress.[39] First, Congress should take control of regulating the banks from the states. Jefferson hoped that the states would voluntarily cede control. Congress would then deny the banks the right to issue banknotes. Second, only hard money and Treasury notes would be acceptable as currency. He thought those states that did not voluntarily cede control would be forced into compliance because the national currency would come to be preferred to banknotes from their states. Jefferson thought this would not only deal with the problem of inflation but that a stable currency would be of more real benefit to American industry than the tariff.[40]

Jefferson's plan, if implemented, would no doubt have reversed the financial revolution that Hamilton had launched thirty years before. In retrospect, it sounds reckless and far-fetched, but it is important to understand clearly what he was attempting to do. Jefferson was attempting to establish a republican political order: a combination of sound money and banking, free enterprise, and small government in which the genuine voice of the people predominates. When put this way, Jefferson's proposed financial regulations were similar in intent to those proposed by Adam Smith. Although Jefferson went beyond Smith in doing away with paper money completely, their goal was the same: to open the way for the free market to operate rather than to curtail it. Rather than stymie economic growth Jefferson's scheme would ensure that the market allocated resources to the most productive uses rather than to speculators and projectors.[41] Jefferson's aspirations and even some of his theories it should be added have a very contemporary ring to them. Jefferson's fears also have a contemporary ring about them: big government, the perils of fictitious wealth, and a loss of democratic control.

To be sure, Jefferson left open the question of how the economic system would deal with the time when the nation ceased to be agricultural. He realized that it catered to farmers more than it did to businessesmen. Some historians have concluded that Jefferson's political economy was ultimately pessimistic in that it was tied to a finite agricultural phase of America's existence.[42] There is some truth to this but it is important not to forget Jefferson's optimism about the prospects for future progress whether it be in the area of the rights of man around the world, the international system, American slavery, or religious toleration. Whatever obstacles stood in the way, Jefferson was confident they could eventually be overcome. With regard to political economy, Jefferson accepted that within certain limits the axioms of that science were uncertain and changing. Here as elsewhere, the progress of science will point the way forward. The trick, as always, would be to ensure that future economic experiments supported the grand experiment in self-government.

THE VIRTUES AND VICES OF JEFFERSONIANISM AND HAMILTONIANISM

There are many instructive ironies in the way the economic debate between Hamilton and Jefferson played out politically.[43] Despite his support for manufacturing Hamilton's Federalist party lost the support of many manufacturers, especially city artisans. This was partly because of the often heavy-handed elitist politics of the Federalists and it was partly because Hamilton's policies did not give small manufacturers what they most wanted, namely, effective protection from British imports. Hamilton rejected the idea of a protective tariff and his policies aimed at financial modernization that would increase access to capital. Hamilton's policies seemed to favor large-scale manufactures and looked forward to an American industrial revolution. Jefferson benefited politically from Hamilton's inability to cultivate support in the cities. Yet, with Jefferson's ascension to power, his Republican party, as we have noted, began quietly and later more emphatically to embrace Hamiltonian ideas, though Hamilton was seldom mentioned. Jefferson's Treasury Secretary Albert Gallatin utilized the spectacularly successful financial system Hamilton had created to pursue Jeffersonian ends. Peace, prosperity, and sound public credit allowed Jefferson to cut taxes, pay down the debt, and at the same time easily finance the expansion of the United States. Gallatin was also less of a strict constructionist than Jefferson over matters such as internal improvements and Gallatin's position, despite the attempts of Jefferson and Madison to hold the line, increasingly became the Republican position. Republicans also warmed to Hamilton's arguments about the importance of a diverse economy for stability, prosperity, and even intellectual progress. Party politics and the need for votes explains some of this shift but it also reflects the Jeffersonian Republicans' recognition, though almost always unacknowledged, of the extent to which Hamilton's policies were reasonable responses to the political and economic realities faced by the United States.

Hamilton would not receive due recognition for his accomplishments until after the Civil War. The Republican synthesis of Jefferson and Hamilton was the first of many to follow. Pure Hamiltonianism of the sort that prevailed in Washington's administration has never recurred, and apart perhaps from the Jacksonian period, nor has pure Jeffersonianism. Instead, grand syntheses have prevailed, chiefly those begun by Lincoln (and fleshed out by post–Civil War Republicans) and Franklin Roosevelt.

These syntheses have combined elements of each man's approach. Let us summarize the main differences in their approaches before turning to the issue of their potential vices. The contrast is starkest in three areas. First, Hamilton and Jefferson disagreed about the role of theory in politics. Hamilton acknowledged that modern political science had made considerable progress, but he was convinced that the world could not be made over. Passion too easily triumphs over reason and enlightened self-interest. Jefferson was more optimistic about the potential for theory rather than self-interest to guide politics. Second, Hamilton saw the Constitution primarily as a grant of power to accomplish national goals. For Hamilton, it was the very structure of that Constitution that would restrain it from abusing its powers. Secondarily, he relied on what he thought was a common understanding of the difference between national and local interests. Jefferson saw the Constitution as strictly limiting the national government to its enumerated powers. He thought that holding the government to the letter of the Constitution, rather than the use of structural incentives, was the key not only to restraining abuses of power but also for resisting the inevitable tendencies toward governmental centralization. Lastly, Hamilton had a more dynamic vision of capitalism than Jefferson. He saw sophisticated financial and industrial systems as not only necessary but as highly compatible with republican government. Partly because of this dynamism Hamilton saw a greater role for government in the economy than Jefferson. Jefferson's vision of capitalism was less dynamic. Capitalism functioned best and was compatible with republicanism when it was based on hard money and the honest industry of the common man.

It is possible, with the benefit of hindsight, to point to the potential vices inherent in each man's general approach. These it should be added are the vices of their general approach and not necessarily the vices that showed themselves when the two men were struggling to shape the future of the nation. Hamilton's approach threatens to abolish constitutional limits on governmental power. His scheme of government support for industry may degenerate into crony capitalism in which government serves the interests of big business. The "top-down" or elitist aspects of government activism risk a loss of popular support not just for the government in power but for government and the Constitution in general. Lastly, the Hamiltonian approach, because of its distrust of theory, risks accommodating itself too easily to the world as it is rather striving for what it might become.

The Jeffersonian approach has a corresponding set of vices. Strict construction threatens to cripple the government in its essential endeavors. Relatedly, Jeffersonianism risks failing to see the positive contributions government and statesmanship might make to the economy and elsewhere. Its valorization of the common man risks slipping into mere populism. Lastly, its penchant for theory invites a preoccupation with formulating policies for a world that does not exist now and might never exist.

CONCLUSION

What is to be done? Let me suggest two further avenues of inquiry important both for answering this question and more generally for shaping a political economy for twenty-first century American democratic capitalism. First, the answer to the "what is to be done" question depends a great deal on how one assesses the current state of American politics. Which vices are most apparent? Are the vices of the Hamiltonian approach more apparent than its virtues today? If so, then this might be a Jeffersonian moment! But the question is complicated. The New Deal brought into being a new and complex set of political and economic arrangements that make discerning what is truly Hamiltonian or Jeffersonian very difficult. Lest the vices of the Jeffersonian system recur, I would suggest that a second avenue of inquiry is needed. Hamilton and Jefferson had two important areas of agreement: both men agreed that there was a distinction between national and local concerns (though they differed as to the scope of each) and both men believed that the end of government is liberty, understood as the protection of natural rights. Both these points of agreement were swept aside in the New Deal synthesis of Hamilton and Jefferson. Recovering these points of agreement might provide a compass for reinvigorating Constitutionalism, for correctly assessing the present political situation, and for a prudent choice as to future policies.

NOTES

1. Ron Chernow (*Alexander Hamilton* [New York: Penguin, 2004]) and Forrest McDonald (*Alexander Hamilton: A Biography* [New York: Norton, 1979]) provide fine accounts of the intellectual influences on Hamilton. These books also provide excellent overviews of Hamilton's economic plans to which I am much indebted. I provide a detailed account of Smith's relationship to Hamilton in *Political Economy and Statesmanship: Smith, Hamilton and the Foundation of the Commercial Republic* (DeKalb, IL: Northern Illinois University Press, 1998).

2. Hamilton to George Washington, April 14, 1974, in *Hamilton: Writings*, Joanne Freeman ed. (New York: Library of America, 2001), 817. Hereafter cited as Hamilton, *Writings*.

3. The full titles of Hamilton reports and the dates they were presented to Congress are as follows: "Report Relative to a Provision for the Support of Public Credit" (his Report on Public Credit), January 9, 1790; "Second Report on the Further Provision Necessary for Establishing Public Credit" (the Report on a National Bank), December 13, 1790; "Report on Manufactures," December 5, 1791. He presented his "Opinion on the Constitutionality of a National Bank" to Washington on January 23, 1791.

4. See especially Richard Sylla, "The Political Economy of Early U.S. Financial Development," in *Political Institutional and Financial Development*, ed. Stephen Haber, Douglass C. North, and Barry Weingast (Stanford: Stanford University Press, 2008), 60–91. For Hamilton's skills handling an economic panic, see Richard Sylla, Robert E. Wright, and David J. Cohen, "Alexander Hamilton, Central Banker: Crisis Management during the U.S. Financial Panic of 1792," *Business History Review* 83 (Spring 2009): 61–86.

5. Hamilton, Report on Public Credit, *Writings*, 533

6. On this point, see Max E. Edling and Mark D. Kaplanoff, "Alexander Hamilton's Fiscal Reform: Transforming the Structure of Taxation in the Early Republic," *William and Mary Quarterly* 62 (2004): 712–44.

7. See Joseph Ellis, *Founding Brothers: The Revolutionary Generation* (New York: Knopf, 2001), 48–80, for a full account of the dinner.

8. Hamilton, Report on Public Credit, *Writings*, 551.

9. Hamilton to Washington, May 28, 1790, in *Papers of Alexander Hamilton*, ed. Harold C. Syrett (New York: Columbia University Press, 1961–1987), 27 vols., 6:438. Hereafter Hamilton, *Papers.*

10. For the importance of opinion in establishing public credit, see McDonald, *Hamilton*, 39–40.

11. Hamilton, Report on Public Credit, *Writings*, 569–70.

12. See Hamilton to Washington Hamilton, August 18, 1792, *Writings*, 767. See also Hamilton, "Defense of the Funding System," *Papers*, 19:29–30, 43.

13. See Chernow, *Hamilton*, 199–202.

14. Hamilton, Report on a National Bank, *Writings*, 602.

15. For a review of Congress's handling of Hamilton's Report, see Douglas A. Irwin, "The Aftermath of Hamilton's 'Report on Manufactures,'" *The Journal of Economic History* 64, no. 3 (September 2004): 800–21.

16. See McDonald, *Hamilton*, 235–36.

17. See Madison, Speech in Congress, February 2, 1791, in *Madison: Writings*, ed. Jack Rakove (New York: Library of America, 1999), 480–90, especially 487–89.

18. Opinion on the Constitutionality of a National Bank, February 15, 1791, in *Jefferson: Writings*, ed. Merrill Peterson (New York: Library of America, 1984), 416–21, especially 416, 418, 420. Hereafter cited as Jefferson, *Writings*.

19. Hamilton, Opinion on the Constitutionality of a National Bank, *Writings*, 614, 618, 621, 624–25, 632, and 644.

20. Hamilton, Reports on Manufactures, *Writings*, 702–03; Hamilton, Opinion on the Constitutionality of a National Bank, *Writings*, 616, 638, and 640.

21. Jefferson to M. D'Ivernois, February 6, 1795, *Writings*, 1024.

22. For Jefferson's personal circumstances, see Herbert E. Sloan, *Principle and Interest: Thomas Jefferson and the Problem of Debt* (Charlottesville: University of Virginia Press, 1995). For Jefferson feigning ignorance of financial dealings, see Ellis's account of the dinner deal over assumption of the state debts in *Founding Brothers*, 48–80.

23. See Jefferson to G. K. van Hogendorp, October 13, 1785, in *Writings*, 834–37, and Jefferson to John Taylor, November 26, 1798, in *The Works of Thomas Jefferson*, ed. Paul Leicester Ford, Federal Edition, 12 vols. (New York: G. P. Putnam's Sons, 1904), 8:479–83. Hereafter cited as Jefferson, *Works.*

24. An important correction to this trend is Joyce Appleby, *Capitalism and a New Social Order: The Republican Vision of the 1790s* (New York: New York University Press, 1984).

25. See Clifton B. Luttrell, "Thomas Jefferson on Money and Banking," *History of Political Economy* 7, no. 2 (1975): 156–73.

26. Hamilton to Edward Carrington, May 26, 1792, in *Writings*, 746. Donald F. Swanson follows up on this observation and speculates on what Jefferson as Treasurer may have attempted in "Thomas Jefferson on Establishing Public Credit: The Debt Plans of a Would-Be Secretary of the Treasury," *Presidential Studies Quarterly* 23, no. 3 (Summer 1993): 499–508.

27. December 20, 1787, *Writings*, 917.

28. Jefferson, *Writings*, 290–91.

29. Jefferson, *Writings*, 300.

30. An important study of this feature of Jefferson's thought is Robert W. Tucker and David C. Hendrickson, *Empire of Liberty: The Statecraft of Thomas Jefferson* (New York: Oxford University Press, 1990). A recent more general treatment of Jeffersonian Republican foreign policy may be found in Gordon Wood, *Empire of Liberty: A History of the Early Republic, 1789–1815* (New York: Oxford University Press, 2010), 620–700.

31. "Report on the Privileges and Restrictions on the Commerce of the United States in Foreign Countries," December 16, 1793, in *Writings*, 445–46.

32. See Jefferson to Lithgow, January 4, 1805, *Works*, 4:86–88.

33. See especially Jefferson to Benjamin Austin, January 9, 1816, *Writings*, 1369–72. Jefferson's continued skepticism about large-scale manufactures is discussed by Drew McCoy in *The Elusive Republic: Political Economy in Jeffersonian America* (New York: Norton, 1980), 223–35.

34. See Jefferson to Madison, September 6, 1789, *Writings*, 959–64. Although he failed to convince Madison of his theory in its entirety, he continued to adhere to it and to try to convince others. See his letter to John Wayles Eppes discussed below.

35. March 4, 1801, *Writings*, 494.

36. Jefferson to Gallatin, July 12, 1803, and December 30, 1803, in *Works*, 10:15–16, 56–58.

37. Jefferson to Gallatin, December 3, 1816, *Works*, 10:57.

38. Jefferson to Charles Yancey, January 6, 1816, *Works*, 11:493–98.

39. See Jefferson to (his son-in-law) John Wayles Eppes, in *Writings*, 1280–86. Jefferson ideas on currency and finance are surveyed perceptively by Donald A. Swanson, "'Bank Notes Will Be As Oak Leaves': Thomas Jefferson on Paper Money," *The Virginia Magazine of History and Biography* 101, no. 1 (January 1993): 37–52.

40. Jefferson to Charles Pinckney, September 30, 1820, *Works*, 12:164–66.

41. See Jefferson to Richard Rush, June 22, 1819, *Works*, 12:128: "The banks themselves were doing business on capitals three-fourths of which were fictitious: and, to extend their profit they furnished fictitious capital to every man, who having nothing and disliking the labors of the plough, chose rather to call himself a merchant to set up a house of 5000 D. a year expence, to dash into every species of mercantile gambling, and if that ended as gambling generally does, a fraudulent bankruptcy was an ultimate resource of retirement and competence." See also Adam Smith's argument for a maximum rate of interest to prevent lending from being diverted to "prodigals and projectors" in *An Inquiry into the Nature and Causes of the Wealth of Nations* (Indianapolis: Liberty Classics, 1981), 2 vols., 1:357.

42. This is a major theme in McCoy, *Elusive Republic.*

43. These developments are chronicled in important essays by Lawrence A. Peskin, "How Republicans Learned to Love Manufacturing: The First Parties and the 'New Economy,'" *Journal of the Early Republic* 22, no. 2 (Summer 2002): 235–62 and Andrew Shankman, "'A New Thing on Earth': Alexander Hamilton, Pro-manufacturing Republicans, and the Democratization of American Political Economy," *Journal of the Early Republic* 23, no. 3 (Fall 2003): 323–53.

9

The Right Kind of Regulation

What the Founders Thought about Regulation

Joseph Postell

The last fifty years have witnessed a striking shift in economic thinking in America. Due in part to the influence of recent thinkers (who are often invoked for causes contrary to their own teachings) and in part to the advance of an unlimited, centralized government, two views of the role of government in the economy have emerged, both equally extreme. One view is that any government intervention into the economic liberties of the citizen is inconsistent with natural rights to liberty and property. The other view asserts that in modern conditions, government must adopt an expansive view of regulation in which no economic activity can be said to be outside of the scope of the government's control. The former view often invokes the Founding as inspiration, whereas the latter view frequently denounces the Founding because it assumes that the Founders were categorically opposed to government intervention in the economy.

In short, the prevailing assumption of both sides is that the Founders' regime was a laissez-faire paradise (or nightmare). In this way of thinking about the Founding, American society was largely unregulated for a century, until a new set of political ideas arrived and government was reformed to meet the demands of modern conditions. These ideas gave government the capacity to do more things in a more efficient manner, and fitted America with the infrastructure it needed to manage its economy (or to destroy individual initiative). The underlying narrative, in short, tends to be one of progress or regress—either progress from an unregulated and unfair economy to a regulated and fairer economy, or regress from an unregulated and prosperous economy to an overregulated and sluggish economic situation.

However, a careful look at the economic policies of early America reveals that both camps rely on an inaccurate picture of what economic policy was like during the Founding period. By taking a close look at how the Founders approached questions of economic policy and regulation, we can start to understand, and therefore revive, the Founders' approach—an approach which allows for regulation, but for the sake of protecting individual rights, promoting opportunity for all, and ordering a complex economy. In other words, the Framers did not promote laissez-faire economic policy, contrary to the views of some, but they also had to deal with a complex economy through regulation, contrary to the views of many others. Therefore, their approach still matters today, because the world of the Founders is not so different from ours as we tend to think.[1]

This chapter has two main purposes. The first purpose is to explain the kinds of regulations that were widely implemented during the American Founding period. For purposes of this chapter, only regulations during the pre–Civil War era will be discussed. The first part of this chapter, therefore, examines the nature and extent of regulation in America from the late eighteenth to the middle of the nineteenth centuries, attempting to provide a brief but comprehensive overview of the kinds of regulations which existed. These regulations have been chronicled in a number of relatively obscure works in economic history, but those accounts tend to be overlooked by political scientists and those who practice politics, though they clearly inform our understanding of American political ideas. We will see that there was indeed a vast array of regulations in place at the local, state, and even the federal level during this period. The world that the Framers encountered was not so alien to our modern, complex economy. They faced difficult questions just as we face today. Thus, the practical decisions made by the Framing generation as they confronted the task of protecting rights and regulating a complex economy offer a worthy comparison to contemporary circumstances.

The second purpose of this chapter is to articulate the justification or rationale which permitted extensive regulation of the economy in a manner consistent with the protection of rights to liberty and property. The second part of this chapter, therefore, examines the writings of various figures from the Founding period to ascertain whether these regulations can be reconciled with the protection of rights to liberty and property, which of course is frequently (and rightly) said to be the primary purpose of government in the view of the Founders. Although it would appear at first blush that there is a strong tension between the protection of rights to property and the existence of extensive state regulation of and intervention in the economy, jurists and thinkers of the Founding period saw no tension between the two. In other words, regulations were understood to be consistent with natural rights, not opposed to them as is now so widely maintained.

The evidence will direct us to the following conclusion: the political economy of the early republic was both regulatory (in the traditional sense) and promotional, and leading Founders and jurists during the antebellum period justified regulations as *protecting*, rather than *restricting*, natural rights to liberty and property. By connecting the Founders' practical task of crafting regulation to deal with the new problems of governance that they confronted, this chapter attempts to shed light on how the Founders reconciled the protection of individual rights with the exigencies of modern government in a coherent fashion. Today, when we are still struggling with how to reconcile the need for regulation with the importance of respecting individual rights, we would do well to consult the experience of our Founders, who thought more clearly about these issues than most of us do today.

REGULATION DURING THE EARLY REPUBLIC

Although not generally discussed by scholars of American politics, interventions of government in the economy during the antebellum period at the local, state, and national levels were prevalent. The scope of regulation was so vast that it defies simple characterization. However, for ease of presentation the activities of government during this period can be divided into two categories: pure service activities and regulatory activities. Service activities are government initiatives which provide tangible benefits to a class of citizens or to the public at large. Provision for welfare, building of roads, and education are typical service activities. Regulatory activities, on the other hand, are government initiatives which control the otherwise private actions of individuals or corporations, and are typically aimed at market transactions where goods and services are exchanged. Examples of regulatory activities include licensing for occupations, setting rates for common carriers, and inspecting goods before they can be sold on the market.

For purposes of understanding regulation during the early republic, the category of regulatory activities is most relevant, but it is nonetheless useful to examine the various service activities performed by government during this period to get a clearer sense of the appropriate role for government activity in society at large.

Service Activities

During the antebellum period, government at the local, state, and federal level engaged in activities which were service-oriented in nature. At the federal level, many of the constitutional powers granted to Congress possess this character, such as the power to establish post offices and post roads, grant patents, provide compensation for veterans of the military, and order the dispensation of public lands.

Other than their explicit constitutional foundation, what unites these powers is that they do not in themselves constrain the decision making of individual citizens. They do not establish rules that control behavior. Rather, they provide goods and services which are public in nature, *or* they provide necessary services that cannot adequately be supplied by a private entity. The powers to grant patents and establish uniform weights and measures supply the standards to facilitate economic activity and exchange of goods and services. Compensation for military veterans, dispensation of public lands, establishment of public spaces, and the delivery of mail are public services which are best, or most conveniently, supplied by a public entity.

Prior to the Civil War, the national government carried out these service activities vigorously. The Post Office was one of the most sophisticated endeavors which the national government undertook prior to the Civil War; it was, in Lawrence Friedman's words, "a large, functioning, federal bureaucracy" during the nineteenth century.[2] By 1831 it employed nearly nine thousand postmasters, comprising "over three-quarters of the civilian federal work force" according to another historian.[3]

Perhaps the most interesting of these activities for present-day purposes is the pension and health programs that were established for military veterans and sailors. Revolutionary War veterans received pensions that were considered to be an entitlement; frequently these veterans would petition the Congress to receive the benefits established by law.[4] Similarly, in 1798 Congress by law imposed a payroll tax on sailors' wages and used the funds to establish sailors' hospitals, known as the Federal Marine Hospital system.[5] These nationally administered programs were extensive and affected the economic situation of thousands of families during the antebellum period.

A final area of federal involvement in service activities was the dispensation of public land. This was a matter of profound controversy in the policy of the early republic, for (as is well known) the possession of land was vital to economic self-sufficiency for families of the period. As Friedman notes, "After 1787, the vast stock of public land was at once a problem and a great opportunity. . . . The issue was as persistent as issues of war, slavery, and the tariff."[6] In part, this is because the government did not seek a purely economic outcome in dispensing the land, maximizing profits in the process of divesting itself of the land. Rather, the national government used the land in its possession to advance policy goals, such as compensating veterans and encouraging the building of colleges and universities.[7]

In 1796, Congress passed the law which would provide the legal framework for selling off public lands. The law created the office of Surveyor General and divided the land into 640-acre parcels for sale. (Public land did not sell well in such large parcels, and thus subsequent acts reduced the sections gradually to 40 acres.)[8] Similarly, under the Northwest Ordinance each state would be divided into counties and townships, the latter of which to be divided into thirty-six sections. Four of these sections would be reserved for government uses such as public and educational buildings.[9] Under the law the land could not be settled until it was properly surveyed. After 1800, government surveys were commonplace through district land offices established after 1803. During the early nineteenth-century lands were auctioned off to individuals to allow for maximum opportunity for all to participate in the purchasing of land.[10] In the case of public land there was thus a legal and administrative framework in place to advance policy goals in the economy, including the widespread distribution of land.

By granting land to citizens in a variety of economic and social stations, the government advanced its understanding of a healthy citizenry. As Friedman argues, "The ideal was a country of free citizens, small-holders living on their own bits of land."[11] Similar to Jefferson's design in eliminating primogeniture and entail, the dispensation of public land was designed to advance republican goals. Thus, land policy was intended to further both liberal and republican goals, allowing for the free acquisition and use of property while also promoting the kind of citizenry conducive to perpetuating republican government. In fact, Jefferson had anticipated the national government's plan to dispense of public lands in a plan he had outlined in 1784.[12]

While the foregoing examples of national government involvement in service activities are important, it is equally important to examine the service activities performed by states and localities during the antebellum period. The provision of welfare, education, and even subsidies to fledgling industries all indicate the importance of state and local government activity in the early republic.

The provision of welfare and education at the state and local level was pervasive during the antebellum period. To be sure, there was considerable debate at the national level about the legitimacy of the national government's role in such activities. At the Constitutional Convention many of the delegates lobbied unsuccessfully for the national government to possess the power to establish a national university. Despite losing that battle at the national level, statesmen such as Washington and Madison continued to press for the creation of a national university in their annual messages to Congress. Also, the debate over Alexander Hamilton's *Report on Manufacturers* demonstrates that there was some controversy about whether the national government should subsidize manufacturing during this period.[13] Furthermore,

Congress regularly allocated money to aid those afflicted by federal disasters. Although the Congress refused to assist Savannah after it was decimated by fire in 1796, in many other cases during the early republic Congress granted money to help citizens affected by such incidents.[14]

In general, however, the overwhelming majority of the provision of welfare and education occurred at the state and local levels of government. Welfare provides an interesting case. By the 1750s Massachusetts required a poor house to be located in every county.[15] Early in American history the defining feature of welfare policy was that it was locally controlled and administered.[16] In 1788 New York's welfare law required that "Every city and town shall support and maintain their own poor."[17] At times this created controversies regarding which locality was responsible for supporting a pauper. In some states litigation was necessary to decide the outcomes.[18] But the principle of support and relief for the poor was never questioned, even when states and localities sought to reduce the size of their welfare rolls.

Government subsidies were also widely present during the antebellum period. The state of New York was a prominent subsidizer of private enterprise through loans and bounties. Over a forty year period between 1785 and 1825 New York spent millions in aid of agriculture and manufacturing.[19] Citing the scarcity of capital available to start up new ventures, the state legislature would regularly pass special acts granting loans to specific manufacturing enterprises.[20] Even western states such as Missouri granted special loans and subsidies to farmers.[21] Subsidization and facilitation of commercial enterprise also extended, of course, to state sponsorship of internal improvements such as roads and canals, which occurred at every level of government and was perhaps the most prominent manifestation of the government's service activities during the early republic.

Regulatory Activities

While the service activities of government were prevalent during the early republic, these were not the only areas in which governments were active during the period. In fact, the regulatory power of government was exercised at every level of government and spanned all areas of economic life, from common carriers to banks and labor.

Two of the most prominent yet lesser-known examples of government regulation involve inspections of goods and licensing of occupations. In Massachusetts before and after the Revolution town selectmen and other elected local officials were empowered to inspect commodities such as beef, pork, and fish before they could be exported from the state. Once inspected to ensure quality, the elected officials were to "imprint, with a burning iron, the following brand or mark, *Mass. RPD.* With the initial letters of his Christian name and his sirname at large, and the letter *P* at the end thereof" so that the commodity was properly labeled as inspected.[22] Inspection schemes such as this persisted in Massachusetts and in many other states, well after the Revolution.[23]

Licensing of occupations, particularly medical professions and common carriers such as innkeepers and auctioneers, was also widely accepted during the Founding period. New York and Massachusetts "gave local medical societies the power to examine and license prospective doctors. Unlicensed doctors were not allowed to collect fees through regular court processes."[24] In Massachusetts, at times, the law went further, prosecuting those who practiced medicine without a license. Laws on the books in Massachusetts and New York levied fines on those who practiced without a license. Howard Gillman and Oscar and Mary Handlin describe cases in which "an unlicensed bonesetter and healer of sprains" and a citizen "selling intoxicating liquors without a license" were prosecuted and convicted; the state supreme court upheld their convictions.[25] At the same time, even the federal government got involved in licensing, requiring the licensing and bonding of private fur traders.[26]

Inspections and licensing were not the only ways in which government regulated the conduct of individuals and corporations during the antebellum period. Through charters of incorporation regulatory duties were frequently handed to corporate entities by state legislatures. Banks were chartered at the state level through special incorporation laws. This meant that state governments could place special provisions in each charter to control the conduct of the bank. In 1833, for example, the legislature of Vermont granted a charter to "The Farmer's Bank" on the condition that the bank charged no more than 6 percent interest on loans.[27] Moreover, states regularly subscribed to the stock of the banks they chartered and capitalized the banks with state funds.[28]

Banks were not the only enterprises which were governed through special incorporation. Transportation companies were often authorized to perform economic services by special charters from state governments. As Friedman explains, "Banks, insurance companies, water companies, and companies organized to build or run canals, turnpikes, and bridges made up the overwhelming majority of these early corporations" which were granted specific charters (permission to carry on their trade) by state governments.[29] As might be expected, in most cases these individual charters came with strings attached in the form of regulatory requirements (and other requirements as well—the state of Pennsylvania required the Bank of Philadelphia to pay a bonus of $135,000 for its charter in 1803[30]). The very use of special incorporation charters meant that the size and function of the corporation were determined by law; otherwise the charter would be indeterminate. With the advent of general incorporation laws, these regulatory tools fell into disuse. As Jonathan Hughes writes, in the nineteenth century "Americans moved from special-action charters, with structure and function prescribed by legislation, to general procedures for incorporation without specific legislative act. General powers left the specific form and structure of the corporation (and changes therein), size and place of business to be determined by the entrepreneurs."[31] Yet the importance of special incorporation acts to regulate and even determine the size and function of corporations cannot be overemphasized.

Common carriers were also regulated, subjected to general police power regulations, regardless of whether and how they were chartered. Chancellor Kent affirmed the regulation of common carriers such as innkeepers, cartmen, and ferrymen, in the state of New York: "As they hold themselves to the world as common carriers for a reasonable compensation, they assume to do, and are bound to do, what is required of them."[32] In the state of Illinois, every ferry keeper was required to keep "a post or board, on which shall be written the rates of ferriage . . . by law allowed."[33] (Passengers in today's taxicabs are certainly familiar with this kind of regulation.) As with banks and other enterprises, moreover, common carriers were often chartered by state governments, which gave the state legislatures another means of instituting controls.

Constitutional law students are familiar with these charters from cases such as *Gibbons v. Ogden* (involving a charter granted by the State of New York and a competing license granted by the national government) and *Charles River Bridge Co. v. Warren Bridge Co.* (involving competing charters granted by the Massachusetts legislature).[34] Examples of state control of common carriers through incorporation charters abound—albeit sometimes for non-regulatory aims. For instance, the state of New Jersey in 1832 received gifts of stock from a transport franchise which it granted exclusive rights to provide transportation.[35] Of course, not every government during the period acted solely for the public good; yet the fact that these regulatory mechanisms can sometimes be "captured" for private purposes does not diminish their legitimacy. Rather, the possibility of regulatory capture, both in the nineteenth century and today, demonstrate the need for regulatory institutions to be local (where possible), accountable, and to operate in accordance with the rule of law.[36]

Of course, no account of regulation during the early republic would be complete without mentioning the widespread morals regulations which existed during the early nineteenth century. Regulation of alcohol through licensing was so pervasive as to amount to outright prohibition in many states. Massachusetts and Maine supply prominent examples of this practice.[37] Prohibition of billiard halls, gaming, and houses of ill repute were also widespread during the antebellum period.[38] In the state of New York puppet shows, rope or wire dancing, and "other idle shows" could not be performed for profit.[39]

When one puts all of this together, a very different picture of the relationship between government and economy emerges than the one we are prone to envision. Even at the national level, government was involved in providing public services, such as granting patents, providing transportation, and even subsidizing manufacturing. These actions, and others such as provision of welfare and education, were even more prevalent at the state and local levels. These service-oriented activities were widespread. Furthermore, government was involved in regulating economic activity at the national, state, and local levels. Licensing of occupations, inspections of goods, granting of specific charters to companies (with strings attached), and regulation of transportation rates on common carriers, are just a few of the many tasks the government undertook during this period.

WERE THESE REGULATIONS COMPATIBLE WITH NATURAL RIGHTS?

The existence of pervasive regulation, in which government at the local, state, and national level dictated conditions of employment, inspected goods to be sold on the market, sponsored enterprise, chartered corporations and banks, and regulated the use of property to prevent a wide array of injurious effects, seems at first blush to be at odds with the idea that the basic purpose of government is to secure basic natural rights to liberty and property. As Jonathan Hughes has explained, because these regulations

> have existed so long in peaceful conjunction with Anglo-American ideas about property rights, their long-lived existence must be considered by the historian as somehow natural, given the reality of our laws and customs. A moment's thought should indicate that this is not a trivial point, since the mainstream view of American economists for so long, a view that is still espoused by a vociferous minority, is that only zero government regulation is fully compatible theoretically with free enterprise.[40]

Hughes clearly overstates the tendency of these economists to anarchism, but the general point is correct: American economists and citizens alike tend to believe that regulation and free enterprise are in tension, almost mutually exclusive.

This was not the view of the Founders, however. If we examine writings and opinions of leading thinkers and jurists of the early republic, on the relationship between regulation and the protection of natural rights, we see that in their view regulation could *enhance* or *expand* natural rights rather than necessarily conflicting with them.

At the outset it is worth noting that many prominent Framers were unsympathetic to the principle of laissez-faire. In his "Report on Manufacturers" Alexander Hamilton confronted the idea of laissez-faire head-on, mentioning the argument that

> to endeavor by the extraordinary patronage of Government to accelerate the growth of manufactures is, in fact, to endeavor by force and art to transfer the natural current of industry from a more to a less beneficial channel. Whatever has such as tendency must necessarily be unwise. Indeed it can hardly ever be wise in a government, to attempt to give a direction to the industry of its citizens. . . . To leave industry to itself, therefore, is, in almost every case, the soundest as well as the simplest policy.

While Hamilton granted that "This mode of reasoning is founded upon facts and principles which have certainly respectable pretensions," there are "numerous exceptions" to these theories, and the theories generally "blend a considerable portion of error with the truths they inculcate."[41] While Hamilton thought that it was generally most beneficial to allow industry to take its natural course without government interference, he also believed that laissez-faire was hardly an infallible rule. Elsewhere Hamilton wrote that "This favorite dogma [of laissez-faire], when taken as a general rule, is true; but as an exclusive one, it is false, and leads to error in the administration of public affairs."[42] For Hamilton, in short, government intervention in economic affairs is not fundamentally hostile to liberty. To apply the rule of laissez-faire universally would in fact be pernicious.

James Madison, often viewed to be a foil to Hamilton's expansive vision for government intervention in the economy, agreed with Hamilton that laissez-faire was not an infallible principle. In an 1819 letter to Friedrich List, a famous German economist, Madison wrote that on the subject of internal improvements,

> the true policy . . . will be found to lie between the extremes of doing nothing and prescribing everything; between admitting no exceptions to the rule of "laissez-faire," and converting the exceptions into the rule. The intermediate Legislative interposition *will be* more or less limited, according to the differing Judgments of statesmen, and *ought to be so*, according to the aptitudes or inaptitudes of countries and situations for the particular objects claiming encouragement.[43]

Even John Locke, a philosopher generally credited with asserting the inviolability of rights to property, granted that "the Prince or Senate" has "the power to make Laws for the regulating of property between the subjects one amongst another," and that individuals give up the pre-political power to do whatever is necessary for preservation "to be regulated by Laws made by the society, so far forth as the preservation of himself, and the rest of that society shall require, which laws of the society in many things confine the liberty he had by the law of nature."[44] Thinkers from Locke, to Hamilton, to Madison were united in their view that laissez-faire was not a guiding principle of government, even if it was correct more often than not.

However, while prominent Founders periodically stated their disagreement with the basic concept of laissez-faire, most of the systematic thoughts on regulation are offered not in theoretical essays or statements of first principles, but in legal cases and writings where the more practical aspects of municipal government are treated. This is likely one reason why such arguments about regulation have gone unnoticed for so long.

Importantly, the Framers' defense of regulation also helps us understand the *limits* on regulation. Some regulations, the Founders argued, protect and preserve liberty and property rights—but regulation which goes beyond this purpose inhibits or violates liberty and property rights. Thus, while it is incorrect to say that regulation and free enterprise are *always* in tension, clearly regulation and free enterprise are *frequently* in tension, particularly when the ends and purposes of regulation are no longer well understood.

The Defense of Regulation in the Early Republic

For the most part, the legitimacy of the kinds of regulations described in the first part of this essay was taken for granted. However, from time to time those affected by regulations challenged them in court, charging that the restrictions violated rights to liberty and property. It is in these judicial challenges where we find a robust defense of the legitimacy of regulation during the early republic. The principles justifying regulation in a society based on natural rights were articulated in particular cases and by jurists who were forced to consider particular questions of municipal law and regulation.

In various cases involving regulation in antebellum America famous and eminent judges explained the justification for regulation. These judges included John Marshall, Joseph Story, Chancellor James Kent, and Lemuel Shaw. The justifications offered in their judicial opinions are consistent with systematic treatments of regulation offered by Founding-era statesmen and theorists such as Nathaniel Chipman and James Wilson. Examining the writings of this impressive collection of legal minds gives us a firm foundation for an understanding of the proper scope of regulation.

In defending the kinds of regulations described in this chapter, these jurists offered three distinct arguments. The first argument was that the exercise of private rights must be subordinated to the common or general good of the society. Chancellor Kent, for instance, wrote that "Unwholesome trades, slaughterhouses, operations offensive to the senses, the deposit of powder, the application of steam power to propel cars, the building with combustible materials, and the burial of the dead" may be regulated "on the general and rational principle that . . . private interests must be made subservient to the general interests of the community."[45] Lemuel Shaw, similarly, justified regulation on the principle that "every holder of property, however, absolute and unqualified may be his title, holds it under the implied liability that his use of it shall not be injurious to the equal enjoyment of others having an equal right to the enjoyment of their property, *nor injurious to the rights of the community*."[46] The legal doctrine which grew out of this argument stated that property becomes "clothed" or "affected" with a public interest when its use affects the general interests of the community.[47] Likewise, the Supreme Court of Vermont upheld a regulation on the grounds that "persons and property are subjected to all kinds of restraints and burdens in order to secure the general comfort, health, and prosperity of the state."[48]

In the South, prior to the Civil War, this power was also exercised and defended in courts of law. The Supreme Court of Alabama in 1841 upheld the power of the city of Mobile to regulate the weight and price of bread, declaring that private property shall not be interfered with "unless such calling affects the public interest or private property is employed in such a manner which directly affects the body of the people." The Court also defended the licensing of innkeepers, and the adjustment of the rates of innkeepers, on this principle.[49]

The second argument offered was that the exercise of liberty and property must be regulated in order to prevent injury to others. Rather than subordinating the right to liberty and property to the good of the community, this justification defended regulation as a means of reconciling one individual's rights to liberty and property with another's, in the event of conflict. The legal maxim *sic utere tuo ut alienum non laedas* was frequently invoked in these cases as a separate argument in defense of regulation. In Chancellor Kent's defense of regulation, cited above, both arguments are offered; the full quote states that regulation is justified "on the general and rational principle that every person ought so to use his property as not to injure his neighbors, *and* that private interests must be made subservient to the general interests of the community."[50]

The third argument, offered occasionally in these opinions, is that regulations do not hinder the exercise of liberty and property. In fact, precisely the opposite is the case: without regulation, the rights to liberty and property would actually be *less* secure. Lemuel Shaw, in *Commonwealth v. Blackington*, argued that inspections support the right to liberty and property, rather than restricting those rights:

> The preamble of the [Massachusetts] constitution announces one of its objects to be, to secure to individuals the power of enjoying in safety and tranquility their natural rights, one of the most important of which is, that of acquiring, possessing and protecting property. . . . *such laws are necessary to define, secure and give practical efficacy to the right itself*. . . . All the inspection laws, providing for the inspecting and marking of the principal products of our agriculture and manufacturers, with a view to benefit our commerce in those articles, at home and abroad; all laws made with a view to revenue, to health, to peace and good morals, are of this description.[51]

Shaw grounded the legitimacy of these regulations not on the principle that consumers must be protected from the potential injury which comes from poorly manufactured goods, but rather on the principle that they are necessary to "give practical efficacy to the right itself." In particular, these regulations were understood to *promote* the right to property by supporting the competition of the market. The view of the Founding generation seems to be that commerce is supported by regulation, because it makes for an orderly system of competition. That is, merchants and traders can exercise their rights to liberty and property more effectively when consumers can trust the products they sell. Thus, a merchant's property right to buy, sell, and trade goods is enhanced by regulations such as inspections and licensing of occupations. Similarly, regulations to protect public health and safety, when crafted for the right ends, enhance rights to liberty and property by protecting citizens from injury. Well-crafted regulations expand liberty and property rather than constricting it, according to this view.

Some of the economic historians who have written on the rationale for justification in the early republic seem to have understood this argument, though they did not emphasize it. Oscar and Mary Handlin explain that the Massachusetts laws were defended by merchants themselves on the grounds that "inspection added prestige to Massachusetts goods in foreign ports."[52] Similarly, Louis Hartz notes that in Pennsylvania "Inspection policy was most heavily emphasized in connection with articles produced for export, since the reputation of Pennsylvania merchants in interstate commerce depended on it."[53] These arguments in defense of regulations such as inspection laws are significant because they belie the notion that such regulations are both in conflict with the protection of natural rights and require a subordination of private interest to the good of the community. In the case of many of the regulations and service activities undertaken during the early republic, no tension was present; the activities both promoted the common good and furthered the protection of natural rights to liberty and property.

Regulation during the Founding vs. Contemporary Regulation

We can therefore summarize the theoretical defense of regulation in a regime dedicated to the protection of natural rights as follows. The protection of natural rights to liberty and property does not require complete non-interference from government. In fact, government's action is necessary to preserve—and even to promote—rights to liberty and property. Government's work must be both regulative and promotional. Government has an obligation to regulate activity in the traditional sense: "regulation" as distinct from "government," where the purpose of government is to provide a framework within which free action can take place (including, of course, the basic duty to protect liberty and property from interference by other individuals), rather than dictating the specific terms of exchange of goods and services.[54] It may also promote economic prosperity through targeted subsidies, sponsorship of joint enterprises relating to infrastructure (including transportation and financial infrastructure), to provide greater opportunity to engage in orderly commerce, thus enhancing the opportunities to acquire and possess property.[55]

Understood in this way, the Founders' approach to regulation, while perhaps *appearing* to be similar to the kind of regulation undertaken by most industrialized democracies today, is in fact profoundly different. There is regulation in the traditional sense described in the previous paragraph, and then there is regulation in the sense of centralized planning of all elements of economic life. The latter view of regulation posits that regulation must be pervasive, and that the purpose of control of economic activity is to subordinate the exercise of individual rights to the common good—rather than seeing regulation as a means to securing individual rights. This latter understanding of regulation tends to prevail today, but it is at odds with the Framers' view.[56] As Sidney Fine writes in his important study *Laissez-Faire and the General Welfare State*, while Federalists and Whigs such as Alexander Hamilton and Henry Clay were more favorable to government regulation and encouragement of the economy than many of their contemporaries, "[n]either man . . . thought the state should act as a regulatory agency. That was an idea alien to the Federalist-Whigs."[57]

For the foregoing explanation to be adequate, however, one final question must be confronted. What about the first argument in favor of regulation stated above, namely that the exercise of private rights must be made subservient to the common good of the whole community? Does this rationale not set the precedent for a more expansive and unlimited understanding of regulation? One might state that if the Founders supported subordinating private rights to the good of the whole community, today's expansive understanding of regulation continues that tradition, merely offering a more centralized system of regulation for the common good of a larger community.

To understand the Founders' response to this problem, we must understand how the Founders thought about the relationship between individual rights and the common good. Today, we are more inclined to think that these two concepts are in tension, and that regulation tramples on individual rights but for a socially beneficial outcome that is good for everyone. By contrast, the Founding generation did not see a tension between individual rights and the regulation of liberty and property for the common good. This is because, as the following section will show, their conception of natural rights was *teleological*—that is, it is oriented toward some social good, and so the exercise of these rights (for the most part) will not be in conflict with the common good of the society.

Individual Rights and the Common Good: Not So Incompatible?

We have seen that an important rationale offered in defense of regulation was the idea that rights to liberty and property cannot give someone the freedom to do harm to the public good. Some might point to these arguments to maintain that, while references to natural rights to liberty and property abound during the Founding period, when dealing with practical governance the Founding generation typically subordinated such rights to the good of the public. However, this presupposes a contrast or tension between the protection of natural rights and the public good. Upon examination it is clear that the Founding generation did not see such a tension, and that their theory offered a reconciliation of these paradoxes and perceived tensions.

For instance, Nathaniel Chipman, a statesman and jurist of the Founding generation, argued that "the laws of nature, rightly understood, are found to aim, as well at the promotion of the individual as the general interests—or rather the promotion of the general interests of the community, *through* the private interests of the individual members;—for the general interest consists of an aggregate of the individual interests, properly estimated. If they ever clash or run in opposite directions, it is owing to some error in the estimate."[58] The argument of Chipman and others of the Founding period is that the promotion of the public good is primarily done through the protection of the rights and "private interests of the individual members" of the community, going so far as to say that "the general interest consists of an aggregate of the individual interests." Chipman's view seems to be that there is no public interest outside and above the protection of the rights of all citizens. To promote the common good, in this view, is to protect the private rights of all.

Yet Chipman refines his treatment of the relationship between individual rights and the common good in a chapter of his *Principles of Government*: "Of natural, political and civil rights and liberty." There, he quotes Blackstone's definition of "natural liberty" which "consists, properly, in a power of acting as one thinks fit, without any restraint or control, unless by the laws of nature . . ." Chipman revises Blackstone's definition to read "unless by the laws of *social* nature," accusing Blackstone of "perhaps inadvertently exclud[ing] the notion of social from his law of nature."[59] In preference to Blackstone, Chipman quotes Burlamaqui's definition of natural liberty, which reads "Moral or natural liberty is the right which nature gives to all mankind disposing of their persons, and property, after the manner they shall judge most consonant to their happiness; on condition of their acting within the limits of the laws of nature, and that they do not in any way abuse it to the prejudice of other men." This definition, Chipman argues approvingly, leads to laws which "not only prohibit the doing of what is prejudicial, but *enjoin* many things to be done, that are beneficial to individuals, as well as to society; they enjoin positive acts as well as restraints." This results in Chipman's final definition of natural liberty, which "consists in the free exercise and enjoyment of that right which nature gives all mankind, of disposing of their persons and property in the manner they judge most consonant to their happiness, on condition of their getting within the limits of the laws of nature, and that they observe towards others, all the moral duties enjoined by that law."[60] In the final analysis, Chipman says, natural liberty involves many positive duties that are morally obligatory. Thus, the exercise of natural liberty cannot conflict with social goods, for natural liberty *involves* acting in accordance with moral and social duties.

In formulating his unique definition of liberty out of the definitions offered by Blackstone and Burlamaqui, Chipman combines the idea of individual liberty with the moral and social obligations that are natural to human beings. The common good and the protection of individual rights, for Chipman as for many others during the Founding generation, were not understood to be in tension. This is certainly one reason why Chipman does not subscribe to the paradoxical position of many prominent Framers, that some "inalienable" rights to liberty are nonetheless sacrificed upon entering the social compact. The view that "man, on entering into civil society sacrifices a part of his natural liberty," Chipman writes, "must have been adopted from a very indefinite and, indeed, very absurd notion of natural liberty," one which is more applicable "to the lion, and the tiger" rather than the human being.[61]

James Wilson's *Lectures on Law* contain the same arguments as Chipman with regard to municipal law, regulation, and natural liberty. Just as Chipman asserted the right to liberty as fundamental, and not inconsistent with the proposition that natural law comprises social duties and a concern for the common good, Wilson argued that "every citizen is, of right, entitled to liberty, personal as well as mental, in the highest possible degree, which can consist with the safety and welfare of the state. . . . our municipal regulations concerning [mental liberty] are not less hostile to the true principles of utility, than they are to those of the superiour law of liberty."[62] Wilson, like Lemuel Shaw, therefore concluded that in obedience to municipal regulations "every citizen will gain more liberty than he can lose by those prohibitions. He will gain more by the limitation of other men's freedom, than he can lose by the diminution of his own."[63] By adherence to the right kinds of regulations, Wilson argues, the liberty and property of all is enhanced rather than limited. Each citizen gains more liberty than he loses by following these regulations.

A correct notion of liberty, according to Chipman, Wilson, and many of the other Founders, involves the moral sense, a faculty which is present in every human being and which serves as "the point at which the social nature of man commences." It is a natural faculty which produces sentiments which "relate to society, to social rights and duties."[64] The freedom that is forfeited in civil government, according to these thinkers, was never a part of natural liberty in the first place, since the moral sense prohibits the use of liberty in a manner contrary to social duties. Regulations both cultivate the natural duties discovered by the moral sense and enlarge the liberty of every citizen by promoting an orderly society in which liberty can be enjoyed. Thus, *the right kinds of regulations* (those which are regulatory in the proper sense, and those which are promotional) *enlarge rather than restrict liberty*, in the Founders' view.

Chipman, Wilson, and the Founding generation were neither attempting to subordinate private interest to the public good, nor eliminate consideration of the common good altogether. Repeatedly, both the protection of individual rights *and* the pursuit of the common good are emphasized. Far from suggesting a tension between the two, the Framers sought the means of allowing both private interest and the common good to be pursued without leading to the utter detriment of either.

CONCLUSION

For the Founders, in both their greatest writings and in their practical tasks of local self-government, no opposition between the protection of individual rights to property and liberty and the regulation of those rights for the sake of the public good was perceived. The public good was not seen to be at odds with individual rights. What does all of this mean for today? It means that, while we may have good reasons to be skeptical about the immense scope of government regulation under which we currently live, this does not give us license to dispense with the idea of regulation altogether. Rather, the Founding generation shows us that, when regulations are designed for certain purposes, and implemented in certain ways, they are not only consistent with the protection of natural rights, but are in fact *beneficial* for the securing of these rights. Regulations for the sake of promoting health and safety, and even for promoting economic development, can in certain situations be justified within the Founders' conception of natural rights to liberty and property.

When modern regulations infringe upon rights to liberty and property is difficult to discern. But this should not dissuade us from trusting government regulation altogether. As we struggle with how to reconcile our dedication to individual liberties with our acceptance of a prominent role for government regulation in twenty-first-century America, we would do well to consider how the Founders reconciled liberal and republican aims in their not-so-distant experience.

NOTES

1. As Lawrence Friedman writes in his definitive *A History of American Law,* "By reputation, the 19th century was the high noon of *laissez-faire*. . . . But when we actually burrow into the past, we unearth a much more complex reality." Friedman, *A History of American Law*, 2nd ed. (New York: Simon & Schuster, 1985), 177.
2. Lawrence Friedman, *A History of American Law*, 439.
3. Brian Balogh, *A Government Out of Sight: The Mystery of National Authority in Nineteenth-Century America* (Cambridge University Press, 2009), 220.
4. Regarding the pension programs for veterans in the early republic, see Laura Jensen, *Patriots, Settlers and the Origins of American Social Policy* (New York: Cambridge University Press, 2003), 1–122.
5. Friedman, *A History of American Law*, 223–224; Brian Balogh, *A Government Out of Sight*, 13, 145–146. One of the most extensive discussions of this federal program is Henry W. Farnam, *Chapters in the History of Social Legislation in the United States to 1860* (Washington, DC: The Carnegie Institution, 1938), 231–251.
6. Friedman, *A History of American Law*, 230–231.
7. Friedman, *A History of American Law*, 232: "Government . . . used land as a lever of policy. . . . Land grants in general were gifts on condition. They were used to advance national policy—to encourage colleges and railroads, for example . . ."

8. Friedman, *A History of American Law*, 231, 233; Louis M. Hacker, *The Course of American Economic Growth and Development* (New York: John Wiley & Sons, 1970), 97.

9. Jonathan Hughes, *The Governmental Habit Redux: Economic Controls from Colonial Times to the Present* (Princeton, NJ: Princeton University Press, 1991), 55.

10. Jonathan Hughes, *The Governmental Habit Redux*, 61.

11. Friedman, *A History of American Law*, 232.

12. Jonathan Hughes, *The Governmental Habit Redux*, 56.

13. Related to both issues—national power related to education and subsidy—consider Madison and Pinckney's resolutions to add to the powers to those listed by the Committee on Detail, "To establish a university," "To encourage by premiums and provisions, the advancement of useful knowledge and discoveries," "To establish seminaries for the promotion of literature and the arts and sciences," "To grant public institutions, rewards and immunities for the promotion of agriculture, commerce, trades and manufactures." See Frank Bourgin, *The Great Challenge: The Myth of Laissez-Faire in the Early Republic* (New York: Harper & Row, 1989), 38–39, citing Max Farrand's *Records* 2:142–144.

14. Balogh, *A Government Out of Sight*, 145; Michelle Landis Dauber, "The Sympathetic State," *Law and History Review* 23 (2005): 394–395. Lawrence Friedman also notes that Congress passed an act in 1815 to assist the citizens affected by a massive earthquake in New Madrid, Missouri. See Friedman, *A History of American Law*, 213.

15. Jonathan Hughes, *The Government Habit Redux*, 48.

16. See Jonathan Hughes, *The Government Habit Redux*, 46 ("local responsibility was the law); Lawrence Friedman, *A History of American Law*, 441 ("In welfare, for example, first came local poor laws, run by country justices and squires of the community"). The emphasis on local control and administration is central to the analysis in Thomas G. West, *Vindicating the Founders* (Lanham, MD: Rowman & Littlefield, 1997), chapter 6.

17. Cited in Friedman, *A History of American Law*, 213.

18. As in New Hampshire and Connecticut in the early nineteenth century; see Friedman, *A History of American Law*, 215.

19. L. Ray Gunn, *The Decline of Authority: Public Economic Policy and Political Development in New York State, 1800–1860* (Ithaca, NY: Cornell University Press, 1988), 101, 114.

20. See Carter Goodrich, ed., *The Government and the Economy: 1783–1861* (Indianapolis, IN: Bobbs-Merrill Co., 1967), 196. A report of the Committee of Ways and Means in the New York State Assembly noted that "the fact of these borrowers applying to the Legislature affords pretty convincing proof, that the property which they offered as security was not sufficient to enable them to obtain loans from private individuals or companies," though their enterprises were "considered matter of public policy to patronize."

21. James Neal Primm, *Economic Policy in the Development of a Western State: Missouri, 1820–1860* (Cambridge, MA: Harvard University Press, 1954), 115–120.

22. Massachusetts *Acts and Resolves*, from law of November 7, 1784, in Goodrich, *The Government and the Economy*, 360–361.

23. In Massachusetts, see Oscar and Mary Handlin, *Commonwealth: A Study of the Role of Government in the American Economy: Massachusetts, 1774–1861* (New York: New York University Press, 1947), 64–66. In Pennsylvania, see Louis Hartz, *Economic Policy and Democratic Thought: Pennsylvania, 1776–1860* (Cambridge, Mass.: Harvard University Press, 1948), 205. In Maryland, as well, William J. Novak notes, "[n]o fish could be exported from Maryland without certification of inspection and an oath by the ship's master that all fish on board had been properly inspected." William J. Novak, *The People's Welfare: Law and Regulation in Nineteenth-Century America* (Chapel Hill, NC: University of North Carolina Press, 1966), 89. Inspection laws during the early republic in Georgia, Connecticut, and New York are discussed by Lawrence Friedman, *A History of American Law*, 183.

24. Friedman, *A History of American Law*, 185. Handlin and Handlin note that Massachusetts law required licenses to keep a ferry, operate a tavern, or become a lawyer or auctioneer. See *Commonwealth*, 69–74. Hartz also explains that Pennsylvania's licensing laws covered innkeepers, liquor merchants, and tavern owners. *Economic Policy*, 206–207.

25. Howard Gillman, *The Constitution Besieged: The Rise and Demise of Lochner-Era Police Powers Jurisprudence* (Durham, NC: Duke University Press, 1993), 52; Handlin and Handlin, *Commonwealth*, 52–53.

26. See Sidney Fine, *Laissez-Faire and the General-Welfare State* (Ann Arbor, MI: University of Michigan Press, 1965), 19.

27. Friedman, *A History of American Law*, 180.

28. Sidney Fine, *Laissez-Faire and the General-Welfare State*, 21; Fletcher Green notes that "By 1850, Maryland chartered 26 banks with a combined capital of $9,225,000; Virginia, 39 with a combined capital of $10,000,000; North Carolina, 22 with a combined capital of $4,225,000; South Carolina, 14 with a combined capital of $11,225,000; and Georgia, 19, with a combined capital of $5,500,000." Green, *Constitutional Development in the South Atlantic States, 1776–1860* (New York: W.W. Norton & Co., 1966), 155.

29. Friedman, *A History of American Law*, 189. He also explains that "In Pennsylvania, 2,333 special charters were granted to business corporations between 1790 and 1860. Of these about 1,500 were transportation companies; less than two hundred were for manufacturing." Ibid.

30. Friedman, *A History of American Law*, 193.

31. Jonathan Hughes, *The Government Habit Redux*, 80.

32. Cited in Jonathan Hughes, *The Government Habit Redux*, 77.

33. Cited in Friedman, *History of American Law*, 187.

34. *Gibbons v. Ogden*, 9 Wheat. (22 U.S.) 1 (1824); *Charles River Bridge Co. v. Warren Bridge Co.*, 11 Pet. (36 U.S.) 420 (1837).

35. Friedman, *A History of American Law*, 193.

36. For a further elaboration of this idea, with examples of the regulatory institutions crafted during the Founding period, see Joseph Postell, "Regulation, Adminis-

tration, and the Rule of Law in the Early Republic," in *Freedom and the Rule of Law*, ed. Anthony Peacock (Lanham, MD: Lexington Books, 2010).

37. See Oscar and Mary Handlin, *Commonwealth*, 252; in Pennsylvania, similar events are described by Louis Hartz, in *Economic Policy and Democratic Thought*, 208.

38. See William Novak, *The People's Welfare*, 155–156.

39. Friedman, *A History of American Law*, 185.

40. Jonathan Hughes, *The Governmental Habit Redux*, 16–17.

41. Alexander Hamilton, *Report on Manufactures*, December 5, 1791, in *The Works of Alexander Hamilton*, ed. Henry Cabot Lodge (New York: G. P. Putnam's Sons, 1904), 4:71–72, 73.

42. Alexander Hamilton, "The Examination, No. III," December 24, 1801, in *Works of Alexander Hamilton*, 8:262–263.

43. Madison, to Friedrich List, February 3, 1819, in *Letters and Other Writings of James Madison* (Philadelphia: J. B. Lippincott & Co., 1865), 4:12. Emphasis in original.

44. John Locke, *Two Treatises of Government* (1690), ed. Peter Laslett (Cambridge: Cambridge University Press, 1960), *Second Treatise*, §§ 129, 139.

45. Chancellor James Kent, *Commentaries on American Law* (New York, 1836), 2: 340.

46. Lemuel Shaw, *Commonwealth v. Alger*, 7 Cush. 84 (1851). Emphasis added.

47. See C.J. Waite, writing for the Court in *Munn v. Illinois*, 94 U.S. 124–126, for a brief synopsis of the development of this doctrine. However, it is unclear whether the Court's decision in *Munn* would have been viewed as legitimate by the Framing generation.

48. *Thorpe v. Rutland & Burlington*, 27 Vermont 149 (1854).

49. *Mobile v. Yuille*, 3 Ala. N.S. 140 (1841).

50. Kent, *Commentaries* 2:340. Emphasis added.

51. *Commonwealth v. Blackington*, 24 Pick. 352, 357 (1837). Emphasis added.

52. Handlin and Handlin, *Commonwealth*, 68.

53. Hartz, *Economic Policy*, 204.

54. For this insight I am indebted to an unpublished manuscript by John Adams Wettergreen (on file with author).

55. The promotional element of government activity and its limits, mainly through service activities but also through regulation, was expressed by Hamilton in his *Report on Manufacturers*: "In matters of industry, human enterprise ought, doubtless, to be left free in the main; not fettered by too much regulation; but practical politicians know that it may be beneficially stimulated by prudent aids and encouragements on the part of government . . ."

56. The latter view of regulation is expressed by Theodore Roosevelt's statement that "We grudge no man a fortune in civil life if it is honorably obtained and well used. It is not even enough that it should have been gained without doing damage to the community. We should permit it to be gained only so long as the gaining represents benefit to the community." Theodore Roosevelt, "The New Nationalism," in *American Progressivism,* ed. Ronald Pestritto and William Atto (Lanham, MD: Lexington Books, 2008), 217.

57. Sidney Fine, *Laissez-Faire and the General Welfare State*, 16.

58. Nathaniel Chipman, *Principles of Government: A Treatise on Free Institutions* (Burlington: Edward Smith, 1833), 36–37. Emphasis added.

59. Chipman, *Principles of Government*, 58.

60. Chipman, *Principles of Government*, 59. Emphasis added.

61. Chipman, *Principles of Government*, 61.

62. James Wilson, *Lectures on Law*, in *Collected Works of James Wilson,* ed. Kermit L. Hall and Mark David Hall (Indianapolis, IN: Liberty Fund, 2007), 2:1132.

63. James Wilson, *Lectures on Law*, 2:1056.

64. Chipman, *Principles of Government*, 70. See also 74: "From what has been said of the origin and progress of the right of property in society, it will be evident to every reflecting mind, that all just conceptions of the legitimate rights of man, natural, civil, and political, are the genuine offspring of the same natural principle, a susceptibility of moral impression. All social rights are founded alternately in the same principles, and, consequently, all the duties corresponding to those rights are enforced by the same moral obligations," 185a: "It is certain that in all political establishments, we ought to follow principles; but we must always remember, that they are the principles of social nature, of social man—that one principle is not to be pursued to the exclusion of others. They are all to be limited and mutually modified and adjusted, as the best interests of the community shall require," and 163: "it is a law of social nature, that each should so direct his conduct in all his actions, that they shall tend to the general utility, the general interest and happiness of man."

10

American Banking from Birth to Bust, and All Points in Between

Larry Schweikart

It was a surreal scene. We were on a barge going down the Danube in 1990, Nobel Prize Winner Milton Friedman and I, and amid the fine hors d'oeuvres we struck up a conversation about banking. No greater advocate of the free market has ever lived than Dr. Friedman, and yet, strangely, I was the one arguing the free market position and he, the position of greater government involvement. The issue was banking: I favored competitive note issue, regulated entirely by consumer knowledge, trust, and the track record of the institution, while he favored a monopoly money in the hands of the Federal Reserve System. Needless to say, neither "won" the argument, but ultimately I left completely unsatisfied with Friedman's defense of government interference in the money and banking system. A few years later, I attended a two-day Liberty Fund seminar oriented around Leland Yeager's book, *The Fluttering Veil* (1997). Although identifying "monetary disequilibrium" as a source of instability in capitalist nations, Yeager did not find this inherent to capitalism, but rather a condition of government involvement in the money and banking systems. Nevertheless, after two full days, a dozen scholars at the table had failed to even agree on a definition of money, let alone whether it demanded any grounding in a gold (or commodity) standard, or could in fact "float" against other currencies based on its perceived value by consumers.[1]

That we still have so little understanding about money—why it is or is not "special" or "different" from any other commodity—has ramifications for our banking system, and was severely challenged in the late 1990s and early 2000s by the appearance of "derivatives" (financial instruments based on a future trade and future value). Instead of money representing a commodity, as it did from 1791 to 1933, when President Franklin Roosevelt first took the United

States off the gold standard, or, to use a later date, President Richard Nixon's de-linking the dollar from gold in 1971, money came to represent people's faith in the value of the dollar. But with derivatives, that relationship was strained further in that money could represent people's faith in *future* dollars. It was all stupefying, even to some knowledgeable insiders and certainly to laymen, who struggled to understand how so many big investment banks could suddenly be broke, especially when the economy was not all that horrible. How we got here, then, is most certainly worth a trip down memory lane.[2]

American commercial banking began in 1782 with the Bank of North America, established to a large degree by the "financier of the Revolution," Robert Morris, who, for all his vision, died broke from speculation in western lands.[3] Chartered in Pennsylvania, the Bank of North America was soon joined by banks from other states. The concept of the "charter" granted by the legislature required not only an application but a justification for how the new bank would benefit the public. It was insufficient that it be merely about profit; consequently all new applications had to be accompanied by petitions from local citizens and businesses stating their need for such an institution. From an early point, then, the states became leading participants in the process to certify and enable banking functions.

In the meantime, however, the young United States of America had struggled with Revolutionary War debts, not just from the federal government under the Articles of Confederation, but from the thirteen states. Dealing with those debts and providing the nation a steady source of credit fell to the Secretary of the Treasury in the administration of George Washington, Alexander Hamilton. Wrongly described as an advocate of debt, Hamilton in reality advocated extinguishing the debt "in the very *first* communication" which he ever made on the subject, and as biographer Ron Chernow notes, "his warnings about oppressive debt *vastly* outnumber his paeans to public debt as a source of liquid capital." Hamilton warned that progressive debt "is perhaps the NATURAL DISEASE of all governments."[4] Debt was a "blessing" only insofar as it provided investment credit for building the American national defense network and remained low, and easy to repay, thus establishing sterling credit.

Part of Hamilton's program called for the creation of a Bank of the United States (BUS), which would serve three main purposes, the most important of which would be to make loans to the U.S. government.[5] Second, it would serve as the location for U.S. government deposits. Last, it would provide nationally circulating money through its network of interstate branches. Highly controversial, the Bank came into existence through a deal with the Jeffersonians to place the capital in a federal district in Virginia. It also involved a questionable use of the "elastic clause" (or "Necessary and Proper clause") of the Constitution, and while this would be decided in the Bank's favor in the *McCulloch v. Maryland* case (1819), it opened the door to massive government mischief in the name of whatever Congress determined was "necessary and proper." Over time, the BUS loaned the federal government more than $13 million, established a sound circulating currency that rarely dipped below par value, and avoided partisanship (despite the fears of the Jeffersonians).

Meanwhile, states began to charter banks rapidly between 1800 and 1830, with the capital stock of American financial institutions soaring from $3 million to $168 million, with New England's banks in particular expanding by 20 percent per year.[6] Commonly, these banks had charters of twenty years in length and all banks had to redeem their notes (money) upon demand in gold or silver coin, known as "specie." Failure to do so could result in forfeiture of the charter. As with any business environment, banks came and went, some sound, some unstable, with a wave of failures greeting the banking community in the Panic of 1819. By that time, the first Bank of the United States had gone out of business (its charter was not renewed in 1811) and a second BUS, similar to the first but with a larger capitalization, was chartered in 1816 thanks to the efforts of Stephen Girard.[7] By the 1820s, the BUS truly was a "national" bank, accounting for a fifth of the nation's loans and perhaps one-quarter of the country's circulating medium. In 1823, a new president, Philadelphian Nicholas Biddle, was brought in and he quickly expanded the BUS even further, turning it into a patronage operation for loyal subordinates. It is doubtful, however, that the BUS ever exercised "central" banking powers that regulated the state banks; and in any event, the state banks, through their petitions and letters, strongly supported the BUS.

HOW BANKS WORKED DURING THE ANTEBELLUM PERIOD

At this point, a review of how banking operations worked during this period is in order. First, it is important to distinguish between types of banks, whose commonly used names are a source of confusion. Privately owned banks chartered by the state in which they resided are typically referred to as "state banks," even though as noted they were not owned by the states but merely *chartered* by them. State banks usually had charters that had an expiration and their level of note (money) issues were "regulated" by the fact that all notes, in theory, were convertible into specie. Thus a bank which issued notes that were not well trusted would have to maintain a high *specie reserve* to ensure that at any time it could pay out gold or silver to noteholders who came through the door. A second set of banks, called "private" banks, added to the confusion, for the state banks were actually privately owned: the difference came in the fact that the so-called private banks were not chartered, and thus could not issue money. They could, however, accept deposits and make loans. Whereas chartered banks could establish branches if permitted to do so by state law (i.e., build office buildings in other towns that nevertheless shared the same assets and liabilities with the main office), state banks could not open branches in other states. However, since private banks were not bound by such documents as charters, they could (and did) branch across state lines.[8] If private banks had an advantage in branching, it did them little good because, lacking a charter, they couldn't issue notes.[9]

A third type of bank that operated was a state-chartered, state-owned bank also called a "state" bank. Usually, in the case of these banks, they had the name "State Bank of . . ." or "Bank of the State of . . ." in their official title, and usually the state only owned a portion of the stock, not all of it. State-owned banks had several advantages over privately owned state-chartered banks. They had large capitalizations, meaning they also had more money to loan. Not all state-owned banks were endowed with a monopoly status, but most faced no, or little, competition (as in Arkansas, Alabama, Missouri, or Indiana), and they usually had the authority to establish branches throughout the state. Such banks also suffered from disadvantages: typically, laws required that some portion of the profits of a state-owned bank go to a designated public use, such as education. More important, because they needed to please politicians to remain in existence, their chief clients often were legislators, not entrepreneurs, and therefore their loans took on the auspices of bribes, with the overall quality of loans held by these banks suffering. Not surprisingly then, when an economic downturn struck, state banks proved particularly vulnerable and often failed (as did the Bank of the State of Alabama, the State Bank of Arkansas, and others). Burned by investments in these institutions, legislators swung 180 degrees in the opposite direction to ban all banks in some states after 1837 (Iowa, Wisconsin, Arkansas, Texas, Minnesota, and Illinois).

Such extreme measures hardly eliminated banking, as it is a necessity for businesses, but instead merely moved banking across state lines into states that permitted banking or led to the creation of banks that operated under other names, such as George Smith's Wisconsin Marine and Fire Insurance Company. Smith, a Scotsman who operated out of Chicago, then Milwaukee, found himself with the *only* circulating money in Chicago when all Illinois banks were liquidated in 1843. Issuing money through its Wisconsin company, Smith's little non-bank bank provided most of the actual currency in Chicago for some time; then, after Illinois adopted a new free-banking law, he opened a bank in Atlanta, which, by 1854, stunningly accounted for 75 percent of *Chicago's* currency, based on Smith's previous name recognition.[10] The three types of banks then—privately owned state banks, state-owned state banks, and private banks—coexisted through much of the antebellum period.

A bank made its money through loans, which it paid out in the form of its own notes. As noted before, since customers could demand conversion of notes to specie on demand, a bank had to maintain a reasonable reserve. Typically, stronger banks held smaller reserves, as fewer people ever demanded specie for their paper money. But what happened when a merchant deposited notes of another bank in the city in his account? At the end of the day, the cashier or an assistant from Bank A would count and bundle up all the notes of other banks, then make the rounds to those institutions—say, Bank B—presenting them for payment in specie. However, since Bank A's notes had also been circulated and wound up in the drawers of Bank B, Bank B could also exchange Bank A's notes for its own, making up the difference in specie. By the late 1853s, New York, with its 52 banks, established a clearinghouse complete with stations and tables for all the banks: at the end of the day, a cashier would walk from station to station clearing all his notes with that particular bank. The New York Clearinghouse Association required that a bank be a member and provide a fund that would serve both as an emergency fund and as a source of extra cash that banks could draw upon (based on a quota) at minimal interest.[11] This Association thus provided a certain amount of regulation as well, using its lender-of-last-resort operations in the Panic of 1857.

When a severe financial panic struck, however, not even intermediaries such as the Clearinghouse or Massachusetts' "Suffolk System" of banking support could help. In such cases, banks found customers seeking to exchange notes for gold or silver in amounts that far exceeded the banks' reserves. It was a standard banking practice called "fractional reserve banking," in which, based on experience, banks kept reserves as low as possible so as to maximize the money they had in circulation as loans. But in times of panic, customers lined up in lobbies and bank owners responded almost universally by "suspending" specie payments for an unspecified amount of time. Most state charters strictly prohibited suspension—which would result in charter forfeiture—but if all banks did it, the only legislative alternative was to close all banks (and, indeed as we have seen [in the case of Illinois], this happened on occasion). Most of the time, the lawmakers allowed banks to use suspension as an emergency tool. Other than that, regulation was handled by the market, and most importantly, by trust in the bank and its owners.

In other words, at the state level the government had a minor role in banking and regulation, with the exception of the state-owned banks that proved almost universally disastrous. A second variant of government involvement at the state level, we might note, involved the creation of exceptionally large banks using state bond issues in Mississippi and Florida, which had the expected similarly disastrous results. In both cases, artificially large banks made no business sense and suffered phenomenal busts during depressions.

THE NATIONAL BANK, THE PANIC OF 1837, AND THE SUCCESS OF FREE BANKING

Matters were different at the national level with the Second Bank of the United States. Trouble arose when Nicholas Biddle, for reasons still unclear, sought to re-charter the Second BUS four years early when President Andrew Jackson was up for re-election. Some contend that Biddle wanted to box Jackson into the position of having to support the re-charter (when there is little evidence, before this, that he did not support re-charter). In any event, Biddle now found himself involved in a war with the president of the United States, who apparently viewed the BUS as a political, not financial, threat. Professor Edwin Perkins has argued that in fact the Bank's supporters missed numerous opportunities to compromise with Jackson.[12] Others, including myself, have noted that Jackson had his own national bank plan—so he was not inherently antithetical to a national institution—and that his agenda involved one of greater, not less, control over the money supply by eliminating all paper money.[13]

Whether the Bank could perform "central" bank operations depended on one's definition of "central bank," but the BUS certainly partially regulated the note emissions of state-chartered banks by presenting bundles of those banks' notes for redemption in much-feared "raids."[14] Most economists agree it lacked the size or scope to police the nation's banking functions, and there is little documentary evidence that the state banks in any way were dissatisfied with the BUS's operations. The conclusion must be, then, that Andrew Jackson saw the Bank as a political threat, and the hard-headed Jackson got in his head that the Bank had to be destroyed. Jackson reveled in being the executioner. After vetoing the re-charter bill twice, the president administered the coup de grace by withdrawing all government deposits in 1833, stripping from the BUS its most significant advantage—federal money. According to the long-held view, popularized by Federal Reserve banker Bray Hammond in 1957, Jackson brought on the Panic of 1837 with these actions as well as the issuance of the "Specie Circular" in 1836 (in which western lands had to be paid for in gold or silver). Bank-induced "inflation" came to a crashing halt and a depression ensued.[15]

As economist Peter Temin noted, this view persisted because it was internally consistent and because no one had disproven it—until Temin himself did so in 1969 in his book, *The Jacksonian Economy*, wherein he showed that the cause of the inflation was, in fact, silver itself. A large and continued influx of Mexican silver served as a specie base for banks to issue more notes (in which case, it wasn't, technically, "inflation" since the money was backed by specie). The Mexican silver dried up, sending shocks around the world that eventually resulted in smaller reserves in English banks, forcing the English to raise interest rates on their American loans. Hence, the panic.[16] Many states, as we have seen, took the wrong lessons from the Panic and banned banks.

Other states, however, finding themselves without the additional credit of the BUS, liberalized their banking policies to do away with the increasingly burdensome legislative chartering process. The solution was passage of general incorporation laws, in which bankers no longer had to demonstrate "public good," but only had to be a business like any other. These were also labeled "free banking laws," because now any investors could start a bank merely by posting with the secretary of state securities approved under the laws. Usually these were specified government bonds. If the bank failed to redeem its notes, the state would sell the bonds and reimburse the noteholders. Although in theory the banks were "less safe," the noteholders were, in fact, "more safe," receiving priority in the reimbursement process.[17] This process also, not surprisingly, strengthened the bonds of the states using their bonds for backing, always a neat trick by governments. At any rate, the term "free banking" really only meant free entry without an extended chartering process. Banks still operated like chartered state banks.

New York, Michigan, and Georgia were among the first to adopt free banking laws, followed by Ohio and Louisiana. The expansion of banks coincided with new gold discoveries in California and Australia, and characterized a period of general prosperity in the United States. There were a few exceptions when "wildcat" banks appeared, mostly in Michigan, Indiana, and Minnesota. So-called wildcat banking involved a decline in the market price of the securities backing the bank's notes. Say the bonds backing the bank's money dropped in value from $100 to $90: one could take $90 and purchase bonds (par value of $100 dollars), issue $100 in notes, rinse, and repeat. On each transaction, the wildcat banker made $5. Wildcat banks also engaged in the practice of avoiding paying specie by setting up their headquarters "where a wildcat wouldn't go," making it difficult to redeem notes. Of course, these shenanigans only worked once, and very quickly states caught on and modified the laws to require *market* valuation of bonds, not just par valuation. If bond values fell below a certain price for a specified amount of time, the banker had to come in and make up the difference with additional bond purchases.[18] In short, the "excesses" of free banking were ironed out remarkably quickly and with minimal economic dislocation. (It also bears mention that Scotland had a powerful network of free banks that operated with an important modification, which was increased exposure of the owners and stockholders.[19])

Indeed, the economy remained healthy and uneventful until early 1857 when a collapse in railroad bonds triggered a run on New York banks and sparked the Panic of 1857. Traditionally, this was blamed on changes in western wheat prices related to the Crimean War, or the failure of an Ohio bank.[20] More recently, though, Charles Calomiris and I have concluded that the panic could be laid entirely at the feet of Chief Justice Roger B. Taney and the Supreme Court's decision in the *Dred Scott* case.[21] Our conclusions were recently reaffirmed by another researcher, Jenny Wahl.[22] The story is this: on the eve of the Court's decision, Kansas and Nebraska had been opened up to settlement based on Senator Stephen Douglas's concept of "popular sovereignty," or allowing the people of a territory to decide whether or not to permit slavery there. Railroad construction began, pro- and anti-slave settlers flooded into Kansas, and before long there was bloodshed, including the infamous "Pottowatamie Massacre" involving John Brown. Both sides claimed they had the majority: there were two capitals, two territorial legislatures, and two constitutions sent to Washington. The shorthand term for the situation was "Bleeding Kansas."

In the *Dred Scott* decision, Taney's court not only ruled that Dred Scott, a slave, could not sue, but was not even a "person" in the eyes of the law. Furthermore, the Court found that the U.S. Congress had no authority to prohibit slavery in a territory, and the people within the territory could not prohibit it—only after a state became a state *with* slavery could it then amend its constitution to abolish it.[23] That the *Dred Scott* decision was horrible law—as many have subsequently pointed out—was bad enough, but it had the dual distinction of touching off the Panic as it became clear to investors that all of the western territories now might become "bleeding Kansas." The notes of east-west railroads plunged, but only east-west roads. Those railroads running north-south barely moved, reflecting the business concerns about the stability of the climate in the western territories.

The reason it is worthwhile to take time with the *Dred Scott* decision is that it accounts for the *only* serious economic fluctuation under the period of free banking, and we have already seen how the first depression—the Panic of 1837—was entirely the result of natural forces such as the amount of silver coming into the United States and not the banking system. Thus, it is entirely reasonable to suggest that the antebellum system from 1820 on, with or without any kind of government bank, and with entirely open and competitive note issue, was a period of exceptional banking stability that challenges the notion that banks "needed to be regulated."

BANKING AFTER THE CIVIL WAR

At any rate, the point became moot with the onset of the Civil War, during which the need for funds drove the Union government toward new policies that would centralize the money supply. In 1863 and 1864, the federal government passed the National Bank and Currency Acts, which set up a new, second "tier" of banks with national charters from the Comptroller of the Currency. As with the free banks, the new system required member banks to put on deposit with the U.S. Comptroller of the Currency bonds in order to emit notes, but in this case, the bonds were entirely United States bonds, thus enhancing the financing of the war. To increase note emissions, all the bank had to do was purchase more bonds. The National Bank notes had a small bonus in that the bank could put its own name on the note, giving it important free advertising. National banks had higher capitalization requirements than state-chartered or free banks and had other restrictions that, over time, led to a surge in state banks over national banks, much to the chagrin of federal authorities. A more immediate problem with the national banks involved the fact that their notes still, at the time, had to compete with the notes of free banks and state-chartered banks. Congress fixed that, as it fixes most everything, with a tax—in this case, a ten-percent tax on all non-national banknotes. In a brief span, then, the U.S. government had permanently ended banknote competition and given the government a monopoly over currency.

Long before the advent of the Federal Reserve System, then, the government had achieved complete control over the paper money supply. It still could not dictate gold values, however, and from 1865 to 1896, a virtual war erupted over the desire of many groups to inflate the money supply by monetizing silver. This was not their first strategy, however: during the Civil War the Union had created a second type of federal money, the Greenback. About $480 million of these were printed during the war. The chief difference between a national banknote and a Greenback lay in a technicality, in which the national banknotes, in theory, were redeemable in gold. But the government had ended all specie payments during the war, so in reality, anyone holding a national banknote couldn't exchange it for gold until the war's end. The Greenback, on the other hand, bore no promise to redeem in gold, but rather had wording similar to the "legal tender" phrase that now graces all of our currency, and included a promise that at some unspecified future date, they would be redeemable in gold. One *could*, however, use Greenbacks to buy U.S. national banknotes, then when the war was over, exchange *those* for gold. After 1865, resumption in gold payments for national banknotes indeed occurred, but it wasn't until 1875 that Congress announced that it would resume payment in specie for Greenbacks . . . four years later! One can see the reasoning, as Greenbacks were being worn out, being lost, or destroyed, so that the amount of gold in 1879 would be sufficient to cover all surviving Greenbacks by that year.

At any rate, politicians revived various Greenback plans calling for a new infusion of Greenbacks into the economy, as exemplified in the Democrats' "Ohio idea." Little came of these schemes, but continual complaints about shortages of money (but not banks) persisted throughout the West and in the South in the post-bellum era.[24] An alternative solution, then, seemed to be to bypass currency altogether and focus on the gold standard. Hence, Democrats made efforts to monetize silver (that is, make both silver and gold that national backing of all money, and denominate everything in either metal), which brought with it additional headaches of having not one, but two metals that not only experienced natural fluctuations (in terms of how much gold or silver was coming out of the ground) but which fluctuated against each other! Agitation increased after Congress, in the "Crime of '73," refused to monetize silver.[25] Pressures from the silverites grew until 1878, when Congress passed a halfway measure, the Bland-Allison Act, that satisfied no one, then mounted further still until 1890 with the passage of the disastrous Sherman Silver Purchase Act. This measure authorized the federal government to purchase virtually the entire output of western silver and required the Treasury to issue new Treasury (Coin) Notes that could be redeemed for silver or gold. Speculators quickly gathered up all the new Coin Notes they could and took gold, which was undervalued relative to silver. It was a very small margin, but then fortunes are made and lost daily on small margins. The result was the Panic of 1893, which nearly bankrupted the nation. In an ironic turn from recent events, banker J. P. Morgan formed a syndicate that bailed out the U.S. Treasury with a massive infusion of gold—and, yes, he made a commission. Even though the Sherman Silver Purchase Act was repealed, the effects of the Panic continued for years. Worse, agitation for silver did not abate, and marked the major issue of the election of 1896.

Famous for William Jennings Bryan's "Cross of Gold" speech, the election of 1896 saw William McKinley, representing the gold standard, defeat Bryan and his bi-metallism platform, essentially sealing the fate of silver as an official banking for currency in the United States. These events also produced a remarkable and highly controversial narrative that Frank Baum's book, *The Wonderful Wizard of Oz*, was an allegory about the Populist movement and silver. After all, we have Dorothy from Kansas (a hotbed of Populism) swept up by a tornado (as the Populist movement seemed in the West), with her house dropped on the Wicked Witch of the East ("Big Business"). To get home, she must go to Oz (the symbol for an ounce of gold) and the Good Witch of the North (i.e., the Populist northern-tier states in the West) tells

Dorothy to take along the Wicked Witch's *silver*—not red, as in the movie—slippers as she "follows the yellow brick road." This is a perfect image of the bi-metallism standard. Along the way she meets the Scarecrow (western farmers) who only needs a brain (if they knew how powerful they were, they would rise up); the Tin Woodsman (who represented Eastern laborers, who only needed a heart to save them from the dehumanizing drudgery of the factory); and the Cowardly Lion (Bryan himself, most likely, who needed courage to oppose the Spanish-American War). The Wizard was likely McKinley, a politician who appeared to be different things to different people; and the Wicked Witch of the West was killed with water. I'm from Arizona and I can testify that water solves all problems in the West.[26]

By 1900, government's role in banking and money was still limited. It established a single (gold) standard and regulated the expansion and contraction of the money supply through the national banks. But that was precisely the problem: the process whereby banks had to buy new bonds before issuing notes was burdensome and time-consuming, and completely inflexible to rapid changes in the demand for money among businesses (a problem economists call "elasticity"). Put another way, by gaining more control over the money supply, the government had made it far less responsive than it was before the Civil War. At the same time, the disadvantages of being in the national system had driven more and more banks to state charters. The Panic of 1873 and 1893 convinced both state and national bank owners that a "lender of last resort" was needed—Morgan himself agreed with this after the next panic, the Panic of 1907, saying that the economy had grown too large for even his syndicates to rescue again—and the influence of New York was viewed with deep suspicion in the rest of the country. Consequently, a reform movement began with the full support of the American Bankers Association, to solve the problem of New York's "money power," find a lender of last resort, and address the "elasticity" issue.[27]

While they worked on that, bankers at the local level still relied on informal means of regulation to ensure stability, not the least of which was the personal appearance of the banker himself and the quality and investment value of the bank building. It was not uncommon for early bankers, such as J. W. "Joe" McNeal of Medicine Lodge, Kansas, to keep his deposits in his money belt while doing business in a tent; or for Arizona bankers to protect their money at night with rattlesnakes.[28] Other bankers made use of wastebaskets and woodpiles as hiding places for their gold; and Oklahoma banks used chicken wire to segregate their safe area from the customers. The Sweetwater County Bank of Oklahoma, unable to find a suitable building, operated out of a barber shop, which retained its name. Once a bank actually acquired a permanent home, however, it is worth noting how virtually all accounts of the day emphasized the details of the physical structure, and that should have alerted banking historians long ago that there was something important about the bank buildings themselves.

Not only did these facilities usually represent a sizeable capital investment, but the specifics of the materials was notable for their representation of wealth. "Stone pillars," "etched glass," "ornate brass," fine wooden counters, rich marble—every aspect of a bank building was carefully crafted not only to protect the contents of the vault but to display the financial solvency of the corporation. Many buildings were designed by famous architects, including Louis Sullivan. The construction of the vault area, which contained the safe, involved the application of years' worth of study as to how best to protect contents from blasting powder, digging, and fire—which constituted a far more dangerous threat to bank deposits than did robbery. Indeed, Professor Lynne Doti and I discovered a remarkable absence of western bank robberies in our study of western banking. Our sample was western states, beginning at the Kansas/Nebraska lines, and excluding Texas and Alaska; and our period of investigation was 1865–1900. We found only a tiny handful of even attempted robberies, let alone successful heists, and after our book was published, a few other researchers brought two or three more to our attention. Nevertheless, the utter absence of western bank robberies is stunning, and is a testament to the fact that a) bank buildings themselves offered daunting challenges to would-be thieves, and b) that the armed population of every town, whose money was in the banks, had more than a small interest in guaranteeing the safety of their money.

In addition to the bank building, another symbol of safety was the banker himself. Bankers rarely opened a bank until they had established a reputation in another business, such as railroading or a general store. Whether it was the earliest banks in Portland, Oregon, or the Kountze brothers in Denver, Colorado, a mercantile operation offered one of the fastest paths to establishing a reputation for honesty and reliability. The "symbols of safety," therefore, were the person and the building, and while individual bank failures certainly occurred, their numbers were minimal until national panics hit.[29] Once again, contrary to popular imagination, many of these panics had unique circumstances that had little to do with the actual stability of the banking system at all. The Panic of 1857, as we have seen, was a political event; the Panic of 1837 was triggered by massive changes in silver mining; and still later, the Panic of 1893 was almost entirely the result of the Sherman Silver Purchase Act, which artificially lowered the price of gold relative to silver and drained the nation's gold supply. Of all the 19th century depressions, only the Panic of 1873 could be laid at the feet of "banking instability" via the failure of the Jay Cooke banking house—and even that resulted from problems associated with government-subsidized railroad bonds. Put another way, the causes of banking instability in the 19th century were overwhelmingly related to government interference in the market, not to any weaknesses in the banking system itself.

BANKING "REFORM" AND THE RISE OF THE FEDERAL RESERVE

Nevertheless, the "reform" momentum of the late 1800s got around to banking. "Sunshine laws" appeared, requiring banks to post their relevant financial data publicly. States' bank examiners rarely conducted more than an annual examination, and even then, it often was superficial. The guardian of public trust was . . . the public. With each successive panic, however, pressure built to "fix" the problems. By the early 1900s, concern about a "money trust" led to the Pujo Hearings (named for Louisiana Congressman Arsene Pujo), whose committee investigated the "Concentration of Control of Money and Credit" in 1912. Virtually all prominent bankers had to testify, including Morgan. His highly publicized appearance resulted in a classic exchange with the committee's counsel, Samuel Untermeyer, described as a "wealthy New York corporate lawyer who had become increasingly anti-big business."[30] Untermeyer asked Morgan if he favored concentration or competition, to which the banker replied that he liked a combination, but added, "I do not object to competition, either. I like a little competition." Asked if commercial credit was based on money or property, Morgan rejected the premise: "the first thing is character. . . . before money or anything else. Money cannot buy it."[31] The committee reported that 21 percent of the total banking resources of the United States were concentrated in New York City, and that through consolidations, trusts, and stock investments New York's twenty largest banks controlled 43% of the nation's money.[32] Ironically, combining the nation's banks had actually reduced the likelihood and intensity of panics, meaning Untermeyer and his cronies were attacking the bankers for strengthening the system and protecting the depositors.

Contrary to conspiracy views that a cabal of financiers gathered on Jekyll Island to concoct the Fed, pressure for reforming the financial system had been building for years, and came from all directions. Populists wanted a looser money supply; businesses wanted a readily available and reliable stream of credit; a large portion of Americans feared a concentration of money in New York; and bankers themselves wanted to eliminate what they saw as "loose cannons" who could trigger runs and bring them all down. The Federal Reserve System was thus born out of one of those rare convergences in American history where almost everyone clamored for change without entirely appreciating the potentially unintended consequences of that change. (Sound familiar?) In fact, the "Fed," as it was called, addressed all the groups' concerns and for a time seemed the correct answer. By spreading out the system through twelve federal reserve districts, it (in theory) reduced the money power of New York. Indeed, nine of the twelve banks were in the West, Midwest, or South. By providing reserves at the district levels, the Fed seemed to establish a lender of last resort that would bail out troubled banks before they collapsed and took others down with them. And by its discount provisions to member banks, it ensured a more "elastic" money supply. Further guaranteeing the entire structure—even though it was not even mentioned in the Federal Reserve Act—the system continued to be based on gold.

Of course, the Fed received enormous criticism for its part in the banking collapses of the 1930s. Milton Friedman and Anna Schwartz complained that the Fed, obsessed with the soaring stock market, engaged in a willful policy of deflation and failed in its most fundamental role of lender of last resort by refusing to rescue the Bank of United States (no relation to the BUS).[33] Barry Eichengreen pointed out that the ineptitude of the Fed only compounded existing problems with the gold standard in the interwar years.[34] Ultimately, the problem came down to this: on the international gold standard, nations had to tolerate rising unemployment until prices fell, which, in theory, should have caused prices to fall and exports to rise. This only worked up to a point, when public pressure over unemployment grew too strong to resist. In Europe, nation after nation abandoned the gold standard, leaving the United States alone paying out gold for dollars, but unable to acquire gold for francs, marks, or other currencies. Like several men holding up a large cement block, as, one at a time, they run off, the last one holding the block, to quote Mr. Miyagi from the movie *The Karate Kid*, "get squish just like grape." For all his, in my view, numerous egregious faults, the one sensible move Franklin Roosevelt made was to take the United States off gold, thus ending the run on gold and restoring confidence to the banking system. It was *not*, as many who lived during the bank crisis, Roosevelt's enactment of Deposit Insurance that saved the system, but abandoning gold—like everyone else in the world.

The purpose of this chapter is not to review Fed policy. Nothing short of the Hobbit walking scenes from *Lord of the Rings* is surer to put one to sleep than a review of Federal Reserve functions, open market operations, and interest rate fluctuation. But one aspect of national banking policy demands some attention, and that is the role of deposit insurance as a "safety" device. Today, this is something people just accept on faith without ever even looking at data. The reality about deposit insurance is much different. While it is true that the FDIC itself has not yet met a bank run it can't handle (leaving aside who should have dealt with Lehman Brothers and the other mega-bank failures in 2008), a much different picture emerges from studies of state data. Charles Calomiris looked at the 1920s and categorized state banking systems as featuring a) mandatory deposit insurance, b) voluntary deposit insurance, or c) some form of branch banking.[35] He found that the system that correlated most strongly with bank instability and failure was deposit insurance, while the system that correlated most strongly with stability and solvency was branch banking. A. P. Giannini, who backed FDR and yet wanted a national branch banking network that was stymied by the Roosevelt administration, possibly could have saved the United States from some of the worst parts of the Depression if Roosevelt had left him alone.

CONCLUSION: CURRENT TRENDS

I will conclude with a very brief review of trends since the Great Depression when it comes to the government's role in money and banking. The famous Bretton-Woods system introduced a dollar-backed international monetary structure, but also produced the World Bank and International Monetary Fund, both of which relied substantially on American funding and support. Since the purpose of those institutions was, in part, to provide loans and financial help to "developing countries," Bretton-Woods essentially committed the United States to a consistently large foreign aid program—to be sure, never the largest component of the federal budget, but an outlay nonetheless. At the same time, it committed the United States to keeping the dollar's value up. This was "Triffin's Dilemma," named for Lionel Triffin, who recognized that as a reserve currency the dollar had to remain stable, but because the United States would be constantly shipping dollars out (through the Marshall plan and foreign aid), the circulation would exceed the amount of gold backing the dollars. Hence, the two goals of Bretton-Woods were incompatible. In August 1971, President Richard Nixon acknowledged the dilemma by closing the "gold window." Although the U.S. government, through the Fed, still had a monopoly on money, however, numerous foreign currencies now existed to challenge that monopoly; and since the dollar was no longer backed by gold, it floated freely against those currencies.

One could then say that, in essence, we have returned to a much-modified form of money competition. The ability of the government to dictate what its money is "worth" has more or less vanished, particularly after the appearance of instantaneous communications and transfer technology. As Citibank chairman Walter Wriston said in 1979, "Mankind now has a completely integrated international financial and information marketplace, capable of moving money and ideas to any place on the planet."[36] Moreover, Wriston said in 1992, in "Wriston's Law," money "will go where it is wanted, stay where it is well-treated."[37]

We are about to test the post-Bretton framework very soon, for in the near future the trillions of dollars in U.S. debt—and they haven't stopped piling it up yet—must in some way come due. It's a fundamental rule of economics, not to mention finance. U.S. dollars will become worth less and less, meaning those holding the dollars will see their investments shrink and shrink. Pressures to use other currencies as the reserve currency, or to fulfill contracts, have already started (mostly among our enemies) but have begun to shake the Chinese. Competitive money has great blessings, the most foremost being that governments cannot indefinitely inflate (or deflate) without consequences. The only question now is when, not if.

NOTES

1. For Friedman's views, see his *Money Mischief: Episodes in Monetary History* (Boston: Mariner Books, 1997), and for Yeager's views, see his *The Fluttering Veil* (Indianapolis, IN: Liberty Fund, 1997).
2. A good overview of the debates among historians about banking appears in Larry Schweikart, "U.S. Commercial Banking: A Historiographical Survey," *Business History Review* 65 (Autumn 1991): 606–61. One traditional survey of American banking is Fritz Redlich, *The Moulding of American Banking: Men and Ideas*, 2 vols. (New York: Johnson Reprint Company, 1968).
3. Ellis Paxson Olberholzer, *Robert Morris: Patriot and Financier* (New York: Macmillan, 1903); Clarence L. Ver Steeg, *Robert Morris, Revolutionary Financier, With an Analysis of His Career* (Philadelphia: University of Pennsylvania Press, 1954); and B. R. Burg, "Robert Morris," in Larry Schweikart, ed., *The Encyclopedia of American Business History and Biography: Banking and Finance to 1913* (New York: Facts on File, 1990), 351–64 (henceforth called *Banking and Finance*).
4. Ron Chernow, *Alexander Hamilton* (New York: Penguin, 2004), 300.
5. Richard H. Timberlake, *The Origins of Central Banking in the United States* (Cambridge, MA: Harvard University Press, 1978); Benjamin Klebaner, *Commercial Banking in the United States: A History* (Hinsdale, IL: Dryden, 1974); and Jeffrey Rogers Hummel, "First Bank of the United States," in Schweikart, *Banking and Finance*, 181–83.
6. J. Van Fenstermaker, *The Development of American Commercial Banking, 1782–1837* (Kent, OH: Kent State University Press, 1965).
7. Donald R. Adams, Jr., *Finance and Enterprise in Early America: A Study of Stephen Girard's Bank, 1812–1831* (Philadelphia: University of Pennsylvania Press).
8. Larry Schweikart, *Banking in the American South from the Age of Jackson to Reconstruction* (Baton Rouge: Louisiana State University Press, 1987).
9. Richard R. Sylla, "Forgotten Men of Money: Private Bankers in Early U.S. History," *Journal of Economic History* 29 (December 1969): 173–86.

10. Alice E. Smith, *George Smith's Money: A Scottish Investor in America* (Madison: State Historical Society of Wisconsin, 1964).

11. Richard H. Timberlake, "The Central Banking Role of the Clearinghouse Associations," *Journal of Money, Credit, and Banking* 16 (February 1984): 1–15, and his "New York Clearinghouse Association," in Schweikart, *Banking and Finance*, 379–82.

12. Edwin Perkins, "Lost Opportunities for Compromise in the Bank War: A Reassessment of Jackson's Veto Message," *Business History Review* 61 (1987): 531–50.

13. Larry Schweikart, "Jacksonian Ideology, Currency Control, and 'Central' Banking: A Reappraisal," *Historian* 51 (November 1988): 78–102; David A. Martin, "Metallism, Small Notes, and Jackson's War with the B.U.S.," *Explorations in Economic History* 11 (Spring 1974): 227–47.

14. Richard H. Timberlake, "The Specie Standard and Central Banking in the United States before 1860," *Journal of Economic History* 21 (September 1961): 318–41.

15. Bray Hammond, *Banks and Politics in America: From the Revolution to the Civil War* (Princeton: Princton University Press, 1957).

16. Peter Temin, *The Jacksonian Economy* (New York: Norton, 1969).

17. Hugh Rockoff, "Free Banking and Wildcat Banking," *Banking and Finance*, 202–5.

18. Arthur Rolnick and Warren Weber, "Free Banking, Wildcat Banking, and Shinplasters," *Federal Reserve Bank of Minneapolis Quarterly Review* 6 (Fall 1982): 10–19; Hugh Rockoff, *The Free Banking Era: A Re-examination* (New York: Arno, 1975); George Selgin and Lawrence H. White, "The Evolution of a Free Banking System," *Economic Inquiry* 25 (July 1987): 439–58.

19. Lawrence H. White, "Scottish Banking and the Legal Restrictions Theory: A Closer Look," *Journal of Money, Credit and Banking* 22 (November 1990): 526–36 and his *Free Banking in Britain: Theory, Experience, and Debate, 1800–1845* (Cambridge: Cambridge University Press, 1984).

20. Huston, "Western Grains and the Panic of 1857," passim, and his book, *The Panic of 1857 and the Coming of the Civil War* (Baton Rouge, LA: Louisiana State University Press, 1987); Melvin Ecke, "Fiscal Aspects of the Panic of 1857," Ph.D. Dissertation, Princeton University, 1951, 80–85, 92–94, 118–20; Peter Temin, "The Panic of 1857," *Intermountain Economic Review* (Spring 1975), 1–12.

21. Charles W. Calomiris and Larry Schweikart, "The Panic of 1857: Origins, Transmission, and Containment," *Journal of Economic History* 51 (December 1991): 807–34.

22. Jenny Wahl, "*Dred*, Panic, War: How a Slave Case Triggered Financial Crisis and Civil Disunion," *Carleton College Economics Department Working Paper no. 2009-1*, located at http://apps.carleton.edu/curricular/econ/workingpapers/.

23. Don E. Fehrenbacher, *Slavery, Law, and Politics: The Dred Scott Case in Historical Perspective* (New York: Oxford University Press, 1981); Andrew C. Napolitano, *Dred Scott's Revenge: A Legal History of Race and Freedom in America* (Nashville, TN. Thomas Nelson, 2009). See also Larry Schweikart, *Seven Events that Made America America* (New York: Sentinel, 2010), ch. 2, pp. 34–60.

24. Larry Schweikart and Lynne Pierson Doti, *Banking in the American West from the Gold Rush to Deregulation* (Norman, OK: University of Oklahoma Press,

1991); Irwin Unger, *The Greenback Era: A Social and Political History of American Finance, 1865–1879* (Princeton: Princeton University Press, 1964).

25. Milton Friedman argued that monetizing silver in 1873 would have been possible, without the horrific side effects of 1890, because the Civil War had temporarily ended the "reign of gold." He argued that the two standards would have competed with each other and adjusted. But the potential for speculative intrigue, particularly since the government was involved, would have doubled. It was difficult enough ensuring that speculators didn't constantly manipulate the gold standard through their schemes. Adding to that would have been a complication the U.S. needed. See Friedman's "The Crime of 1873," Working Papers in Economics E-89-12, http://hoohila.stanford.edu/workingpapers/getWorkingPaper.php?filename=E-89-12.pdf.

26. For the discussion about the Wizard of Oz as a parable on Populism, see Henry M. Littlefield, "The Wizard of Oz: Parable on Populism," *American Quarterly* 16 (Spring 1964): 47–58; Hugh Rockoff, "The 'Wizard of Oz' as a Monetary Allegory," *Journal of Political Economy* 98 (August 1990): 739–60. Over a decade ago, I met Frank Baum's great-grandson, who completely denied that the book had any political or monetary references.

27. Eugene N. White, *Regulation and Reform of the American Banking System, 1900–1929* (Princeton: Princeton University Press, 1983).

28. Schweikart and Doti, *Banking in the American West*, 36; Larry Schweikart, *A History of Banking in Arizona* (Tucson: University of Arizona Press, 1982).

29. Schweikart and Doti, *Banking in the American West*, chapter 8, passim.

30. Larry Schweikart and Lynne Pierson Doti, *American Entrepreneur* (New York: Amacom Press, 2009), 241.

31. Vincent P. Carosso, *The Morgans: Private International Bankers, 1854–1913* (Cambridge: Harvard University Press), 632–33.

32. Henry C. Dethloff, "Arsene P. Pujo," in Schweikart, *Banking and Finance*, 397–98.

33. Milton Friedman and Anna J. Schwarz, *A Monetary History of the United States, 1863–1960* (Princeton: Princeton University Press, 1964). For a full review of all the various criticisms of the Fed, from the Left and the Right, see Schweikart, "U.S. Commercial Banking," passim.

34. Barry Eichengreen, *Golden Fetters: The Gold Standard and the Great Depression, 1919–1932* (New York: Oxford, 1992).

35. Charles Calomiris, *United States Bank Deregulation in Historical Perspective* (Cambridge: Cambridge University Press, 2000), and his "Deposit Insurance: Lessons from the Record," Federal Reserve Bank of Chicago *Economic Perspectives,* May 1989, 10–30 and "Is Deposit Insurance Necessary? A Historical Perspective," *Journal of Economic History* 50 (June 1990): 283–95.

36. Paul Johnson, *Modern Times: A History of the World from the Twenties to the Nineties* (New York: HarperCollins, 1991), 664.

37. Rich Karlgaard, "Wriston's Law Still Holds," July 21, 2009; Walter Wriston, *The Twilight of Sovereignty: How the Information Revolution Is Transforming Our World* (New York: Scribner, 1992).

Index

About the Editors

Joseph Postell is Assistant Professor of Political Science at the University of Colorado Colorado Springs. He received his Ph.D. in Politics from the University of Dallas. From 2007–2010 he was the Assistant Director of the B. Kenneth Simon Center for American Studies at The Heritage Foundation. He has published articles on the Bill of Rights and regulation during the American Founding, and his writing has appeared in the *Washington Times* and the *Claremont Review of Books*.

Bradley C. S. Watson is Professor of Politics at Saint Vincent College in Pennsylvania, where he holds the Philip M. McKenna Chair in American and Western Political Thought and is Co-Director of the Center for Political and Economic Thought. He is also Senior Scholar at the Intercollegiate Studies Institute and a Fellow of the Claremont Institute. He has held visiting faculty appointments at Princeton University and Claremont McKenna College. He has authored or edited many books, including *Living Constitution, Dying Faith: Progressivism and the New Science of Jurisprudence*, and *The Idea of the American University*. He has published in both professional and general interest forums including *Armed Forces and Society*, *Claremont Review of Books*, *The Intercollegiate Review*, *Modern Age*, *National Review*, and *Perspectives on Political Science*. He was educated in Canada, Belgium, and the United States, and holds degrees in economics, political science, law, and philosophy.

About the Contributors

Bruce Caldwell is a Research Professor of Economics and the Director of the Center for the History of Political Economy at Duke University. He is the author of *Beyond Positivism: Economic Methodology in the 20th Century*, first published in 1982. For the past two decades his research has focused on the multi-faceted writings of the Nobel Prize–winning economist and social theorist Friedrich A. Hayek. Caldwell's intellectual biography of Hayek, *Hayek's Challenge*, was published in 2004 by the University of Chicago Press. Since 2002 he has been the General Editor of *The Collected Works of F.A. Hayek*, a collection of Hayek's writings published jointly by the University of Chicago Press and Routledge. Caldwell has held research fellowships at New York University, Cambridge University, and the London School of Economics. He is a past president of the History of Economics Society, a past Executive Director of the International Network for Economic Method, and a Life Member of Clare Hall, Cambridge. In 2011 he will begin serving as President of the Southern Economic Association.

Samuel Hollander was born in London, UK, in 1937. He is an Officer in the Order of Canada (OC) and a Fellow of the Royal Society of Canada (FRSC). He holds a Ph.D. from Princeton University and an honorary LLD from McMaster University, Canada. He has held Ford Foundation and Guggenheim Fellowships. He taught at the University of Toronto 1963–98, retiring as University Professor Emeritus; was Research Director at the Centre National de la Recherche Scientifique (CNRS), France 1999–2000; and has been affiliated with the Department of Economics, Ben Gurion University of the Negev, Israel since 2000. He is the author of a series of studies on the classical economists, the latest concerning *The Economics* *of Karl Marx,* Cambridge University Press, 2008. A companion volume, *Friedrich Engels and Marxian Political Economy*, is to be published shortly by Cambridge University Press.

Alan Levine is Associate Professor of political theory in the Department of Government at American University. He has held fellowships from the National Endowment for the Humanities and at the James Madison Program at Princeton University; the Hoover Institution at Stanford University; and the Institute of US Studies, School of Advanced Study, University of London. He is the author of *Sensual Philosophy: Toleration, Skepticism, and Montaigne's Politics of the Self*, editor of *Early Modern Skepticism and the Origins of Toleration*, and co-editor of *A Political Companion to Ralph Waldo Emerson*. He has also published on Machiavelli, Nietzsche, Chinua Achebe, Judith Shklar, and European views of America. Dr. Levine received his Ph.D. from Harvard University.

Peter McNamara teaches political theory. He specializes in early modern and American political thought. He is the author of *Political Economy and Statesmanship: Smith, Hamilton and the Foundation of the Commercial Republic* and the editor of *The Noblest Minds: Fame, Honor and the American Founding*, and, most recently (with Louis Hunt), *Liberalism, Conservatism and Hayek's Idea of Spontaneous Order*. His current research projects include essays on Jefferson on federalism and Franklin on religion and a book on "Liberalism and the Problem of Human Nature." In the Fall of 2008 he was the Hayek Visiting Scholar at the Clemson Institute for the Study of Capitalism at Clemson University, South Carolina.

John D. Mueller is Director of the Ethics and Public Policy Center's Economics and Ethics Program and President of the forecasting firm LBMC LLC, both in Washington, D.C. Mr. Mueller has advised American and foreign economic policymakers on monetary, income-tax, welfare, and Social Security policies since 1979. He was Economic Counsel to the Republican Party caucus in the U.S. Congress under Rep. Jack Kemp during both Reagan Administrations. Mr. Mueller is a Fellow of The Lehrman Institute, Princeton University's James Madison Society, the Jack Kemp Foundation, Senior Fellow of the Intercollegiate Studies Institute, and author of *Redeeming Economics: Rediscovering the Missing Element* (ISI Books, 2010).

Larry Schweikart, a professor of history at the University of Dayton, was a rock drummer before obtaining a Ph.D. from the University of California at Santa Barbara. Author of two dozen books on finance, banking, and business history, in 2004 he and Michael Allen wrote the *New York Times* #1

Bestseller, *A Patriot's History of the United States*. In 2010 he became a film producer with the documentary film, *Rockin' the Wall*, about rock music's part in bringing down the Iron Curtain.

Rev. Robert A. Sirico received his Master of Divinity degree from the Catholic University of America, following undergraduate study at the University of Southern California and the University of London. Fr. Sirico co-founded the Acton Institute in 1990. His writings on religious, political, economic, and social matters are published in a variety of journals, including the *New York Times,* the *Wall Street Journal, Forbes*, the *London Financial Times*, the *Washington Times*, the *Detroit News*, and *National Review.* Fr. Sirico has provided commentary for members of the broadcast media such as CNN, ABC, the BBC, NPR, and CBS's *60 Minutes*. Fr. Sirico has received an honorary doctorate in Christian Ethics from the Franciscan University of Steubenville and an honorary doctorate in Social Sciences from Universidad Francisco Marroquin. He is a member of the Mont Pelerin Society, the American Academy of Religion, and the Philadelphia Society, and is on the Board of Advisors of the Civic Institute in Prague. Fr. Sirico also served on the Michigan Civil Rights Commission from 1994 to 1998.

Richard Wagner is the Holbert L. Harris Professor of Economics at George Mason University. He is also the Director of Graduate Studies in the Department of Economics. His scholarly writings span a broad range of topics on political economy and public affairs, and he has authored or edited over 25 books and monographs and over 150 scholarly articles. His books include *Democracy in Deficit* (with James Buchanan), *To Promote the General Welfare*, and *Public Choice and Constitutional Economics* (co-editor). Professor Wagner also serves on such organizations as the Public Interest Institute (where he serves as Senior Fellow and Chairman of the Academic Advisory Board), the Independent Institute, the James Madison Institute for Public Policy Studies, and the Virginia Institute for Public Policy. He received his Ph.D. in Economics from the University of Virginia.

Thomas West is Professor of Politics at Hillsdale College, and a Senior Fellow of the Claremont Institute. He is the author of *Vindicating the Founders: Race, Sex, Class, and Justice in the Origins of America*. His recent publications include "Freedom of Speech in the Founding and in Modern Liberalism," "The Transformation of Protestant Theology as a Condition of the American Revolution," and "Progressivism and the Transformation of American Government." He is also the author of *Plato's Apology of Socrates: An Interpretation*, and he is co-translator (with Grace West) of *Four Texts on Socrates: Plato's Euthyphro, Apology, and Crito, and Aristophanes' Clouds.*